Changing Big Business

Changing Big Business

The Globalisation of the Fair Trade Movement

Anna Hutchens

Director of the Fair Trade Program, Centre for Governance of Knowledge and Development (CGKD) and Postdoctoral Fellow, The Regulatory Institutions Network (RegNet), The Australian National University, Canberra, Australia

Edward Elgar
Cheltenham, UK • Northampton, MA, USA

Published by
Edward Elgar Publishing Limited
The Lypiatts
15 Lansdown Road
Cheltenham
Glos GL50 2JA
UK

Edward Elgar Publishing, Inc.
William Pratt House
9 Dewey Court
Northampton
Massachusetts 01060
USA

A catalogue record for this book
is available from the British Library

Library of Congress Control Number: 2008943833

Mixed Sources
Product group from well-managed
forests and other controlled sources
www.fsc.org Cert no. SA-COC-1565
© 1996 Forest Stewardship Council

ISBN 978 1 84720 971 9

Printed and bound in Great Britain by MPG Books Ltd, Bodmin, Cornwall

Contents

Acknowledgements

The publishers wish to thank the following who have kindly given permission for the use of copyright material:

The United Nations Development Programme (UNDP) Human Development Report Office for Figure 2.2, 'Coffee prices and production in Ethiopia', in Human Development Report (2005), *International Cooperation at a Crossroads: Aid, Trade and Security in an Unequal World*, New York: UNDP, p. 141.

Dr Bill Vorley and the International Institute for Environment and Development (IIED) for Figure 2.3, 'The "bottleneck" in the global coffee industry', in B. Vorley and the UK Food Group (2003), *Food, Inc.: Corporate Concentration from Farm to Consumer*, London: IIED, p. 49.

Professor Raphael Kaplinsky for Figure 2.4, 'Coffee value chain', in R. Kaplinsky (2006), 'How can agricultural commodity producers appropriate a greater share of value chain incomes?', in A. Sarris and D. Hallam (eds), *Agricultural Commodity Markets and Trade: New Approaches to Analysing Market Structure and Instability*, Cheltenham, UK and Northampton, MA, USA: Edward Elgar, p. 366.

Professor Raphael Kaplinsky for Table 2.1, 'Share of coffee in total export receipts', in R. Fitter and R. Kaplinsky (2001), 'Who gains from product rents as the coffee market becomes more differentiated? A value-chain analysis', *IDS Bulletin*, **32**(3), 8.

Zed Books for Table 2.2, 'World commodity price changes since 1980', and Table 2.3, 'Recent profit record of major traders and processors of tropical commodities', from P. Robbins (2003), *Stolen Fruit*, London and New York: Zed Books, pp. 9 and 16.

Sage Publications for Figure 3.1, 'Fairtrade in the coffee supply chain', from A. Nicholls and C. Opal (2005), *Fair Trade: Market-Driven Ethical Consumption*, London: Sage Publications, p. 83.

The Fairtrade Labelling Organizations International (FLO) for the figures of FLO's governance structure 2004/05 (Figures 3.2 and 5.2) and new governance structure (as of 2007) (Figure 7.4).

AgroFair for the figure of AgroFair's corporate governance structure (Figure 6.1).

CTM Altromercato for the figure of CTM Altromercato's corporate governance structure (Figure 6.5).

Equal Exchange for the figure of Equal Exchange's governance structure (Figure 6.6).

The International Fair Trade Organization (IFAT) for the figures of the IFAT governance structure (Figure 7.1), the IFAT Fair Trade Organization (FTO) Mark (Figure 7.2) and the FTO registration process (Figure 7.3).

Every effort has been made to trace all the copyright holders but if any have been inadvertently overlooked the publishers will be pleased to make the necessary arrangements at the first opportunity.

Abbreviations

AFN	African Fairtrade Network
AFTF	Asia Fair Trade Forum
AGICES	Assemblea Generale Italiana del Commercio equo e Solidale
AGM	annual general meeting
ATO	alternative trading organisation
CLAC	Latin American and Carribean Network of Small Fair Trade Producers
COE	circle of enrolment
COFTA	Cooperative for Fair Trade in Africa
CPAF	Cooperative Producers' AgroFair
CSR	corporate social responsibility
ECLA	Evangelical Lutheran Church in America
EFTA	European Fair Trade Association
EU	European Union
F.I.N.E.	FLO, IFAT, NEWS!, EFTA
FLO	Fairtrade Labelling Organizations International
FTF	Fair Trade Federation
FTO	Fair Trade Organization (IFAT)
GATT	General Agreement on Tariffs and Trade
GCC	global commodity chain (analysis)
GEPA	Gesellschaft zur Förderung der Partnerschaft mit der Dritten Welt mbH (Society for the Promotion of Partnership with the Third World)
GSP	Generalized System of Preferences
GVC	global value chain (analysis)
ICA	International Coffee Agreement
IFAT	International Fair Trade Association
IPRs	intellectual property rights
KCU	Kagera Cooperative Union
KEFAT	Kenya Federation for Alternative Trade
LI	Labelling Initiative
LWR	Lutheran World Relief
MNC	multinational corporation
MoM	Meeting of Members (FLO)

NAATO	North American Alternative Trade Organization
NAP	Network of Asian Producers
NCA	National Coffee Association of America
NEWS!	Network of European Worldshops
NI	National Initiative
SCAA	Specialty Coffee Association of America
SERRV International	Sales Exchange for Refugee Rehabilitation and Vocation
TM	trade mark
TNC	transnational corporation
TRIPs	Trade-Related Aspects of Intellectual Property
TWIN	Third World Information Network
UCIRI	Unión de Comunidades Indigenas de la Región del Istmo (Union of Indigenous Communities of the Isthmus Region)
UN	United Nations Organization
UNCTAD	United Nations Centre for Trade and Development
UNDP	United Nations Development Program
UNICEF	United Nations Children's Fund
USFT	United Students for Fair Trade
WTO	World Trade Organization

With deep gratitude to my mentor, Professor Peter Drahos, and in dedication to my loving parents, Diane and Graham

Introduction

Until the lions have their historians, tales of hunting will always glorify the hunter.

(African Proverb)

For a long time, the history of power has told of an all-powerful sovereign state and its legitimate exercise of force over a passive citizenry. While social scientists' more modern translations maintain the hunter's perspective, the 'hunter' is now the global corporation. In this narrative, citizens, producers and consumers worldwide play the perennial 'lion'; they are mere pawns in a chess game between corporate giants.

So something is amiss. Since 1997 a community of 46 000 small-scale cocoa farmers in Ghana has co-built and produced high-quality cocoa for the increasingly successful chocolate brand Divine Chocolate Ltd in the UK (and now US) market, in which they hold directorship responsibilities and own 45 per cent of the shares. Aside from their dividends, the farmers receive above-market prices for the cocoa they produce plus a social premium for community development needs and business capacity-building. Divine's trading arm, located in the UK and now the USA, invests increasing amounts in technical assistance, using the business process as a vehicle for development and market demonstration of how 'fair' business can be; Divine operates in a broader context in which 14 million atomised and exploited cocoa producers fiercely compete in the global cocoa industry for declining prices from a handful of global brand multinationals including Nestlé, M&M/Mars and Cadbury.

Another case is the farmer-owned fruit company, AgroFair, which sells bananas (and other fruits) under the Oké label across Europe. Competing successfully in a corporatised market, AgroFair's small-scale fruit farmers hold 50 per cent of its shares and receive 50 per cent of profits, in addition to further systematic funding for community and business development. The farmers also make decisions over an increasing number of AgroFair's international operations – including traditional 'Northern' competences such as marketing. Situated among behemoth rivals including Chiquita, Dole and Del Monte, AgroFair has reversed the Northern-oriented oligopolistic ownership structures common to the global banana industry in favour of the small producer.

Divine Chocolate Ltd and AgroFair are two 'fair trade' companies that do not conform to the kind of power most social science is suited to explain. This book seeks to show how these unconventional models of market power relationships – that confer power on the weakest market actors – and the movement for fair trade that promotes them have been possible and successful. To do so, the book tells two stories. One is about fair trade – the evolution of the global movement responsible for unique and progressive companies such as Divine Chocolate Ltd and AgroFair, and the product certification system that offers 'mainstream' consumers (mainly food) products made under 'Fairtrade' conditions. Flowing from this is a story about power – an evolving concept within the social sciences which in both its more traditional and modern interpretations has largely neglected the capacity for, and complexity of, social agency.[1]

THEORIES OF POWER

Early theorists such as Hobbes (1991) and Weber (1978) viewed power in terms of the state's monopoly on the legitimate use of force. Power was conceived as an instrument of coercion and domination that enabled the state to execute its will irrespective of resistance. In the last several decades, however, the world has changed remarkably. Many actors, state and non-state, influence the process of governance, and rarely by means of force or coercion (Braithwaite and Drahos, 2000). In fact, the workings of power are rarely overtly identifiable; power rears its head in contexts other than in win–lose bargaining at the decision-making table, and even there, in ways not often assumed. Rather than 'visible', power can be 'hidden', even 'invisible': who speaks and who is silent, who is present and who is absent, who defines and who is defined, whose interests count and who does the counting – all these are matters of power. For Foucault, this is the power of discourse: internalisation of knowledge regimes reproduces social structures. While he believed in the productive – and thus emancipatory – potential of discourse power, Foucault was preoccupied with the over-whelming influence of knowledge regimes and neglected the theoretical development of agency. In fact, in a Foucauldian reading, the 'empower-ment' of disfranchised groups serves to expand liberal Western capitalism rather than advance genuine social and economic justice.

A number of scholars have pursued this latter, incipient intellectual agenda of a 'post-liberal' power and form of agency. In this context, power reflects principles of cooperation, deliberation and critical awareness rather than liberal principles of competition, bargaining and individual-ism. The traditional dichotomy between domination and resistance is also dissolved to capture greater complexity and 'situated'-ness in expressions of agency than is commonly reflected in theory (Bevir and Rhodes, 2005; Nygren, 1999). For instance, in recent work on 'defiance' (Braithwaite, 2009), 'resistance' is but one of a number of ways that different individuals and social groups attempt to overcome institutional and structural constraints in their lives. 'Game-playing' is another type of defiance of authority structures (which is arguably capable of social transformation). Through an investigation of the fair trade movement's attempts to realise social justice in global post-industrial/post-Fordist markets (particularly agriculture), this book examines the complex space of agency, integrating the concept of (post-liberal) power to articulate the micro-processes by which weak actors bring about change in the structures and institutions of global markets. As can be discovered through the story of fair trade, the answer lies in the power(s) and strategies of 'game-playing' – the subject of this book.

POWER IN MODERN MARKETS . . .

In the shift from an industrial to a post-industrial economy (Toffler, 1980; Drucker, 1969; Bell, 1978), the hegemony of the state has shifted to the hegemony of global corporations. In recent decades this power base has expanded Northern firms' power over world markets through the consolidation of an international 'free' trade regime and rise of global 'commodity'/'value' chains of production. The basis of corporate power in this context is the brand – an image of the trade mark (an abstract object). Trade marks are a form of intellectual property that have strengthened in the last 50 years in unprecedented – and global – proportions. Trade mark ownership enables established brand owners to heavily influence consumer subjectivities, and, through this mind-control, confers on them oligopolistic market power over the terms and conditions of international production and trade with developing-country producers.

. . . AND THE POWER OF FAIR TRADE

In this context the fair trade movement has sought to reshape relations of power in markets in favour of the weakest actors: small-scale developing-country producers clustered in the production of agricultural commodities. Based on alternative trading links between small producers and politically active 'Alternative Trade Organisations' (ATOs) in Northern markets, the movement has articulated principles that both address market failures affecting marginalised producers' ability to participate in markets, and construct terms and conditions of international trade that serve producers' economic and developmental interests. These principles include stable commodity prices, direct purchasing from, and long-term trading partnerships with, democratically organised producer organisations, and a social premium for investment in social development projects, producer capacity-building and technical assistance. The fair trade movement has promoted this alternative discourse within 'mainstream' production and trade routes over the last two decades via a system of product certification and labelling for products made under the above-mentioned 'Fairtrade' conditions, as well as more recent experiments in commercial ATO 'brand' companies. The movement's rapid 'mainstream' market growth – powered by a consumer movement that in 2006 spent US$1.6 billion on labelled and non-labelled fair trade goods – has nevertheless provoked numerous political tensions and challenges for the movement that pivot on a perception (and very real empirical concern) about fair trade's market absorption.

OUTLINE OF THE BOOK

Through a rich, in-depth analysis of the fair trade movement, this book offers a new theory about power, one that synthesises, fills gaps in and extends the interdisciplinary contributions of other writings on the subject. The complex organisational development of fair trade makes for a dense yet grounded thesis about power and evolutionary change in markets. As a whole, the book promises to engage both those interested in fair trade and social movements that generally challenge modern global market processes, and those interested in theories of power and social change.

Chapter 1 provides the theoretical framework for examining power. It charts the development of thought from power as domination ('power over') to a broader, more liberating and politicised notion as an individual and collective capacity ('power with', 'power to', 'power within'). Chapter 2 demonstrates the operation of 'power over' in the corporatised landscape of global commodity markets, specifically the global coffee market. For the benefit of those unfamiliar with fair trade, Chapter 3 provides a brief sketch of the fair trade movement. Chapters 4–7 then bring this movement to life through the voices of its practitioners – its organisational development, market growth and political and institutional challenges. These chapters aid the development of an inductive understanding of how alternative discourses evolve in the process of economic change and the role of different social movement actors in the evolutionary process.

Chapter 4 documents how the 'grassroots' movement has achieved expansion of fair trade markets, providing insight into how atomised actors within global market structures collectively trigger large-scale market outcomes. Chapter 5 explores the fair trade actors seeking to institutionalise Fairtrade-certified products – the Fairtrade Labelling Organizations International (FLO) and its Labelling Initiatives (LIs) – and the particular organisational structures they have evolved. This account enables an analysis of power in the context of resistance and the risks this unique evolutionary trajectory poses to a movement's ultimate survival. Chapter 6 then turns to consider several of fair trade's pioneers' strategic response to corporate capture: (re-)innovations in radical commercial fair trade businesses. This illuminates how the evolutionary strategy of 'game-playing' (re-)liberates alternative discourses (such as fair trade) from corporate hegemonic absorption. Chapter 7 considers the evolution of the movement's two governing institutions, FLO and the International Fair Trade Association (IFAT), and the challenges to cooperation and coordination that the two dynamics – of resistance and game-playing – pose for the movement's overall survival. This story enables the elucidation of how game-players ensure institutional survival and effectiveness in a hostile market environment. The Conclusion draws this story of the emergence and evolution of fair trade to a close and outlines the elements of a theory about the power of 'weak' actors.

NOTE

1. This book is based on Hutchens (2007).

1.   'Game-playing': rethinking power and empowerment

For social scientists, the exercise of power has traditionally been an instrument of domination, involving coercion, struggle and force. This view of power – as 'power over' – prevailed in the social sciences in the twentieth century (Clegg, 1989; Lukes, 1974). More recent scholarship has advanced our understanding of how power is exercised in the modern world (see especially Foucault, 1977, 1979). In contrast to the traditional 'power over' perspective, contemporary social theory creates space for individual agency, but until recently this space has lacked theoretical development. An emergent research agenda now questions how disempowered groups exercise agency positively to achieve empowerment (see O'Malley, 1996; O'Malley et al., 1997; Townsend et al., 1999; Rowlands, 1995, 1997; Bevir and Rhodes, 2005; Eyben et al., 2006). Braithwaite's (2009) conceptual framework of 'defiance' extends this incipient intellectual programme with a typology of individual psychologies and behaviours for defying institutional and structural constraints. Elaborating Braithwaite's psychological framework to the level of collective action and transnational structure, the chapter focuses on one type of defiance, game-playing, and develops a conceptual scheme of empowerment through which game-playing can be understood to trigger global transformations.

'POWER OVER': A LEGACY AND ITS LIMITATIONS

According to Steward Clegg (1989: 22), twentieth-century thought on power has been grounded in a notion of 'human agency' that is 'expressed through causal relations measurable in terms of mechanistic indicators'. For Dahl (cited in Lukes, 1974: 16) for instance, 'A has power over B to the extent that A can get B to do something that B would not otherwise do'. Similarly Weber (1978: 53) viewed power as 'the probability that one actor within a social relationship will be in a position to carry out his own will despite resistance', or to put it another way, 'the power of one person or group to get another person or group to do something against their will' (Townsend et al., 1999: 26; Rowlands, 1995, 1997; see for example Dahl,

1961). In this tradition, power is a 'product of conflicts between actors to determine who wins and who loses on key, clearly recognised issues in . . . clearly established decision-making arenas' (Gaventa and Cornwall, 2001: 70). It is located in decision-making processes, conflict and force, and is zero-sum by nature. As Rowlands (1995: 101) observes, 'power over' implicitly suggests a finite resource in which 'the more power one person has, the less the other has'. 'Power over' is thus an 'instrument of domination' (ibid.).[1]

While still predominant, this construction of power has received criticism. In his signal work *Power: A Radical View*, Steven Lukes (1974) defines 'power over' as only one (limited) dimension of power, and a negative one at that. Other dimensions of power include 'hidden' power and 'invisible' power.

HIDDEN POWER

'Power over' is traditionally associated with visibility, specifically, visibility in decision-making processes (Lukes, 1974; Clegg, 1989). Critics argue that power is more subtle, 'hidden' and diffuse, taking place anywhere, not just in overt power plays at the decision-making table (see also Bachrach and Baratz, 1970). Indeed, 'hidden power' determines who is at the decision-making table, what is on the agenda (VeneKlasen and Miller, 2002) as well as who gets to define, and make decisions about, agenda issues (see Gaventa, 1993). As Gaventa and Cornwall (2001: 70) claim, 'if certain voices are absent in the debate, their non-participation is interpreted as their own apathy or inefficacy, not as a process of exclusion from the political process'. 'Power over' is thus weak on analysis of the distribution of power between social groups, portraying power and powerlessness as static relational states, and the powerless as helpless victims (Hartsock, 1990; Starhawk, 1987; Rowlands, 1995: 101).

INVISIBLE POWER

Critics also argue that 'power over' theories ignore the subtle operation of 'power over' within the self through which the social order is maintained (Townsend et al., 1999; Kabeer, 1994; VeneKlasen and Miller, 2002). Termed 'invisible power', this dimension of power manifests itself as an acceptance of, or belief in, one's subordinate position and a denial of the problems one faces in one's environment; it shapes the ideological boundaries of individual and group beliefs, wants, interests and identity. In this context, 'power over' is an internalised oppression of both the oppressor and the oppressed because it circumscribes the bounds of individual thought and imagination. As Kabeer (1994: 227, citing Shklar) suggests, at a pragmatic level individuals

> subscribe to accounts of social reality which deny that . . . inequalities exist or else assert that they are due to individual misfortune rather than social injustice . . . it prevents conflicts between dominant and subordinate groups . . . by shaping wants, needs and preferences in such a way that both accept their role in the existing order . . . both [groups] . . . are unaware of their oppressive implications or incapable of imagining alternative ways of 'being and doing'.

In addition to both the 'oppressors' and the 'oppressed' conforming to their respective roles, as VeneKlasen and Miller (2002: 45) point out, 'in the absence of alternative models and relationships, people repeat the *power over* pattern in their personal relationships, communities and institutions . . . [they] imitate the oppressor'. A long-standing proponent of 'invisible power', Gramsci (1971) emphasised its role in maintaining social order with his theory of hegemony – the individual internalisation of ruling ideas. Foucault (1977) theorised the same process in terms of the commingling of power and knowledge and their operation in the form of 'discourse'.

Foucault's subsequent emphasis on micro-politics – a 'micro-physics' of power (1977: 26) – has represented a significant contribution to the history of ideas about the localised, capillary- or network-like nature of modern power (see for example Allen, 2003; Lukes, 2005; McLaren, 2002; McNay, 1992; McWhorter, 1999; Sawicki, 1991). Foucault's (1977) critique of macro 'power over' theories ('meta-power' analysis) highlighted the attachment of power to the coercive strategies of a sovereign state. He argued that modern power is a force constructing subjective discourses, through which power – derived from the authority of that discourse (truth) – can flow throughout the social body.

In Foucault's view, the traditional Hobbesian position that the essential tool of governance involves the state's monopoly over the legitimate use of force becomes obsolete. Instead, the essential tool of contemporary governance involves the ability to monopolise the construction and evolution of discourse (see Chapter 2). Discourse power is enmeshed in the production of systems of knowledge that define the boundaries of truth and, through this, the possible field of individual action. Individuals become complicit in the regulation of their own behaviour by internalising discourses and adhering to the behavioural norms embedded within them, thus setting up the power relations that operate in society (Foucault, 1977). Viewed this way, Foucault (cited in Allen, 2005: 6) described power as 'everywhere, not because it embraces everything, but because it comes from everywhere'.

Foucault presupposed that power is produced by widespread participation, much like Latour's (1986) notion of power as 'enrolment' (Wood and Shearing, 2007: 9) (see below). To have 'power' or be 'powerful', social actors must build constituencies for particular subjectivities, by means of 'an intense activity of enrolling, convincing and enlisting' (ibid.). In this light, 'strong' actors in modern society are those with a capacity to enrol others (Braithwaite and Drahos, 2000).

MOVING BEYOND 'POWER OVER': AGENCY AND EMPOWERMENT

Foucault viewed power as fundamentally positive or constitutive, whereby power and resistance 'create conditions of possibility for each other' (Simons, 1995: 81). This alternative proposition – the idea of power as positive and the capacity for individual agency within power structures – was premised on two theoretical assumptions. First, that wherever there is power there is resistance – an individual capacity to respond to the influence of power; power is a resource that 'endows subjects with some capacities required to be agents, even when it is oppressive' (Foucault, cited in Simons, 1995: 81). Second, for Foucault, power relations refer to 'the means by which individuals try to conduct, to determine, the behaviour of others' and thus relations of power 'do not solidify into states of complete domination' (ibid.). As Simons (1995: 82) argues, the 'recalcitrant actions of free subjects resisting attempts to direct their conduct are a necessary condition for the exercise of power'.

Despite creating the potential for agency ('resistance'), Foucault portrayed modern regimes of power/knowledge as 'tools of repression', frequently triumphant in disciplining social behaviour, thereby creating 'a sense of entrapment' for subjects of power structures (see O'Malley, 1996; O'Malley et al., 1997: 510; Simons, 1995: 83; Townsend et al., 1999; Benhabib, 1992; Benhabib et al., 1995; McNay, 1992). As Simons (ibid.) observes, 'Foucault's optimistic assertions about the possibility of resistance are unconvincing in comparison with his portrayals of domination' (see also Townsend et al., 1999; Hartsock, 1990; Fraser, 1989: 29; Mouffe, 1992).

Foucault's theoretical marginalisation of agency has led a number of contemporary theorists from various disciplines to pay central attention to agency, analysing how relatively powerless groups change, and even transform, their lives.[2] As a concept located in our very understanding of power, the notion of 'empowerment' is a contested one. On the one hand, empowerment is conceived in terms of Western liberalism and thus achieved through the marketplace: enterprise equals empowerment (Rowlands, 1995, 1998: 12; Mayo and Craig, 1995; Onyx and Benton, 1995; Hulme and Turner, 1990). This is an instrumentalist's view of empowerment: empowering the 'weak' is a strategic means to consolidating and expanding Western liberal capitalism (Rowlands, 1995).

Given the importance of power in institutions for determining how markets operate, a liberal view inadequately explains how markets deliver genuine empowerment (see for example Bhagwati, 2005). Obscuring structural inequalities (Townsend et al., 1999: 21), a liberal view of empowerment does not involve a structural change in power relations – empowerment is 'given' or 'delegated' to a person or group and can just as easily be taken away from them (Rowlands, 1995).

On the other hand, a post-liberal theorisation of empowerment envisages empowerment in structurally meaningful (i.e. non-liberal) terms (see Townsend et al., 1999: 30; Eyben et al., 2006; Chambers, 1997; Nelson and Wright, 1995; Hartsock, 1990; Hulme and Turner, 1990; Alcoff, 1990; Benhabib, 1992; Held, 1993; Allen, 2003). Power, or empowerment, takes the form of critical awareness, organisation, cooperation and deliberation, rather than the liberal tenets of individualism, bargaining and competition and the 'forms of rule' associated with it (see Eyben et al., 2006: 8; Townsend et al., 1999: 102; O'Malley, 1996: 312; Mouffe, 1997). As Townsend et al. (1999: 24) explain,

> Neoliberalism speaks of 'empowerment', but with reference to the electoral rights of the individual in the nation state . . . not empowerment of the community or the group, let alone a right to critical awareness. Postliberals . . . understand power as dispersed throughout human society. The micromechanisms of power at the local level produce local criticisms which, if organized politically, develop into strategies to resist the mechanisms of power.

Empowerment through this lens is 'a force exerted by an individual or group' (ibid.: 30), as a 'capacity to produce change' (Miller, 1982), and an 'affecting and transforming power but not a controlling power' (Hoagland, 1988). In this context, as Alsop (cited in Chambers, 2006: 100) argues, empowerment refers to 'enhancing an individual's or group's capacity to make purposive choices and transform that choice into desired actions and outcomes'. In this post-liberal reading – where Foucault's belief in 'power from below' is given central theoretical attention – dominant regimes are capable of being destabilised by, and subject to, a 'transformational' and 'indigenous' politics (O'Malley, 1996).[3] Not only is this latter alternative narrative capable of triggering change; it also exhibits decided heterogeneity, comprising as it does multiple 'situated knowledges'[4] (Nygren, 1999: 282) (see Chapters 5 and 7).

In essence, the emergent post-liberal movement in theorising empowerment reflects an evolution in the sociological quandary of agency and structure – the extent to which individuals make meaningful choices and act purposively within the confines of social structures. Traditionally, agency and structure have been portrayed in dichotomous terms, where *either* human freedom prevails and is unrestricted by social structures (humanism/liberalism) *or* structures determine social actors' circumstances and opportunities (structuralism/Marxism). Giddens (1984) dislodged this debate from its *impasse* with the idea that agency and structure have an iterative or mutually constitutive relationship whereby the notion of structure refers to a 'set of rules and resources integral to the conduct of individual and collective actors'.[5] From this perspective, people act on the basis of their knowledge of pre-existing structures, and, in so acting, reproduce those structures. In this sense, structures are not stand-alone forms, but rather are embedded in social interaction: structures are not static states, but mutually constitutive processes.

Social structures thus form the backdrop conditions for individual actions by presenting actors with options that are both enabling and constraining. When constraints – values, norms, rules and so on – are universal and in place for a long time, they tend to go unnoticed, leading to the durability of tradition (Bevir and Rhodes, 2005; Braithwaite, 2009). At the same time, as Bevir and Rhodes (2005: 4) point out recently with their concept of 'situated agency',[6] it cannot be assumed that all individuals are similarly affected by, or even recognise, the influence of 'tradition' and inherited rules, norms or values:

> We can accept that people always set out against the background of a social discourse or tradition and still think of them as agents who can act and reason in novel ways to modify this background . . . When we defend the capacity for agency . . . we do so recognising that it always occurs within a social context that influences it. Agency is not autonomous. It is 'situated'.

This evolution in thinking about the relationship between agency and structure underpins post-liberal ideas on power in the sense that they emphasise the capacity for agency and its diversity in the process of evolution. Post-liberal scholars work with three primary forms of individual and collective empowerment: 'power with', 'power to' and 'power within'.

'POWER WITH'

The 'power with' is a form of empowerment that describes 'the capacity to achieve with others what one could not do alone'. 'Power with' connotes a cooperative relationship in which individuals work together to 'multipl[y] individual talents and knowledge' (VeneKlasen and Miller, 2002: 45). As Gaventa (2006a: 24) argues, 'power with' means 'the synergy which can emerge through partnerships and collaboration with others, or through processes of collective action and alliance building'. 'Power with' thus relates to a group-oriented concept that Zapata (cited in Townsend et al., 1999: 150–63) sees as 'active at many levels, in joint projects, in the village, in the region, in the country and in the world'. Follett (1942) likewise proposed that 'power with' is a collective ability derived from reciprocal relationships among group members.

The idea of reciprocal and cooperative relationships runs counter to a liberal view that human beings will seek to dominate, out-compete or annihilate others to maximise their personal gain. 'Power with' assumes a positive-sum outcome whereby everybody gains from the operation and exercise of power and thus is largely 'dismissed as an impractical socialist ideal' within the context of a 'competitive world' (Townsend et al., 1999: 31). Other social scientists also differentiate postliberal notions of 'power with' from liberal notions of power:

> whereas the former [associational power] rests upon enablement and tends to stress the possibility of collective, integrative action, the latter term [instrumental power] refers to an instrumental ability to gain at the expense of another. Where one sees the possibility of collaboration, the other sees the potential for domination. (Allen, 2003: 51–2)

> Those who assume that power has only a distributive dimension ['power over'], and thus regard it as having a fixed volume, see little possibility for cooperative action and anticipate that existing powerholders will resist or co-opt any organisational initiative . . . The generative dimension of power ['power with'] points to the possibility that all members of a society or other social unit may benefit from an increase in its power if the increments in power are broadly shared within the group . . . this suggests an alternative to the economist's concept of economic man, based on individualism, selfishness and competitiveness. (Hulme and Turner, 1990: 214–15)

Latour (1986) takes a radical stance with the idea that by increasing the number of people involved, the generation of power is also greater. In 'The powers of association', Latour (1986) questions the guiding assumption in the social sciences that power is a tangible 'possession' of a person or institution. He argues that if nobody obeys an order, the person who issues it has no influence or power; the person or group 'in charge' is not powerful. As Latour (1986: 273) phrases it, power is not the 'cause of people's behaviour but . . . the consequence of an intense activity of enrolling, convincing and enlisting'. Or to put it another way, power can only be attributed to a person *ex post facto*, and the power is one born from collective action. In her early work on power in *The Human Condition*, Hannah Arendt (1958, cited in Allen, 2003: 53) stressed this idea:

> Power corresponds to the human ability not just to act but to act in concert. Power is never the property of an individual; it belongs to a group and remains in existence so long as the group keeps together. When we say of somebody that he is in power, we actually refer to his being empowered by a certain number of people to act in their name. The moment the group, from which the power originated to begin with disappears, 'his power' also vanishes.

A Latourian and Arendtian perspective on power adds insight into what sustains power over time: collective action. The implication is that exercising power to cause effects becomes an intense process of enrolment. Even dominant institutions, actors and groups depend on enrolling collective support for their ideas or actions (Braithwaite and Drahos, 2000).

'POWER TO'

Another type of empowerment is the 'power to'. This power is a form of agency and purposive choice (Chambers, 2006: 100). It is an additional capacity or ability, 'the capacity to empower or transform oneself and others' (Allen, 2005: 8). The 'power to', according to Townsend et al. (1999: 33), involves 'accessing a full range of human ability and potential'. 'Power to' is the strength and ability to act, to build new capacities and skills in order to 'build a future different from that mapped out by custom' (see also Nussbaum and Sen, 1993). For VeneKlasen and Miller (2002: 45), this form of power 'refers to the unique potential of every person to shape his or her life and world'. The capacity to act and relate in new ways and do new things implicitly challenges *status quo* relations and roles. As Zapata (cited in Townsend et al., 1999: 163) suggests, the 'power to' refers to 'the power to change relationships in the direction the individual [or group] wishes'.

'POWER WITHIN'

The ability to free up alternative discourses and imaginativeness involves a third dimension of power. Empowerment theorists describe it as 'power within' and view it as a 'precondition for action' (Gaventa, 2006a: 24). 'Power within' manifests as a form of internal strength, a 'confidence', self-awareness and sense of identity. According to Moser (cited in Townsend et

al., 1999: 30), this power 'is central to empowerment . . . [as it] seeks to identify power less in terms of domination over others . . . and more in terms of
the capacity . . . to increase . . . self-reliance and internal strength' (see also
Hartsock, 1990; Hoagland, 1988; Bandura, 1982, 1986). The 'power within'
contrasts with 'invisible power', the latter being a type of 'tyranny we exercise over ourselves' (Townsend et al., 1999: 131). Indeed, 'power within' is
the product of the defeat of 'power over' internal to the self and involves the
growth of self-esteem (Zapata, cited in Townsend et al., 1999).

Encouraging 'power within' can lead to broader social change, but liberation from 'invisible power' and the growth of 'power within' requires
awareness-raising to enable people to critically evaluate the norms, beliefs,
attitudes and values they hold to be true (Freire, 1996).[7] In this way, social
movements and minority groups can be seen to have long played the role of
encouraging the development of 'power within' for broader social change
to occur, and to do so in increasingly novel ways.[8] As Crano (cited in
Moscovici et al., 1994: 18) suggests,

> by its very existence, a minority transgresses group norms, thereby suggesting
> alternative ways of thinking . . . the minority causes cognitive conflict merely by
> making its position known. The conflict . . . can provoke people to re-examine
> their beliefs and actions . . . and such re-examination may result in attitude and
> behaviour change . . .

While feminists in this post-liberal orientation distinguish 'power with',
'power to' and 'power within' as different forms and levels of empowerment, they recognise that these categories are interconnected, 'overlapping'
processes of capacity-building that build on one another (Townsend et al.,
1999: 26). As scholars from other disciplines such as Chambers (2006: 100)
suggest, 'power with' and 'power within' combine as 'power to influence
and change . . . power over'. Proponents of these ideas see these forms of
power as enabling the realisation of greater freedom to change existing
structural and institutional constraints. Table 1.1 categorises the foregoing
overview of theorising power.

PUSHING THE EMPOWERMENT AGENDA:
'DEFIANCE' AND ENTREPRENEURSHIP OF NORMS

Despite the evolution of interdisciplinary knowledge about power, it
remains unclear how markets produce a post-liberal form of empowerment. On the one hand, the operation of markets is significantly determined by the exercise of institutional power. On the other hand, however,
evolutionary economists tell us that markets *do* transform, and the

Table 1.1   Two primary theoretical traditions in theorising power in the social sciences

Power as:	Form	Definition	Nature
Domination	'Power over'	The power of an institution, group or individual to carry out their will despite resistance, or to get others to act against their own will. Takes 'visible', 'invisible' and 'invisible' forms	Disempowering, instrumental, zero-sum, private gain, exclusive
Empowerment	'Power with'	The power to achieve with others what one could not achieve alone	Empowering, collaborative and cooperative, mutual gain, inclusive
	'Power to'	The power to act or do something, whether as a group or as an individual	Enabling, a capacity, empowering, agentic, inclusive, transformative
	'Power within'	Self-empowerment	Creative, self-confidence, self-awareness, a source of internal strength

transformation is triggered by specific actors: entrepreneurs (Schumpeter, 1934, 1943). In order to illuminate the possibility of structural change and genuine empowerment through markets, this chapter develops a post-liberal version of empowerment in a way that integrates an analysis of power into the process of market transformation.

THE REVOLUTIONARY ENTREPRENEUR

A prominent theorist in evolutionary economics, Schumpeter (1934) viewed entrepreneurship as the cause of revolutionary change in the marketplace.[9] For Schumpeter, the entrepreneurial act involves materialising 'new combinations' (innovations) in enterprise, including: the introduction of a new good or new quality of good; the introduction of a new method of production; the opening of a new market; the conquest of a new source of supply; and the creation of new organisational systems within an industry through structural adjustments (Schumpeter, 1949: 63–84).[10] 'New combinations' can therefore have structural implications: innovation – the exploitation of new knowledge (Harper, 1996) – disrupts stable market structures in 'sudden' and 'discontinuous' ways, overturning settled patterns and relationships instead of reaffirming them (Goyder, 1998: 13). In short, entrepreneurs can stimulate revolutionary change by exploiting new discourses to replace accepted practice. They are the cause of 'gales of creative destruction' that break up market concentration and move the economy forward: capitalism is dependent on entrepreneurship in order to evolve (Schumpeter, 1934).

In a Schumpeterian world, economic evolution pivots explicitly on the individual entrepreneur's capacity to eschew and revolutionise traditional ways of being, doing and thinking. However, Schumpeter did not examine the causes and preconditions of this key element in economic evolution – only its effects (Binks and Vale, 1990). He only hinted at the entrepreneur's evident capacity for critical reflection on, and rejection of, market norms, coining the term 'horizon' to suggest a broader-than-average 'range of choice' within which the entrepreneur 'moves freely' and makes the 'decision for a course of action'. The entrepreneur's 'horizon' had profound economic implications:

> there is [a] kind of change . . . which arises from within the system, and this kind of change is the cause of so many important economic phenomena that it seems worthwhile to build a theory for it, and . . . to isolate it from all other factors of change. . . . what we are about to consider is the kind of change arising from within the system which so displaces its equilibrium point that the new one cannot be reached from the old one by infinitesimal steps . . . (Schumpeter, cited in Binks and Vale, 1990: 23–4)

Subsequent economic theorising about the entrepreneur has not explained the mysterious agency and power of entrepreneurship that seems capable of rendering existing ideas, technologies and skills obsolete and rapidly replacing them with new market institutions and structures. For McGrath and MacMillan (2000: 94) for instance, entrepreneurship 'disrupts the rules of the game', leading to a 'breaking down [of] the barriers that cause the current market to be structured as it is'. For Robert and Weiss (1988: 5), innovation is an offensive, not a defensive, weapon in the process of change.

Telling descriptions though these are, evolutionary economists tend to neglect the role of power in determining the 'rules of the game' and structuring markets as between those business models that prevail, and those that are weak (see Chapter 7). In fact, evolutionary economists liken innovation to the Darwinian notion of genetic variation and view the market as a value-free mechanism for selecting the 'fittest' among competing species (see Nelson and Winter, 1982). Selection mechanisms 'favour one variety over another, from which one species is eliminated and the other prevails based on its adaptability' (Casson, 1999: xvii). Innovation (genetic variation) is a source of selection pressure, in response to which weaker species adopt the comparatively superior traits of the 'fittest' species (Casson, 1990: xvii; Foster and Metcalfe, 2001: 1–2).

The consequence is that it is not clear how power operates in the context of entrepreneurship. It is obscure how the entrepreneur is capable not only of creating thriving business innovations, but also of triggering transformation to existing market structures and institutions with those business models. Nor is it clear how and why the entrepreneur is constrained by power in the market such that his/her innovations are deemed 'weak' in, or even eliminated from, the marketplace. These unknowns about power in market evolution are all the more significant with respect to the unique type of entrepreneurship addressed in this book: entrepreneurship of norms. Entrepreneurs are traditionally conceived of as innovating in new products and doing so within capitalist market institutions for the purpose of profit (see Binks and Vale, 1990: 24). While the game-player is akin to Schumpeter's entrepreneur, he/she innovates not for profit-maximising reasons but rather for the specific purpose of transforming the normative basis of market structures (see Chapter 6). Hence the entrepreneurship in question here embodies an act of agency and positive power to change the prevailing neoliberal market regime: entrepreneurship of norms to reconstitute and transform the normative basis of markets, their values and processes. Entrepreneurship of norms is embodied in Braithwaite's notion of 'game-playing'.

DEFIANCE

'Defiance' is a term Braithwaite (2009; see also Braithwaite et al., 2007: 290–96) uses to describe the psychology of defying social structures and institutional constraints. It is an attitude or behaviour that social actors adopt when in a conscious process of questioning or rejecting 'the path laid out for them by an authority'. Defiance is a particular outlook on the world that may be expressed through words or actions, sometimes both. Defiance is deliberative: individuals have thought about their position and intend to convey the message that they reject blind acceptance and subservience to rules or authority. Defiance is a rational and healthy response that any individual is capable of making to the demands of society; it does not refer to abnormal or pathological psychological states or behaviours. As Braithwaite observes, when institutions cease to serve citizens well and when they dominate individual lives to the point where they cause distress or destruction, defiance by social actors is necessary for forging a path to institutional change. Defiance is thus a healthy micro-response of individuals to macro-social conditions that are harmful to, or destructive of, qualities that are important for individuals' self-definition or self-worth.

In support of a research agenda concerned with the 'situated' nature of agency and knowledge (Bevir and Rhodes, 2005; Nygren, 1999), 'defiance' explores and captures the heterogeneity in the dimensions and expressions of agency available to actors. Probing the complexity of 'defiance' supports the development of a more sophisticated theoretical account of how agency and power operate and interact in the process of change (see especially O'Malley, 1996; Nygren, 1999; see also Bevir and Rhodes, 2005: 4–5).

Along these lines, Braithwaite argues that engaging in defiance can take a number of different forms, or 'motivational postures' (see Braithwaite et al., 2007: 290–91). Motivational postures describe the internal beliefs and attitudes that determine the degree and nature of an individual's engagement with an authority. The analytical framework for posturing derives from large Australian empirical studies of the sociology of regulation (see Braithwaite, 1998, 2009; Braithwaite et al., 2007). Individuals assume postures when they have reason to express their belief in the dysfunctional nature and impact of existing institutions and structures on their social environment. These 'postures' include (but are not limited to) 'resistance' and 'game-playing'.

In Braithwaite's research, 'resistance' involves active defiance, and resisters want their criticisms heard and want to play a part in changing the system for the better. Resisters challenge regulations and regulatory administrators, yet not by creating new norms or rules. Rather, resisters work to inject the new ideas of others into the system. In order to do so, they 'yield' to the norms and constraints imposed by the existing order. As Braithwaite et al. (2997: 292) describe, 'resisters often lose the argument and succumb to become a compliant citizen of the regulatory order over time'. The resistance posture achieves only limited and incremental gains, or what Berlin (1958) would term 'negative liberty'.[11]

Game-playing is a more 'imaginative' and 'bold' form of defiance than resistance. It involves defying or transcending regulatory constraints through 'moving around or redefining the rules' (Braithwaite, 2009). This response involves 'keen engagement with the regulatory code', and 'using the code to dismantle or change the regulatory system'. Game-players innovate where there is an absence of recognition of authority: they think 'outside the square' rather than acknowledge, let alone work within, the confines of convention. The 'game-player' is a creative and visionary individual seeking transformation of his/her regulatory environment to realise a Berlinian 'positive liberty'.[12] Furthermore, the game-player exhibits an 'entrepreneurial mindset'[13] (see Chapter 6) and qualities of the classic entrepreneur who 'is rendered by the notion of a creative, convention-defying individual entrepreneur, making innovative decisions . . . in the face of a hostile, or at the least a passively resistant, environment' (Cauthorn, 1989: 15). The game-player personifies this portrait in his/her attempt to transform market norms.

On the one hand, then, resistance and game-playing occupy opposite ends of a spectrum of agency – one is conservative, the other radical (though these two categories are by no means rigid or homogeneous; see Chapter 5), thereby achieving different degrees of structural freedom. Endowed with different 'horizons' or degrees of 'situated agency' (Bevir and Rhodes, 2005: 4), individuals have diverse styles of challenging dominant narratives, based on different constraints from which they perceive, and interact differently with, institutional structures. These various forms of institutional engagement cause different institutional impacts. Game-playing involves not only the rejection of norms and institutional structures, but also the creation of new structures liberated from their institutional moorings. In this regard, and as this book aims to show, game-playing appears to hold the potential for agency and empowerment of both self and others by freeing structures from their traditional institutional anchors, producing new structures and institutions (see Chapter 7).

On the other hand, resistance and game-playing share a symbiotic existence in the context of social movement politics (see Braithwaite, 1998). The motivation underpinning resistance lies in the resisters' structural location in capitalist market institutions.[14] Resisters institutionalise alternative models or regimes into those capitalist institutions rather than seek institutional transformation. Resisters do the 'hard sell and execute model implementation', transporting game-players' radical models from the periphery to the centre (see Chapter 4) to make money out of the propagation of the model (see Chapter 5). In other words, resisters exploit game-players' innovations in social movement politics (see Chapters 5–7), turning game-players' 'toeholds into footholds'.

In the process of institutionalisation, resisters seek engagement with conventional actors; a process of negotiation and compromise which tends to result in resisters' capture (see Ayres and Braithwaite, 1992) and the modification of game-players' radical models (see Chapter 5). Resisters do not aim to change institutional actors' motivations, but simply to convince those actors of the attractiveness (political, economic, cultural or otherwise) of the model. Game-players by contrast refuse to play within the rules of the game and instead invent new rules as a means of enabling an evolution in the normative basis of markets (see Chapters 6 and 7).

With an analytical typology of different dimensions of expressing agency and strategies for its exercise, Braithwaite's defiance framework offers a more sophisticated lens for probing the array of individual psychologies for challenging authority structures. This yields an opportunity to understand more deeply and processually how, and to what extent, different social actors exercise agency and influence social structures. 'Game-playing' is of particular interest in this book, and explaining how power operates in the game-playing context contributes theoretical knowledge about power in the process of market evolution. Beyond the level of individual psychology with which Braithwaite deals, there are two levels of game-playing that are of significance in the process of causing large-scale change through markets. These are the levels of agency (primarily collective agency) and structure (transnational structure), discussed in turn below. Through this elaboration, a conceptual model of empowerment is developed to illustrate and explain how game-playing operates at these levels (see Figure 1.1).

'DEFIANCE GROUPS': SOCIAL CONNECTIONS FOR COLLECTIVE AGENCY

Game-players are cognisant of the intersection between collective agency and structure, whereby collective action spawns new structural patterns. Defiance is more sustained and threatening to social order when it is supported by others and is socially organised (Tajfel, 1978). Game-players have a worldview that sees the potential for power as residing in 'social connections' between otherwise disconnected social actors.

The term 'social connections' was coined by Iris Marion Young (2004), who suggests that social actors can engage in the process of social change in different ways and at different levels of the social structure.[15] Young suggests that structural injustice persists because of an absence of questioning and challenging the *status quo*. In other words, it persists because of the influence of 'invisible power':

> Most of us contribute to a greater or lesser degree to the production and repro-
> duction of structural injustice precisely because we follow the accepted norms
> and expected rules and conventions of the communities and institutions in
> which we act. (Young, 2004: 29)

Given Young's suggestion that structural inequity is maintained because 'we follow the accepted norms and expected rules and conventions' – i.e. defiance is absent – Braithwaite's framework becomes particularly relevant

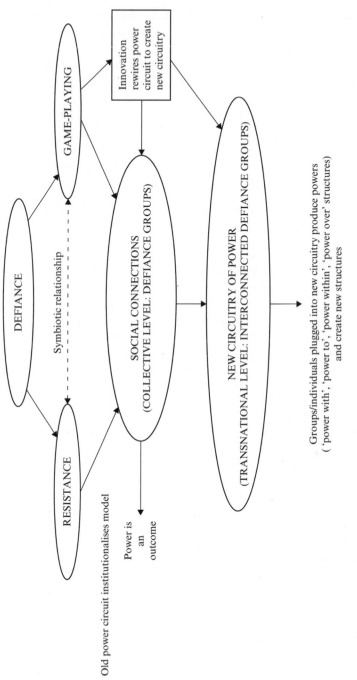

DEFIANCE

GAME-PLAYING

RESISTANCE

Symbiotic relationship

Innovation rewires power circuit to create new circuitry

SOCIAL CONNECTIONS (COLLECTIVE LEVEL: DEFIANCE GROUPS)

NEW CIRCUITRY OF POWER (TRANSNATIONAL LEVEL: INTERCONNECTED DEFIANCE GROUPS)

Old power circuit institutionalises model

Power is an outcome

Groups/individuals plugged into new circuitry produce powers ('power with', 'power to', 'power within', 'power over' structures) and create new structures

Figure 1.1 A conceptual model of empowerment

for understanding how the processes of structural change are triggered at the micro-level. From Young's perspective, since all individuals participate 'in the diverse institutional processes that produce structural injustice', only collective action can overcome the creation and reproduction of structural injustice:[16]

> millions of agents contribute by our actions in particular institutional contexts to the processes that produce unjust outcomes . . . responsibility consists of changing the institutions and processes so that their outcomes will be less unjust. None of us can do this on our own . . . The structural processes can be altered only if many actors in diverse social positions work together to intervene in them to produce different outcomes. (Young, 2004: 32)[17]

Young's 'social connections' framework is a useful starting point for conceptualising how game-players navigate and harness power strategically in complex systems to produce large-scale outcomes. Modern governance[18] involves far more than the existence of a sovereign state (see Rose and Miller, 1992; Scott, 2004; Slaughter, 1997; Rhodes, 1997). Rather, governance refers to a phenomenon that is deeply complex and networked in the production of outcomes, much more so than regulatory and socio-legal theories accommodate (Burris et al., 2005; Castells, 1996, 2000; see for example Hayek, 1960).[19] In the context of multiple actors, levels and mechanisms, conceptualising how power is commanded, distributed and produced becomes far more challenging an exercise and one that finds scholars often 'cling[ing] to the old [theoretical] models, working ever harder to fit the phenomena we observe into the forms of the past' (Burris et al., 2005: 32).

Young's social connections model reflects this search for more empirically accurate tools for explaining the micro-processes by which order and outcomes are produced in modern society. Her model blends the notion of structure with the dynamic and complex processes of change. For this reason it is a useful framework for considering how game-playing affects markets in structurally significant terms. Figure 1.1 sets up the inductively based conceptual model of how game-playing operates at the collective and transnational level, which we shall see brought to life in the book's exploration of the fair trade movement.

At the level of collective agency, this model explicates game-players' worldview of power as distinctly Latourian, interpreting power as an outcome of collective action (Youngian 'social connections' between group members). Game-players make new social connections obtainable for social actors and groups through innovation. Innovation destabilises organisational and knowledge hierarchies (see Achrol and Kotler, 1999; Schumpeter, 1934), and game-players exploit the opportunities afforded by networks to expand new models of social and economic organisation (see Chapters 4, 6 and 7).[20] Game-players' innovations make new social connection possible, rewiring circuits of power to create new circuitries that move around 'old' or institutional circuits. Based on Latour's insight that power is the product of collective action/support, innovative models have the capacity to generate power (in terms of freedom and new capacities for actors) if sufficient numbers of people link up with or 'buy into' the model.

By innovating in new models of organisation that build new bridges between social actors and foster new collectivities of action, group members tap their collective knowledge and capacities as well as gain new capabilities. In Figure 1.1, these groups of individuals are referred to as 'defiance groups'. Defiance groups produce power through collective action (Chapters 4, 6 and 7). From a Hayekian (1960) perspective, such groups contribute influence or value by way of concentrating the diffused knowledge and capacity residing in many decentralised sites of activity and decision-making. When coordinated and facilitated, this concentration of contextual resources and 'wisdom' (Braithwaite, 2004: 308) is enabling and enhancing. The notion that mobilising localised knowledge and capacities is of benefit to the entire network is analogous to Putnam's (2000) idea of social capital as a valuable resource generated by and accessible to networked individuals.[21]

For Shearing and Wood (2003) and Burris et al. (2005), these localised sources of knowledge are 'nodes' along networks that are both conceptually and practically more important than networks themselves for explaining the augmentation of diffused knowledge and resources, and how outcomes are thereby produced. The conceptualisation of empowerment in Figure 1.1 adds to these ideas an understanding of the entrepreneurial actors (game-players) who deploy networked governance arrangements strategically as a means of producing power to trigger transformation. In short, coordinated group action becomes a powerhouse of new capacities and strengths from which members benefit. This reciprocal nature of the power generated by game-playing becomes important at the structural level. Indeed, this mode of organisation can liberate new knowledge systems, which in turn can challenge dominant discourses (see Chapter 7).

INTERCONNECTED DEFIANCE GROUPS: NEW CIRCUITS OF POWER FOR TRANSNATIONAL STRUCTURAL CHANGE

The multiple social connections between disparate defiance groups, the power from whose action coalesces at the transnational level, produces new 'circuits' of power from which new power flows forth. New power is produced only if many people hook up – and continue to hook up – to form and expand new circuitries of power. This point is important: the model (or circuit-board) does not presuppose power but it does presuppose people plugging into it. Power does not precede or cause macro-diffusion. Rather, the amount of power produced is directly proportional to the number of actors enrolled in the composition (Latour, 1986; Arendt, 1958). This essential process of groups mimicking or 'modelling' (Braithwaite, 1994) others by 'plugging in' to the model is a recognised strategy by which micro-action causes macro-change (see also Braithwaite and Drahos, 2000; Braithwaite, 2004). Enrolling many 'defiance groups' concentrates dispersed pockets of power to create new circuitries of power at the transnational level.[22]

The macro-dimension of game-playing develops when players engage multiple groups to participate in new transnational relations. Game-players make connections realisable through their innovative models. The operation of game-playing at the collective and transnational level has a double effect: it mobilises capacities and knowledge, and harnesses them at the transnational level to produce outcomes and new power flows. In turn, these new flows benefit and liberate the myriad of groups that collectively produce it. 'Weak ties' (Granovetter, 1973) link together widely dispersed, heterogeneous groups (geographically or culturally). From a Putnamian (2000) perspective, heterogeneous connections build bridges or generate 'bridging social capital' between diverse groups in the sense that they encourage the spread and percolation of ideas, resources and opportunities in society.[23] Linked at the macro-level by game-players' models, groups co-produce transnational circuitries of power as a result of the mobilisation of their group resources and capacity. Interconnected participation in an alternative structure and set of institutional processes has transnational effects: interconnected defiance groups bring together individuals to participate in defying structures that make a difference to collectivities and foster new structural patterns.

EXPANDING THE BOUNDS OF EMPOWERMENT: THE LENS OF DEFIANCE

This book takes a primary interest in game-playing as it manifests defiance in a form that brings about radical change and leads to the creation of new institutions and structures at the transnational level. While not explicitly addressed, the issue of power underscores the above conceptualisation of the freedom and power in game-playing, and the game-player's structural significance. The following questions help to structure this enquiry into how agency is able to shift structure when the reverse is normally true:

1. How do social actors cause large-scale market outcomes? (Chapter 4)
2. How do power and agency operate in the institutional sequence of resistance? (Chapter 5)
3. How do power and agency operate in the context of game-playing? (Chapter 6)
4. How does game-playing change the institutional environment? (Chapter 7)

The book is based on an in-depth empirical analysis of the fair trade movement; therefore the categories of power used in the book carry meanings specific to this analysis. These include 'power over', 'power with', 'power to', 'power within', 'power beyond'.

'Power Over'

'Power over' refers to a process by which a person, organisation or group restricts the options, abilities and capacities of others through certain mechanisms. These various mechanisms include 'power over' in its visible, hidden or invisible forms. 'Power over' is exercised through control, manipulation, exclusion or invalidation of others, whether via knowledge production, information, scale or legal ownership. 'Power over' is activated when actors or organisations exploit its instruments to protect their influence and control over outcomes and thus preserve the *status quo*. These mechanisms deny or subvert the inclusion of weaker actors and their ability to access or own the resources of power.

'Power With'

'Power with' refers to a process by which individual people, organisations and groups together create capacity in order to bring about certain objectives and processes that are collectively shared and beneficial. This is a group-centred and process-oriented concept. 'Power with' is generated by interconnected social units (families, workplaces, schools, businesses, universities, communities), connections that are established on the basis of tools imbued with, or created for the purpose of nurturing and expanding, a supported philosophy. These tools include websites, trade marks, businesses, markets, local activities, events or practices. 'Power with' is switched on when individuals, groups and/or organisations engage in habitual support of these tools (see 'power to').

'Power To'

'Power to' refers to the performance of an action or actions through which individuals, groups and/or organisations gain new capacities, skills and abilities to trigger change. It is a concept of an infinite nature, and occurs at individual, collective and interconnected levels of action. The 'power to' is activated when models are created by game-players and then activated by social networks that support the expansion of those models. They are designed to benefit diverse groups, affirming group values and building group capacities to effect change. Exercising 'power to' is empowering; it is an avenue for new behaviours and ways of thinking that lead to change (see 'power within').

'Power Within'

'Power within' refers to a unique psychological outlook and set of behaviours embodied in the game-player (an entrepreneur of norms). 'Power within' is an internal power or strength and an acute critical awareness of dominant social structures and institutional constraints. Although it is an individual power, in this thesis the game-player's 'power within' is exercised for distinctly collective and pro-social ends. That is, game-players exercise 'power within' (manifest in creativity, vision, persistence and determination) to empower those who are disadvantaged by dominant market power structures. 'Power within' involves more than the rejection of the authority of the *status quo*. In particular, it involves exploiting, or innovating in, alternative discourses that unleash new rules, norms, institutions and structures, and destabilise 'power over' in its visible, hidden and invisible forms.

GAME-PLAYING, 'FREE STRUCTURES' AND 'POWER BEYOND'

As the story of fair trade reveals, by working around – and independently of – institutional politics to build new structures, game-players do not rely on 'winning over' those who control traditional power circuits. The new configurations are a creation of their creator, and not subject to formal/traditional regulation. Instead, game-players make possible the exercise of 'power beyond' old power circuits (the 'powers that be'), utilising network opportunities and connections, and rewiring circuits of power to build new, 'free' structures. The foregoing formulation of how game-playing initiates structural change processes construes structures as 'free'. The concept of 'free structures' injects into the notion of structure greater fluidity, latitude, opportunity and potential for ingenuity than is readily accommodated in existing accounts of power.

'Power beyond' ('power over' structures) refers to the cumulative effect of new structural processes. No one can alone create 'power beyond', and it cannot be created by or through existing institutional constraints and interests. Hence 'power beyond' is realised not through resistance but through game-playing. In resistance, power is pulsed through 'old wires' of power. Old wires are already under the control of authority structures. When resisters institutionalise the new configurations in old circuits, once-free structures are rendered 'unfree' by those power circuitries. As threats to the *status quo*, 'free structures' face the perennial possibility of capture. For this reason, 'free structures' are in the process of constant creation, or 'creative destruction' (Schumpeter, 1934); perpetual new acts of entrepreneurial rewiring of power circuits enable the pursuit of freedom to continue.

NOTES

1. 'Power over' underlines realist thought in international relations. For realist theorists such as Carr (1946), Morgenthau (1948), Gilpin (2001) and Krasner (1991), the world is anarchic, and relies upon a hegemon to provide stability in world order. The hegemon today, the USA (in the nineteenth century, the UK), is able to exert utmost influence over other state actors and act in isolation from them to achieve its objectives (these objectives being tied to national security). Yet it will also defect and cooperate when its self-interest depends on doing so in order to achieve its desired outcomes (based on the 'prisoner's dilemma' theory). For an alternative perspective focused on post-hegemony and international cooperation, see Keohane (1984) and Keohane and Nye (2000). This conceptualisation of power can also be found in several strands of feminist theory, principally phenomenological, radical, socialist and poststructuralist feminist theories (see Allen, 2005).
2. Two classic writers in this mould are de Certeau (1984) and Scott (1985).
3. Indigenous governance refers to 'forms of government that arise in, and are endemic to, the everyday lives of subjects' (O'Malley, 1996: 313). It is unlike liberal governance, which imposes governance 'from without'. In this sense, indigenous governance is also an endogenous system of governance.
4. 'Situated knowledges' refers to an analytical orientation that assumes that social actors' representations of the world will be highly diverse and fluid, and thus overlooked by sharply defined conceptual categories (such as 'Western science' versus the 'people's science', 'modernity' versus 'tradition', or 'local' versus 'global'). Portrayed in such a way, 'totalising theories' that construct crude boundaries between local and dominant discourses become inadequate for enhancing social scientists' knowledge about those they study and their influence upon the discourses that permeate their lives (Nygren, 1999).
5. Structures comprise and include the roles of different institutions; surrounding physical structures; the use of resources; and allocated routines, all of which form the historical givens for individual action and reflection. For a critique of Giddens, see Archer (1990).
6. 'Situated agency' portrays agency as, on the one hand, contextualised by social actors'

background (i.e. the social background influences individual beliefs and subjectivities), and on the other hand, a meaningful and novel capacity for actors to modify, even transform, their social background (Bevir and Rhodes, 2005: 4–5).

7. The idea of popular education was popularised by Paulo Freire (1996) in Latin America in his work with the poorer classes, viewing them as holding the key to their own liberation once having learned of the *status quo* norms and patterns maintaining their oppression.

8. Contemporary business/marketing theorists discuss the notion of 'social marketing' as a novel way in which social organisations are challenging 'ruling ideas' to shift societal values, attitudes and behaviour (see Golding and Peattie, 2005: 160). Social marketing draws on commercial marketing principles for the purpose of 'changing behaviour to increase the wellbeing of individuals and/or society' and to promote a social aim or 'proposition' (ibid.), to benefit the broader collective/society (Andreasen, cited in ibid.). Young and Welford (cited in Nicholls and Opal, 2005: 166) view contemporary social movement work as exemplary social marketing – a mix of 'marketing, education and campaigning'.

9. Of all the key modern economists, only Schumpeter focused his energies on entrepreneurship and the entrepreneur's impact on capitalism (Drucker, 1985: 13). Leading contemporary economists studying entrepreneurship and innovation include Howard Stevenson (with others, 2006, 1991, 1986) and Peter Drucker (1985). The study of entrepreneurship is divided into two primary camps (see Berger, 1991). The former, from the school of economics, views entrepreneurship as a variable dependent on economic factors – as a response to exogenous forces. This camp proposes that entrepreneurial activities will occur spontaneously when economic conditions are favourable. They emphasise the crucial role of the availability of capital, access to markets, labour supply, raw materials and technology. Social scientists other than economists view entrepreneurship as a variable deeply embedded in culture (see for instance Weber, 1958), simultaneously produced by and productive of it. The unique psychological attributes of the class of actor referred to as entrepreneurs also fit within this latter camp (Berger, 1991: 20; on the psychology of the entrepreneur, see McClelland and Winter, 1964).

10. McGrath and MacMillan (2000: 93–7) observe that entrepreneurs create 'radical' and 'revolutionary' reconfigurations of markets that can force existing business models, reliant on 'business-as-usual' structures, to become obsolete. Radical reconfigurations involve the creation of a new business model, which renders obsolete conventional business models of unacceptable or lesser-valued attributes. Revolutionary reconfigurations reshape current business models entirely, delivering a product or service with 'completely new and different attributes'.

11. According to Berlin (1958), actors who seek 'negative liberty' aim to preserve the existing range or field of action available to them and to prevent further restrictions to that range.

12. In contrast to negative liberty, 'positive liberty' is an attempt to expand one's capacities and liberties – to express self-mastery and self-determination – by seeking a broader field of action than institutions allow (Berlin, 1958).

13. The 'entrepreneurial mindset' is the name McGrath and MacMillan (2000: 2–3) give to their book on entrepreneurial thinking and behaviour, in which they attempt to define the characteristic attitude of the entrepreneur.

14. A striking similarity can be drawn between Val Braithwaite's (2009) resisters and John Braithwaite's (1994) 'model mercenaries'. As John Braithwaite (1994) explains, the motivations of model mercenaries are rooted in their structural location in capitalist market institutions. Their role in the process of model diffusion is to transport radical models from the periphery and institutionalise them in the centre for the purpose of 'cashing in' on the propagation of the model. As he describes them, model mercenaries 'do the hard sell' and 'execute model implementation'. Chapter 7 shows the similarity between model mercenaries' motivations and strategy and that of the 'resisters' in this book.

15. Young's (2004) reconceptualisation of structure and agency within transnational structures offers a particularly contemporary framework for considering the expression of individual and collective agency within global market structures.

16. Young (2004) distinguishes different social actors/groups as regards their responsibility in terms of varied levels of power/influence, privilege, interest and collective ability. The purpose of the model is to conceptualise the complexity of responsibility in the production and reproduction of structural injustices, and the means by which action at all levels may be taken to change them.

17. In her conceptualisation of socially structured actors as endowed with different capacities to trigger change processes, Young envisages a process of change in which 'different kinds of issues and directions for action' are taken by individuals. A Bourdieuian conceptualisation of 'fields' (social, political, economic, cultural) is a useful way of thinking about the different spatial locations in which change processes may be enacted or power exercised by actors of different social positions.

18. Governance is taken here to mean the influence on and management of the 'flow of events' (see Burris et al., 2005; Parker and Braithwaite, 2003; Wood and Shearing, 2007: 6).

19. Analysing the market as a basis for understanding how order is produced out of the tacit and diffuse knowledge and dispersed action of many market agents, Hayek (1960) argued that centrally planned, top-down control of markets was highly undesirable. In his view, this type of governance frustrated and interfered with the market's own capacity to produce 'spontaneous order'.

20. Numerous authors, Castells (1996, 2000) in particular, observe the global networking of information and its value on the internal or organic ordering of contextual complexity over the managerial competence attributed to yesteryear central planning (see Braithwaite, 2004: 305–9; Rhodes, 1997; Slaughter, 1997). In a world of networked governance, strong business models and nations are those that take advantage of networked arrangements of governance and organisation.

21. Social capital describes 'the collective value of all social networks and the inclinations that arise from these networks to do things for each other' (Putnam, 2000).

22. From a Hayekian (1960) perspective, this transnational-level circuitry of power (interconnected defiance groups) is the ordering produced by coordination of the diffused knowledge and capacity located at and generated by the collective action level (defiance groups).

23. While Putnam's concept of social capital was developed to explain national-level phenomena, it can be extrapolated to the international level of networked communities that transcend national boundaries and wherein the collective activity and connection between a community benefits not only that community but also another, more distant, community (or set of communities) (see Nicholls and Opal, 2005: 174).

2. 'Power over' as global power in world markets

A key theme in the history of ideas about power is 'power over': the ability to get one person or group to get another person or group to do something against their will (see Chapter 1). In the shift from an industrial to a post-industrial economy (Toffler, 1980; Drucker, 1969; Bell, 1978), 'power over' can be seen as having shifted from the hegemony of the state to the hegemony of global corporations. The brand is the basis of corporate hegemonic power. It is an image of the trade mark, itself an abstract object that embodies a set of legal rights of ownership that have recently been deepened and globalised (Drahos with Braithwaite, 2002; Bellman et al., 2005). This chapter outlines how corporate 'power over' has become global power: through the ownership of abstract objects in world markets (see Drahos, 1996). A psychological theory of the image explains how the image – and therefore the brand – works to influence consumers' subjectivity. Added to this is a theory of abstract objects and intellectual property (ibid.) that explains how the image is the subject of exclusive proprietorial control. The modern history of the global coffee market – a vignette of transformations in North–South agricultural trade relations and the broader economy – brings to life these psycho-social and legal machinations of corporate hegemonic power.

A MODERN HISTORY OF THE GLOBAL COFFEE MARKET

After World War II and until a quarter of a century ago, agro-industrial development and trade in tropical agricultural commodities between the South and North were premised on Keynesian economics and international commodity agreements. This system of mass production of undifferentiated products for mass consumption in Western markets effectively stabilised prices and production levels, but over the course of the 1980s was aggressively superseded by the now-dominant global economic doctrine of neoliberalism. Consider coffee. From the early 1960s until 1989 the coffee market had been managed effectively under the International Coffee

Agreement (ICA). The ICA was designed to maintain relative market stability and high prices: aside from a few price spikes due to Brazilian frosts, the world price for coffee (the 'C' price) fluctuated between US$1.00 and US$1.50 (Jaffee, 2007: 42), and producer and consumer nations together set quotas for producing countries to maintain stable supply levels. Unless the price of coffee rose above this range, in which case producing countries were permitted to increase their supply levels, producing countries kept within their fair share of production levels (Oxfam, 2002: 17).

Until its collapse at the end of the 1980s, the ICA created favourable conditions for producing countries in the coffee trade (Talbot, 1997a: 71). The ICA was an amicable arrangement for the major market stakeholders involved: it enabled producer countries to organise collectively at the international level and thus secure higher export incomes from coffee; it facilitated consumer countries' 'somewhat disguised' provision of economic assistance to strategic Third World allies; and it stabilised both supplies and prices of coffee as well as enabling healthy profits for multinational coffee companies.

It has been written that the abolition of the ICA (on 4 July 1989) symbolised the death of an old era (of Keynesian economics) and the birth of a modern free market era (Dicum and Luttinger, 1999: 95). It was no coincidence that the ICA dissolved simultaneously with the collapse of the Soviet Union (Wild, 2005: 3). At the time of the ICA's disbanding, the Soviet Union had collapsed, multinational corporations (MNCs)[1] had gained control over key markets, and *laissez-faire* economics was being widely embraced (Talbot, 1997a: 71). The final straw for the ICA was the irreconcilable disagreements between the ICA's members and pressure from the then Reagan administration for trade liberalisation (Fairtrade Foundation, 2002: 7; Renkema, 2002: 59–60).

Immediately after the ICA's collapse, coffee prices plummeted to US$0.49/pound and remained there for the following five years – their lowest record in history and well below producers' production costs. Subsequent price increases in 1994/5 and 1997 (resulting from frosts in Brazil, the world's largest coffee producer) only aggravated a growing oversupply of coffee as Vietnam became a leading exporter (second only to Brazil).[2] The massive glut in supply devalued the two types of coffee bean, robusta and arabica coffee,[3] causing high-quality coffee typically sold at US$1.60/pound to drop to only 48 cents (Fairtrade Foundation, 2002: 16), and the 'C' price to drop to US$0.41/pound in 2001. By 2002, coffee was trading at its lowest levels in three decades (see Figure 2.1).

The cumulative consequences of the all-time low in the price of coffee have been severe and long-lasting. According to one estimate, in the six years between 1994 and 2001 coffee-producing countries lost around

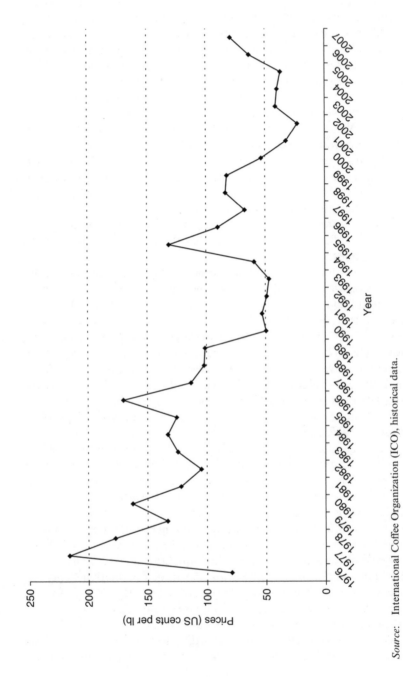

Source: International Coffee Organization (ICO), historical data.

Figure 2.1   Fluctuation in world 'C' price between 1976 and 2007

Table 2.1   Share of coffee in total export receipts (average 1995–99)

	Share of total exports (1995–99 average)	GNP/capita ($) (1995–99 average)
Burundi	76	146
Ethiopia	68	106
Rwanda	62	274
Uganda	60	310
El Salvador	26	1886
Guatemala	26	1608
Honduras	25	734
Colombia	17	2424
Brazil	5	4684

Source: Fitter and Kaplinsky (2001: 8).

US$32 billion. Equally revealing, a report estimated that whereas a decade ago producing countries received US$10 billion from a US$30 billion world market, these countries collectively receive less than US$6 billion from a market now doubled in its value (Oxfam, 2002: 20; see also Renkema, 2002: 59).[4] This loss is significant in developmental terms – coffee is produced in over 60 countries, employing more than 25 million farmers and up to 100 million worldwide in the industry. As one of the most valuable primary commodities in global trade (second only to oil), coffee is a significant source of foreign exchange and a vital commodity for national economies, as can be seen from Table 2.1.

POST-FORDIST MARKETS AND COFFEE: CORPORATE 'POWER OVER' PRODUCERS, PROFITS AND PRICES

The lift in the market price to around US$0.95 in 2006 has done little to eliminate price fluctuations – and the more consistent and pervasive problem of highly exploitative market relations. Producers' economic conditions have been structurally worsened by deeper processes of de-industrialisation and market concentration in the North, and increased industrial capacity in the South. Not isolated to coffee, the real price of primary commodities (and manufactures) has progressively declined alongside an exponential rise in the value of intangible assets (Gereffi, 1994; Piore and Sabel, 1984; Kaplinsky and Morris, 2001). Tables 2.2 and 2.3 demonstrate this paradox of declining commodity prices alongside

*Table 2.2   World commodity price changes since 1980, taking inflation
             into account ($US/tonne)*

	1980s prices adjusted for inflation	2002 prices	2002 as % of adjusted 1980
Copra	904	260	28.8
Coconut oil	1439	420	29.2
Palm oil	1345	312	23.8
Sugar	553	126	22.8
Cocoa	6174	1190	19.2
Coffee	8696	1234	14.2
Tea	4061	1920	47.3
Pepper	4303	1550	36.0
Groundnuts	2060	650	37.5
Jute	804	400	49.7
Cotton	3656	793	21.1
Rubber	3117	650	20.9

Source: Robbins (2003: 9). Copyright © Peter Robbins, 2003. By permission of Zed
Books, London and New York.

*Table 2.3   Recent profit record of major traders and processors of tropical
             commodities*

Date announced	Company	% profit increase	Account period
16/08/02	Cargil	131	2002 fiscal
15/02/02	Cadbury	12	2001
02/08/02	Unilever	33	1st half 2002
23/08/02	Nestlé	79	1st half 2002
19/07/02	Kraft	17	2nd quarter
02/08/02	Starbucks	20	3rd quarter fiscal
11/10/02	Sara Lee	21	1st quarter fiscal

Source: Adapted from Robbins (2003: 16). Copyright © Peter Robbins, 2003. By
permission of Zed Books, London and New York.

significant profit increases among dominant firms processing, distributing
and trading agricultural commodities.

Dominant in agricultural commodity production and dependent on it
for socio-economic development, developing countries have been forced
on to a track of immiserising growth – increasing their export volumes
in return for less (see Figure 2.2). In Ethiopia, the birthplace of coffee,

Index (1985 = 1, harmonic scale)

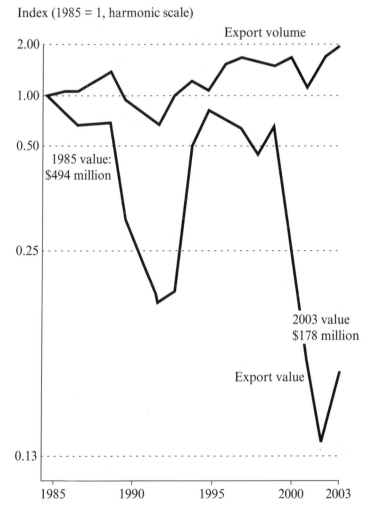

Export volume

1985 value:
$494 million

2003 value
$178 million

Export value

Source: Cited in UNDP (2005).

Figure 2.2   Coffee prices and production in Ethiopia

coffee export volumes have increased by two-thirds since mid-1990, yet
export earnings have fallen steeply over the same period. In markets such
as cocoa, producers' share of value-added has declined from 60 per cent
to 28 per cent in the last three decades (Vorley, 2003: 22), while chocolate
prices have risen by 300 per cent since 1980 (Robbins, 2003: 16). In a rising
consumer market worth more than US$75 billion per year, the world's 14

Consumers

Retailers   30 grocers = 33% of global market

Roasters   3 companies (Philip Morris, Nestlé and
                                                   Sara Lee) = 45% of global coffee market
                                                   (2001)

International traders   4 companies (Neumann, Volcafe,
                                                   ECOM, Dreyfus) ~ 39% of global market

Domestic traders

Smallholder/estate   25 million farmers and workers

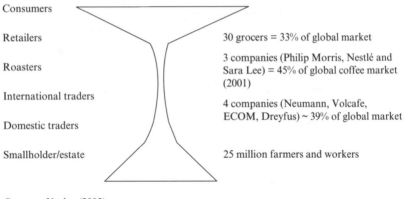

Source: Vorley (2003).

Figure 2.3   The 'bottleneck' in the global coffee industry

million cocoa producers receive just US$4 billion and cocoa prices have declined by 50 per cent since 2003 (*The Economist*, 4 April 2007).

Increasing market concentration among brand manufacturers and (more recently and rapidly, retailers) in the North has enabled these market actors to play a dominant role in controlling agricultural markets and prices via the development of new, fragmented structures of production called global commodity chains (Vorley, 2003; Gereffi, 1994). It is through these chain structures that global retailers, traders and brand companies connect the world's producers and consumers. These actors not only put significant downward pressure on commodity prices, but are also formidable gatekeepers to agricultural producers seeking market access. In 2002, the 30 leading retailers accounted for 33 per cent of global sales in contrast to 29 per cent just three years earlier (Vorley, 2003: 28).

The global coffee industry offers a stunning example of these trends in corporate concentration and expansion, particularly among brands (roasters) (see Figure 2.3). Since the 1970s, a small number of multinational corporations (MNCs) has come to dominate over 80 per cent of global coffee consumption (Talbot, 1997b: 119). In 1992, only four MNCs controlled 70 per cent of the global coffee market, including Sara Lee Corporation (USA), Proctor & Gamble (USA), Nestlé (Switzerland) and Kraft Foods Inc. (USA) (Hudson and Hudson, 2003: 2). This 'bottleneck' has produced an extreme power imbalance between these companies and the 25 million small-scale coffee producers[5] who produce 50 per cent of the world's coffee supply, and impacts enormously on international coffee prices (see Green, 2005; Morisset, 1997).[6] Between 1975 and 1993 the world market price for coffee dropped by 18 per cent but the consumer price increased by 240 per cent (Talbot, 1997b). Coffee farmers received roughly US$12 billion in export income from coffee at the end of the 1980s, yet by 2003, despite increasing their export volumes, they received only US$5.5 billion (UNDP, 2005: 140). During this time, retail coffee sales mushroomed from US$30 billion to US$80 billion (ibid.: 140).

Global commodity chain (GCC) analysis,[7] now global value chain (GVC) analysis, has sought to account for this dramatic redistribution of value (Daviron and Ponte, 2005), addressing barriers to entry and rent, governance and variation in value chain structures (Kaplinsky and Morris, 2001; Gereffi et al., 2005). This framework considers each component or unit of the production process and how value chain actors vie for greater power *vis-à-vis* others in terms of seeking higher returns or lower production costs. In terms of value distribution, Schumpeter's theory of 'rents' is used to suggest that a firm's competitiveness and value-adding capacity depends on its ability to insulate itself from competition through possession of scarce resources (which can be created) (Kaplinsky, 2006); hence the unit value of any economic activity in a production chain is indirectly proportional to the level of competition at that particular stage of production (Schrank, 2004).

In a post-industrial context, agricultural commodity production is associated with high competition and low returns whereas knowledge-intensive activities, namely branding, marketing and advertising, are associated with minimal competition and very high returns. It is with brand-name advertising that the highest barriers to entry exist (see below) due to the high – and increasing – levels of expenditure required. High expenditure is warranted because the returns are exclusive to the owner and are legally protected (under trade mark law) for an indefinite duration (see below).

The structure of the coffee market value chain can vary significantly in terms of the financial return and conditions for producers, but typically, and similar to tropical agricultural commodities more generally, coffee production occurs in 'buyer-driven' chains:[8] a small number of (typically Northern) corporate buyers lead centrally coordinated but internationally dispersed production networks, setting the terms and conditions of production (e.g. geographical source, market price and production time-frames) (Gereffi, 1994; Gibbon and Ponte, 2005). The coffee chain structure also involves many units of value-adding – as many as 150 (Slob, 2006: 128) – including coffee-growing, picking, processing, sorting, grading, exporting, shipping, distribution, roasting, redistribution, transportation, packaging, brewing and drinking. Chain actors jostle for participation in higher-value activities in the chain yet producers' opposition to do so is

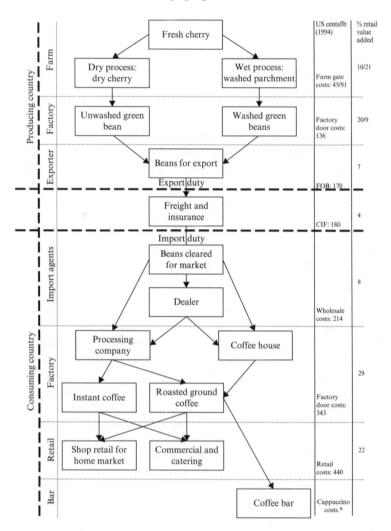

Notes: * Costs variable but very high. Include: overheads, advertising, other products (i.e. milk), and the 'experience' of the coffee bar. (See breakdown of the price of a cup of coffee.) CIF: cost, insurance, freight; FOB: free on board.

Source: Kaplinsky (2006). Figures cited in Dicum and Luttinger (1999: 132).

Figure 2.4   Coffee value chain

systematically and structurally denied (see Figure 2.4).[9] As Talbot (1997b: 124) has observed, 'as the coffee producers attempted to gain control of the processing stages of the chain with higher value added, the transnational corporations attempted to lower production costs by locating plants closer to the sources of their raw materials'.

Producers' returns vary according to different national production costs, interest rates, labour and land prices (Dicum and Luttinger, 1999: 106), as well as the quality or grade of the bean (i.e. arabica or robusta) (Slob, 2006: 131). Not all producers can grow the higher-quality arabica bean – they are grown only in particular regions and conditions, and presuppose higher levels of producer organisational capacity, capital and intense buyer governance over suppliers' compliance with quality standards and industry codes and requirements. In fact, the coffee market comprises two markets, both highly concentrated and corporate-centred. One, for robusta, is typified by the standard 'bulk commodity' chains of the agrifood system (highly competitive, undifferentiated) and is for canned or instant coffees and traded on the London Commodity Exchange. The other, for arabica, exhibits 'buyer-driven' supply chains for highly differentiated foods (i.e. 'gourmet' or 'specialty' coffee) that are traded on the New York Coffee, Sugar and Cocoa Exchange (Vorley, 2003). Despite the higher price of arabica beans, the glut in robusta beans has devalued the price of arabica since roasters can vary the blend of the two beans in the roasting process (Jaffee, 2007: 45).

While existing wisdom suggests that struggling coffee producers should diversify into other production activities so as to lessen their dependence on coffee, such 'wisdom' has been unrealistic for smallholder producers. Local economic activity has stagnated due to the lack of income in coffee-growing regions, making it hard for farmers to sell their produce to local markets. Also, alternative agricultural commodities such as cotton and sugar are unviable options because they are heavily subsidised and undercut local producers' prices (see Osterhaus, 2006: 30, 37–8; see Chapter 3).[10]

The impact of both the coffee crisis and above-mentioned market relations in the industry on coffee-producing communities has been deleterious and intergenerational. Farmers' inability to repay loans and to pay high rates of interest makes their economic situation highly precarious, forcing them to sell their assets or land (if they actually own it) in order to feed their families. Many have ultimately been forced off their land through lost income and economic uncertainty (Oxfam, 2002). Without sustainable incomes and financial security, farmers have been unable to feed or clothe their families, educate their children, access health care services or purchase basic necessities or essential drugs.[11] Poverty, hunger and malnutrition have reached severe levels in coffee-growing regions.[12]

With growing economic desperation, crime and theft, some farmers have turned to dangerous yet lucrative commodity trades such as coca,[13] which has contributed to the incidence of violence, assault, suicide, guerrilla activity and rape in local areas (Oxfam, 2002: 12; Fairtrade Foundation, 2002: 15). Others have resorted to selling their furniture, taking on extra employment where available, and sending their children to live with extended-family members. Women are most exposed to the problems created by social unrest and economic disaster. They go without medical treatment to prioritise children's medical expenses, often work in the field with children while their husband works in other regions, and are responsible for nursing sick children and possibly elderly family members (Oxfam, 2002).

Conditions are equally harsh, if not worse, for seasonal workers, who are vulnerable to unstable and exploitative working conditions and contracts on coffee plantations (which make up only 30 per cent of production). They are prevented from collective bargaining, their labour rights are typically unrecognised (with or without official national labour laws), and they often inhabit slum-like boarding-houses. Female casual/seasonal labourers suffer most – they are typically paid less than men for identical forms of labour, are victims of sexual harassment, and face employment discrimination if pregnant. Workers' contracts are often non-existent, and wages, overtime pay and social security payments are often precarious or non-existent (Oxfam, 2004).

Small-scale coffee producers and workers have been losing out to large corporations in the last several decades especially, but so have consumers: consumers have not shared in the drop in coffee prices but instead have forked out significantly more for packaged and served coffee. Part of the reason why brand companies have been able to *increase* their coffee prices amidst historic lows in world coffee prices – and for so long – owes to information asymmetries and consumers' attraction to brands (Oxfam, 2001: 26). This in turn requires a deeper analysis of the evolution of the modern corporation and the central role of the brand in its transformation and survival.

THE BRAND-BASED NATURE OF GLOBAL BUSINESS

Industrial historian Alfred Chandler has described the period between 1897 and 1902 as 'the first and most significant merger movement in American history' (Chandler et al., 1968: 270; see also Barsamian, 2000; Bakan, 2004). A crucial time in US corporate legal history, the turn of the century saw control and coordination of national production and distribution undergo rapid centralisation.[14] Before 1880 the US industrial market was rather unspectacular. Decision-making was decentralised and uncoordinated among thousands of small, localised firms. And factory production – the backbone of industrial enterprise – was owned and managed by many different individual manufacturers (Chandler et al., 1968). Modelling their organisational innovation on the US railroad business of the 1850s, the pioneers of the modern corporate era (DuPont, General Motors, Jersey Standard and Sears, Roebuck) built centralised, hierarchical and bureaucratic managerial and administrative structures to execute strategies of accumulation and rapid scale (see Chandler, 1962). With accompanying innovations in production – Ford's production 'assembly-line' – these firms influenced the emerging corporate era of mass production and consumption that prevailed until the 1970s (see for example Fligstein, 1985).

In agriculture, industrial development prevailed in the period following World War II. Intense chemical and technical inputs, environmental appropriation and corporate concentration underpinned the mass production of standardised ingredients and homogeneous products for mass consumption in Western markets (Freidmann, 1982; Goodman et al., 1987). In the 1980s and 1990s, however, neoliberal management of markets gave rise to a post-Fordist model of production and consumption, as the recent evolution of the coffee industry illustrates. Until the end of the nineteenth century, the majority of consumers were drinking coffee in coffee houses or doing their own roasting within their own homes. The flavour of the coffee – bought from local grocers – was either 'excellent' or 'foul and suspect' (Dicum and Luttinger, 1999: 122), and often accompanied by unpleasant surprises such as dirt, dried blood or figs (ibid.).

In 1865 John Arbuckle responded to the problem of unreliable quality with a new packaged ground, roasted coffee that made a more consistent product available to consumers beyond his roasting facility. Arbuckle, along with emerging competitors such as Hills Bros, Maxwell House and Folgers, continued to develop the new concept of consistent quality and convenient purchase. By the 1920s coffee in this form had become a 'universal beverage' with 'democratic appeal'. In keeping with the growing persona of universalism came increasing product homogenisation and technification, and market consolidation and production technologies. As Talbot (1997b: 119) writes, 'instant coffee was on the cutting-edge of the "durable foods" introduced into the US market during the 1950s . . . along with other new convenience foods like frozen orange-juice concentrate, Birdseye frozen vegetables and "TV dinners" '. From the 1940s to 1960s and beyond, the modern coffee market spread to Switzerland, France, Australia, New Zealand, Canada and Japan.

The capital-intensive nature of manufacturing instant coffee encouraged market concentration. In their expansion in the USA, regional roasters developed into national enterprises, driving out smaller competitors. National companies were then bought out by even larger conglomerates. The year 1962/3 was a zenith year for coffee consumption in the USA, with Americans consuming close to 40 gallons of coffee each (Dicum and Luttinger, 1999: 130). This dovetailed with a 'buying spree' among coffee conglomerates and their increasing political influence through the National Coffee Association (NCA).

Soon after, and signalled by declining real prices and consumption levels, Northern industrialisation began to wane (Piore and Sabel, 1984). Instead of passing cost reductions on to consumers through lower retail prices, the corporate giants of the modern corporate era shifted to oligopolistic forms of competition in order to survive – substituting price competition for 'product differentiation through advertising, trade names and styling' (Chandler et al., 1968: 276). Investing heavily in brand advertising, firms attempted to build 'value' around their brand to ensure profits (see Barber, 1966). The subsequent shift from marketing generic goods to marketing brand-based products (from Fordist to post-Fordist consumption) has since altered the content and purpose of advertising over the last century (see Gardner and Levy, 1955) and driven a deep shift in society away from close-knit geographically proximate 'iron' bonds and community-oriented identification to weak 'gossamer'-like social ties predicated on brand use and identification (Boorstin, 1974).

Reflecting these economic transformations, coffee companies developed into profitable assets for parent companies, competing almost exclusively on brand advertising (see Table 2.4) rather than on price – creating a 'parody of a functioning free market' (Dicum and Luttinger, 1999). In a 'race to the bottom' on quality with ever-cheaper and harsher-tasting coffee beans, the competitive strategy of brand advertising was short-sighted. Price spikes in the mid- to late 1970s and a growing concern in the USA over the effect of coffee consumption on human health saw consumer demand drop away in the mass market (Dicum and Luttinger, 1999).

By the early 1990s, coffee consumption levelled out. Mass-marketed coffee owned by giants such as Procter & Gamble, Nestlé and Kraft became associated with low-price and low-quality coffee and a 'ubiquitous staple' and 'unexciting drink for fogies' (Dicum and Luttinger, 1999: 144). This sentiment articulated a growing public disaffection with mass commercialisation and commodification, and the squeezing out of local businesses and farmer markets well known to local communities and reputed for their quality produce and individual character (ibid.). Sellers of mass-marketed

Table 2.4   Importance of advertising to major coffee brand companies in the US coffee market (in fiscal terms)

Company	Level of expenditure on advertising (1996)
Starbucks	$2 million
Chock Full o' Nuts	$3 million
Nestlé	$16 million
Colombian Coffee Federation	$18 million
Others	$75 million
Procter & Gamble	$95 million
Phillip Morris	$135 million

coffee quickly abandoned advertisements of mass-produced, homogeneous goods designed for the vague 'masses' in favour of smaller 'segmented' markets. Marketing became more heterogeneous and 'less cookie-cutter', and the message 'much more subtle' (Dean, 2004: 361). Seizing the market opportunity for a counter-corporate, 'specialty coffee' revival, a then-small company, Starbucks, emerged and positioned itself as an alternative – and 'alternative' identity – to the mass-market norm. As Starbucks owner, Howard Schultz, observed:

> Americans are so hungry for a community that some of our customers began gathering in our stores, making appointments with friends, holding meetings, striking up conversations with other regulars . . . People don't just drop by to pick up a half-pound of decaf on their way to the supermarket . . . they come for the atmosphere and the camaraderie. (Cited in Dicum and Luttinger, 1999: 152)

The emergence of the Starbucks 'alternative' reflected a wider turn away from the homogeneous, undifferentiated products of Fordist 'mass-production' to those of post-Fordist 'mass-customisation' (Kaplinsky, 2006) and its distinctive relations of production and consumption (see Kumar, 1995: 36–65). In the food industry this evolution was manifested in the growth of 'niche' value-added markets for highly differentiated, non-traditional, off-season and 'exotic' foods, and foods labelled or certified as 'healthy', 'organic' or 'fair trade' (Goodman and Redclift, 1991; Raynolds, 2002, 2004). The sophistication and pervasiveness of advertising has intensified under post-Fordist consumption, representing a multi-billion-dollar industry and the brand itself has become the *raison d'être* of the modern corporation. As Naomi Klein (2000) writes, the brand has become 'the core meaning of the modern corporation, [and] advertising is one vehicle . . . to convey that meaning to the world'.

Advertising continues to expand and morph into new forms, with contemporary marketing research suggesting that 'marketplace communities' and 'brand communities' can foster greater consumer loyalty (see McAlexander et al., 2002). Some analysts predict that fostering consumer loyalty in future will involve greater penetration of social spaces – turning social spaces into 'branded' ones – to gain 'share of mind' rather than (or as a route to) market share (see Solomon, 2003; Dean, 2004). Solomon (2003) calls this the era of 'consumerspace', where social space is redefined and experienced as branded: the brand *is* the experience; it *is* the product (Solomon, 2003; Dean, 2004; Klein, 2000; Hamilton, 2003). Consumers' homes, workplaces and cultural spaces become 'saturated' with the brand logo in the process of engineering an 'idealised version of reality' (e.g. Disneyworld or Niketown) (see Solomon, 2003; Dean, 2004).

Above all else, the success of Starbucks in the coffee industry has been its emphasis on the intangible 'Starbucks' experience – in-house services, ambience and 'camaraderie'. It is here – in the value-added in immaterial parts of the value chain – that Western multinational firms focus their resources and ensure their ownership (Daviron and Ponte, 2005). Although it has shrugged off its independent specialty coffee roaster image, Starbucks' 'success' in highly concentrated markets now stems from business strategies that match those of established global brand giants. With staff backgrounds in multinationals such as 7-Eleven, McDonalds, Burger King and Nike, Starbucks' 'tricks of the trade' include 'co-branding with the big boys . . . PepsiCo, Anheuser-Busch, United Airlines, Marriott, and Barnes & Noble' (parent companies of convenience food and beverages; beers; international carriers; hospitality; and online and retail books, music and media respectively), aggressively buying out smaller independent café stores – or their buildings – in order to determine consumers' 'choice' of coffee (Dicum and Luttinger, 1999: 154–5).

Starbucks' brand-based strategy for market share exemplifies the 'brand extension' era. Although takeovers are nothing new to modern corporations, increasing concentration in global markets is encouraging the trend towards 'bundling' multiple brands from different markets under a diminishing number of conglomerate enterprises. Klein (2000: 160) calls this business strategy one of 'bundling', 'brand extensions', 'mergers' or 'synergy', in which parent companies own and cross-promote a multiplicity of 'competing' brand companies. Effective in blocking competitors in any one industry or market, this development has blurred the distinction between sectors and industries so that branded products and services in media, music, entertainment and computer software industries are owned by the one global corporation. In the US coffee market, for instance, 'the largest coffee brand in the country is owned by a soap company, while its major competitor is owned by a combined cereal and cheese company that is owned by a cigarette company' (Dicum and Luttinger, 1999: 128).

The emphasis on the brand for modern market competitiveness brings into question the basis of its power. The answer to this question lies in the link between brands and trade marks. Behind the brand image that consumers recognise lies a cluster of proprietorial rights known as intellectual property rights (IPRs). IPRs are unlike conventional property rights (see Drahos, 2005) in the sense that they refer to abstract or intangible forms of property ownership (see Braithwaite and Drahos, 2000: 39–40).[15] Brands fall within the category of IPRs known as trade marks. The brand is at once the image of the trade mark and the subject of exclusive proprietorial rights held by the trade mark owner.

THE ECONOMICS OF TRADE MARKS

Economists view trade mark protection as a necessity in a competitive market economy and of value to consumers (see Table 2.5). Trade marks (TMs) operate for consumers as signs of the trade source from which the good or service has derived or is connected in some way.[16] A 'sign' includes 'any letter, word, name, signature, numeral, device, brand, heading, label, ticket, aspect of packaging, shape, colour, sound or scent' (Ricketson and Richardson, 2005: 987). Trade marks enable consumers to distinguish the 'origin' of a good or service from others in the market. Trade marks are also thought to reduce consumers' 'search costs' by enabling quick selection between numerous available products, whose differences would take

Table 2.5   The economic functions of trade marks

Function of trade mark	Definition
Origin function	TMs operate for consumers as signs of the trade source from which the good or service has derived or is in some way connected
Quality/guarantee function	TMs enable consumers to link goods and services with a range of personal expectations about quality, expectations guaranteed based on advertising, recommendation or prior experience
Investment/advertising function	TMs protect the asset value of goodwill, which MNCs invest millions to promote. This asset value is also one that consumers and shareholders often consider in their own spending and investment decisions

time to understand and whose features or quality cannot necessarily be tested prior to purchase (Landes and Posner, 1987).

Which brand a consumer actually decides to purchase derives primarily from trust in, or personal expectation of, the quality of a brand; the consumer has either seen an advertisement, had a recommendation from someone they know, or knows from prior experience of purchasing the brand. This is 'goodwill': a perceived intangible asset that consumers will buy based on the reputation of that brand. It is thus a form of competitive advantage.[17] The importance of goodwill in consumer decision-making cannot be overstated. Consumers frequently choose brands with well-known or established reputations over unknown brands (Economides, 1988). For this reason, economists view businesses as having an incentive to produce consistently high-quality goods and services while being protected against lower-quality imitations (Landes and Posner, 1987). Trade marks therefore serve a 'quality' or 'guarantee' role for consumers (Cornish and Llewelyn, 2003: 587). In turn, investment in brand reputation creates an *ex ante* argument for protecting trade marks: a strong brand reputation enables companies to anticipate profits. Established trade marks thus acquire significant investment and advertising value which warrant protection from imitation or defamation (ibid.).

THE PSYCHOLOGY OF TRADE MARKS

When consumers purchase a product, they look for a brand, not a trade mark. The brand is the image of the trade mark, which itself is an abstract entity. In one sense, then, trade marks appear to have nothing to do with brand consumption. In another sense, they have everything to do with it. This is because of the direct and intentional role that owners of well-known brands play in creating consumer attachments to their brand. The psycho-emotional basis of this strategy sits at odds with the above-mentioned economic theories of the consumer and the market function of trade marks.

Psychologists have long understood the influence of the image – and therefore the brand – on individuals (see Forrester, 2000). In the contemporary advertising culture, consumer decision-making is influenced at a sub-conscious and emotive level rather than at a conscious and factual information-based level (see Jung, 2006). Psychologists call this reflex response 'classical conditioning',[18] in which a stimulus that elicits no response can be made to elicit a positive response in a reflex-like manner after it has been associated numerous times with a second stimulus that already elicits a positive response (Gray, 1999).

Classical conditioning underpins modern advertising methods. Advertisers pair their company's brand (a neutral stimulus) with evocative symbols, scents, scenes, shapes, colours or sounds (a response-inducing stimulus). When this sequence is seen or heard numerous times (i.e. through repetitive and aggressive advertising), consumers develop reflex-like responses towards the brand in the absence of the advertisement (see Cheskin, 1959). This sophisticated manipulation of the human mind through advertising began in the early twentieth century as part of the growing recognition and exploration of the non-rational basis of consumption (see Packard, 1981). Advertisers refashioned themselves as 'hope merchants', idealising values of 'beauty', 'sophistication, 'wealth', 'popularity' or 'youth' in connection with their brand. The consumer becomes persuaded that he/she can obtain those socially desirable attributes through the brand's consumption now that the brand is associated symbolically with those values (ibid.: 15). Nowadays, exploiting the emotional and sensory drivers of consumption is a *sine qua non* for marketing power (O'Shaughnessy and O'Shaughnessy, 2002). Critic of consumer culture, Clive Hamilton, expresses this idea in the following way:

> In the marketing of margarine . . . the consumer does not buy something to spread on bread but a concatenation of feelings associated with idealised family relationships . . . In a world of social disintegration, modern consumers have a powerful need for family warmth, and humans, just like Pavlov's dogs, make unconscious associations. Unmet emotional needs and unconscious association are the twin psychological pillars of the marketing society. (Hamilton, 2003: 84–5)

In the 'marketing society', or as Galbraith (1976) calls it, the 'affluent society', advertising itself generates the 'demand' it seeks to satisfy: 'few people at the beginning of the nineteenth century needed an adman to tell them what they wanted' (ibid.: 2). Now, 'the institutions of modern advertising and salesmanship . . . cannot be reconciled with the notion of independently determined desires, for their central function is to create desires – to bring into being wants that previously did not exist' (ibid.: 124). In the manufacturing of a product, modern firms prioritise the manufacture of demand for the product over the manufacture of the product itself (ibid.). This is where market value lies: creating markets for products, not products for markets. With brand advertising, firms distort perceptions of not only the 'need' for, but also the 'value' of, branded goods to charge a higher premium than would otherwise be warranted. The non-rational, socially constructed consumer and the real-world influence of firms on that consumer are omitted in an economic view of markets and market prices (see Hanson and Kysar, 1990). As van Caenegem (2003: 705) says:

brands or trade marks . . . in reality, do not inform the rationally maximizing consumer, but rather influence the emotionally-driven consumer by enabling 'perception advertising'. The brand or mark is manipulated by its owner, shrewd perception advertising imbues the brand, and by association the product, with properties the consumer imagines to be desirable. This allows the trade-mark owner to set a higher price for the marked goods, generating higher returns. The consumer is prepared to pay more, not because she discerns, via the brand or mark, the higher quality of the underlying goods, but because the goods are rendered subjectively more desirable by their association with a heavily promoted brand or mark.

It is not simply that firms use advertising to create markets for new/existing brands, but to inhibit competition in those markets. The economic justification for trade mark protection as fulfilling a basic and value-free function becomes problematic from this perspective since economic theory omits to explain how, in practice, companies exploit brands to insulate themselves from competition and obtain exclusive access to trade mark rents. More problematic still is the degree to which trade marks have become protected. Trade mark law now provides unprecedented leverage to the 'apparently autonomous existence' and 'immense influence' of modern perception advertising, which, in its effect on consumer preferences, advances monopoly/oligopoly 'power over' global markets.

A (CRITICAL) LEGAL VIEW OF TRADE MARKS

The aim of intellectual property law is to protect 'applications of ideas and information that are of commercial value', examples being copyright, patents and trade marks (Cornish and Llewelyn, 2003: 6).[19] As subjects of IPRs, ideas and information are the bread and butter of the modern knowledge economy.[20] Problematically, because these abstract objects (intangible forms of property) are subject to exclusive proprietorial control (Drahos, 1996),[21] information markets pose distinct challenges for a knowledge economy (Drahos, 2005: 140). Legal scholars acknowledge the 'negative characteristic' of intellectual property law which is detrimental to innovation and its public utilisation: IPRs legally empower one actor to stop others, such as new market entrants or users of innovation, doing certain things. In the case of patents, for example, this includes even a third party who, unaware of the first party's innovation, makes a simultaneous and identical innovation or discovery (see Cornish and Llewelyn, 2003).

While trade marks 'do not owe their existence to some act of invention, discovery or novelty' (Graham and Peroff, 1987: 33) (unlike copyright and patents), they none the less function much like other forms of

IPRs by obstructing market competition. Indeed, the 'monopoly nature' of IPRs (Drahos, 2005: 147) is amplified in the case of trade marks, causing a greater 'impact across industry' than other forms of IPRs (Cornish and Llewelyn, 2003). While trade mark law tends to reflect an economic view of markets, more critical (particularly critical cultural) legal perspectives share an affinity with a sociological/psychological view and explain how the evolution of contemporary trade mark law – which neglects the realities of actual market behaviour – enables large firms to exploit market monopolies premised on 'share of mind'. This body of legal scholarship also offers insight into the escalating market and cultural significance of trade marks from the mid-twentieth century onwards (see for example Lunney, 1999; Coombe, 1998; Bellman et al., 2005).

The legal power conferred on trade mark owners has not always been as extensive as it is today (see Braithwaite and Drahos, 2000; Bellman et al., 2005). In the USA – where primary leaders of the global IP industries are based (Braithwaite and Drahos, 2000) – two particular changes have redefined – and enlarged – the scope and capacity for trade mark owners to control markets (Lunney, 1999). The first change expanded the definable subject matter of trade mark protection to include features not affixed to the product, such as advertising slogans, trade dress and trade names. Over time, product packaging, designs and features (such as words, names, symbols or devices) have become matters of proprietorial control. The second change extended the bundle of rights conferred on trade mark owners to protect the mark as a desirable property in its own right rather than as a source of identification of indiscernible product information:

> Originally, trade mark law was justified on grounds of preventing consumer deception. Ownership was assigned to the person who adopted the mark for her trade, not because she had created it or its favourable associations, but because such [a] person was conveniently placed and strongly motivated to vindicate the broader public interest in a mark's ability to identify accurately the source of the goods to which it was attached. While the mark was its owner's property, it was her property only in the limited sense that she held the legal right to seek a remedy should another adopt a mark sufficiently similar to threaten the mark's ability to indicate product source . . . a mark's owner did not have the right to control every use that might reduce, or capture for someone else, some part of 'her' mark's value, nor did she have the right to exercise dominion over 'her' mark in whatever way she desired. (Lunney, 1999: 417–18)

Based on the trade mark's modern interpretation, courts now 'prohibit the imitation of desired product features even where a defendant is

careful to identify the imitation as its own' and condone 'an almost irre-
buttable presumption of infringement drawn simply from the imitation
of a successful original' (Lunney, 1999: 388). Trade mark protection
as property-based protection thus presents a more significant threat
to market competition than misrepresentation-based protection, since
the former 'goes too far towards prohibiting imitation as imitation [i.e.
mere competition], rather than limiting itself to imitation as material
deception' (ibid.: 486):

> anti-competitive risks associated with protecting a mark valued for its own
> sake increase. When a word, or something else that might serve as a trade-
> mark, has value to consumers for its own sake, aside from its role in connect-
> ing information to [a] precise product, protecting the mark will require others
> to expend additional resources replicating the mark's attraction as product,
> without imitating the mark too closely. Such protection will therefore increase
> the costs and risks associated with introducing a competing product. Such
> protection will also lessen the extent to which consumers will consider such
> 'competing' products perfect substitutes for the original, not merely because
> the information readily available concerning the products will differ but
> because the products themselves will differ. Because protection renders direct
> competition both more expensive and more difficult, it will tend to increase
> the market power, prices and rents associated with popular brands. (Ibid.:
> 437)

Since competition in oligopolistic markets is predicated on marketing
to establish and sustain a brand's value to consumers, firms with the
largest advertising budgets wield a powerful weapon for controlling
markets (Barber, 1966; see also Chandler, 1964; Lunney, 1999). Joe
Bain's (1956: 216) seminal study of the characteristics and consequences
of barriers to new competition showed that the reputation (goodwill) of
established brands is the single most significant barrier to the entry of
competitors. Without the capacity to produce lavish advertising campaigns, smaller or newer competitors are eclipsed by dominant brand
names. For instance, of the 16 000 products launched on the US market
each year, 95 per cent are brand extensions of existing brands (Murphy,
cited in Lury, 2004: 71). Bolstered by a legal framework that condones
'consumer lock-in' as a form of (exclusive) competitive advantage,
aggressive advertising enables dominant firms to protect their oligopoly/
monopoly power.

Despite – or rather, because of – the excessive market power that strong
trade mark protection enables, the WTO's Agreement on Trade-Related
Aspects of Intellectual Property (TRIPs) amplified and globalised a pro-
monopoly trade mark regime as part of its introduction of controversial
changes to the laws of intellectual property relating to international trade

(Bellman et al., 2005; Drahos with Braithwaite, 2002: 4). For instance, the TRIPs definition of a trade mark extended ownership rights to 'anything perceptible to a human being that could serve as a signalling device – visually perceptible words, designs, sounds, scents, tastes or textures' (Bellman et al., 2005: 214). With this broad array of elements over which to claim exclusive ownership, dominant firms now have unprecedented scope to block competition.

TRIPs also removed the precondition that registration for trade mark protection be conditional on the mark being in use. This requirement interfered with the 'modern marketing strategies' that enable firms to build markets for products, not products for markets (Bellman et al., 2005: 233). This legal precedent has legalised the formation of market monopolies in future market segments.

TRIPs rules on licensing also recognised – and reinforced – at a global level the concept of the trade mark as a protectable property in its own right, a 'stand-alone commodity' (Bellman et al., 2005: 249). This amplifies the anti-competitive effects of trade marks to a global-market level since, as discussed earlier, 'protection [of the trade mark as property] renders direct competition both more expensive and more difficult . . . [and so] will tend to increase the market power, prices and rents associated with popular brands' (Lunney, 1999: 437).

While economic theory holds that trade marks are vital in a competitive market, the foregoing story about trade marks tells of brand control on a global scale. That is, it has highlighted the especial relevance of trade marks as a vehicle for brand control, not as tools of legal protection that encourage market competition and protect consumer sovereignty. Despite their heavy lobbying for stronger trade mark protection at the global level, global corporations are only interested in the trade mark as a vehicle for controlling markets with their brand. TRIPs globalises a version of trade mark law that is consistent with the global protection of brands and

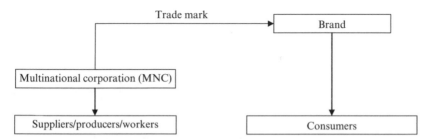

Figure 2.5   The trade mark as a vehicle for control in world markets in the post-industrial context

favours those companies with large advertising budgets.[22] By strengthening the rules of trade mark ownership, brand companies have a formidable legal weapon to exert more pervasive oligopolistic control in the global marketplace. Figure 2.5 illustrates the means by which corporations exercise global power over consumers and producers in world markets.

CONCLUSION

Developing-country agricultural producers, like Western market consumers, have become subject to global corporate 'power over', which is achieved by shaping and reinforcing consumers' subjectivity with brand images that act as discreet proxies for securing exclusive market control. In the agricultural industry, brand companies' control of consumer markets via brand advertising facilitates market oligopoly. The modern history of coffee demonstrates the devastating effects of such power on the smallest actors in the coffee market: growers and workers. Assuming that this is indeed how global power works, the constituent elements of the dominant power complex must be addressed if those dominated by it wish to seek alternatives – alternatives that give better expression to their values. Drawing insight from the fair trade movement, the chapters in this book develop a theory of how global markets can be used to liberate the different value 'preferences' of consumers and producers. First, however, we turn to consider the history, governance and constituent groups of the movement.

NOTES

1. The terms multinational corporation (MNC) and transnational corporation (TNC) were used in an interchangeable fashion in the literature and by respondents. Both terms refer to a corporation that deals in at least two countries. Hereafter the term MNC will be used in the book.
2. Loans from the government and from the World Bank (1995 and 2000) facilitated the rapid development of Vietnam's coffee sector (now producing 10 per cent of the world's coffee).
3. Because the price has drastically depreciated and farmers are receiving less than enough to cover their production costs, the rational response has been to produce even more coffee to make extra income from higher volumes. Other developments have compounded this, such as technology that makes produce more resilient to disease and insects (FLO, 2005a).
4. The volatility of the market can also be attributed to futures markets and speculative market activity in the world coffee market, wherein close to 90 per cent of trading in coffee comprises 'paper deals' between Northern traders and the remaining 10 per cent is made up of the real commodity itself (Fairtrade Foundation, 2002: 10; Oxfam 2002).
5. Those with less than five hectares of land.

6. These are characteristic ways in which large multinational corporations are able to establish monopoly strength in the global marketplace (Heydon, 1978).

7. A commodity chain refers to a whole range of activities involved in the design, production and marketing of a product (Gereffi, 1994). Gereffi (1994, 1999) defines 'buyer-driven' supply chains as international supply chains in which large retailers, marketers and branded manufacturers are central, dominant actors in establishing decentralised production networks in exporting countries (primarily developing countries). These foreign buyers dictate product specifications to a global network of contractors/ producers. Buyer-driven chains typify labour-intensive industries such as garments, agriculture, toys and footwear. This power structure contrasts 'producer-driven' chains, coordinated by large transnational manufacturers and predominate in capital- and technology-intensive industries such as the automobile and airline industries.

8. Buyer-driven commodity chains predominate in labour-intensive sectors where production functions are typically outsourced and market information, product design and marketing/advertising costs set the barriers to entry for would-be lead firms (Gereffi, 1994).

9. Furthermore, government tariffs protecting processing industries in wealthy countries create strong disincentives and barriers to developing-country producers to export processed goods (Osterhaus, 2006: 45).

10. According to an Oxfam report, in 2000 the US government's subsidisation of its agricultural industries totalled US$245 billion, and the import tariffs of the USA and EU intended to protect their own agricultural industries cost developing nations roughly US$43 billion per year (Oxfam, 2002: 37).

11. Essential drugs are critical in these regions where HIV/AIDS and malaria outbreaks are likely.

12. The rate of UN emergency programmes has increased throughout Central America and other regions affected by the impact of the coffee crisis on producer communities (Fairtrade Foundation, 2002).

13. Coca is the colloquial term given to the shrub *erythroxylon coca*. Chewing the dried leaves of this shrub has a stimulating effect. The plant is also a source of cocaine and some alkaloids, which are extracted and sold.

14. US antitrust legislation and its interpretation by the courts permitted for the first time large consolidated firms to operate (Chandler et al., 1968: 278–9) and changes to corporate governance laws gave firms freedom of incorporation and rights of 'personhood' (Bakan, 2004). US industrialisation peaked in the period before 1890 until 1913, bringing the nation status as both a global leader in manufacturing and a source of one-third of the world's goods (Chandler et al., 1968: 270).

15. According to Drahos (2005: 139), the differences between standard property rights and IPRs are to do with the object to which those rights pertain. For intellectual property rights, the object of IPR protection is information of some kind.

16. This is referred to as the 'origin function' of trade marks (Cornish and Llewelyn, 2003). For instance, a trade mark in Australian law is defined as 'a sign used, or intended to be used, to distinguish goods or services dealt with or provided in the course of trade by a person from goods or services so dealt with or provided by another person'.

17. This intangible quality can and should be distinguished from a company's tangible assets (e.g. stock).

18. Classical conditioning was pioneered in the work of Ivan Pavlov (1849–1936). John Watson later tested classical conditioning in terms of the ability to condition human emotional responses to certain stimuli, which he subsequently proved (Gray, 1999).

19. According to Drahos (2005), the number of IPRs is growing constantly.

20. Peter Drucker (1969) coined the term 'knowledge economy' to highlight a fundamental shift from an economy driven by industrialisation in the twentieth century to knowledge, information and creativity/ideas as the productive elements in a modern economy (see also Toffler, 1980). In a knowledge economy, high-value enterprise deals in the production, management and distribution of intellectual products and services. This work is the preserve of the 'knowledge worker' (see Drucker, 1966).

21. A theory of abstract objects and intellectual property is developed in Drahos (1996).
22. Drahos (2005) observes that the content of TRIPs was 'heavily influenced by owners of intellectual property'. In this case of trade mark rights, trade mark owners with the biggest and most valuable brands in world markets stand to gain the greatest benefits from those rights.

3. The history of fair trade

Since the mid-twentieth century the fair trade movement has sought to bring about a fairer trading system that empowers small-scale producers in international markets. Operating initially within alternative niche markets serviced solely by religious, charity and non-profit alternative trading organisations (ATOs), fair trade was pursued through a system of product certification and labelling in the late 1980s. Designed to enable any company to sell fair trade products to consumers provided they met certain criteria, fair trade expanded into dominant or 'mainstream' commercial supply, distribution and retail channels. While the ATO movement has remained vital during the system's growth, a number of ATOs also reinvented the traditional ATO with a commercial twist – a for-profit brand company – to take the ATO model of fair trade into the 'mainstream'. The certification model and ATO model of fair trade are respectively governed by Fairtrade Labelling Organizations International (FLO) and the International Association for Fair Trade (IFAT). The movement's continued and rapid market growth worldwide has introduced multiple challenges and provoked a deep discord between its two major constituencies and models, reflected in the evolution of their different governance institutions. This chapter introduces the groups, models and institutional structures that have underpinned the movement's development and form the basis of the analysis in later chapters in the book.

FAIR TRADE IN CONTEXT: FREE TRADE THEORY, FREE TRADE REALITY

More than two-thirds of those living on less than US$1 per day (one-fifth of the world's population) are located in rural areas and work as either small-scale farmers or agricultural labourers (UNDP, 2005: 129). They, as part of half the world's population living on less than US$2 per day (Shah, 2006), are losing out under free trade. Free trade advocates, on the contrary, believe them, and the rest of the world, to be better off under a system of free trade than any other, 'less efficient' model of international exchange in goods, finances and services. According to free trade theorists, the principle of comparative advantage will determine that two parties (country A and country B) will export what each is most efficient at producing and import goods each is comparatively inefficient at producing (Ricardo, 1976). India, for instance, grows aromatic basmati rice while Australia has vast amounts of iron ore. Under international trade, Australia can enjoy India's fragrant rice and India can use Australia's iron ore; both Australia and India are better off. Focused on whether trade liberalisation or autarky is better in an international trading environment in which a variety of goods and services is available (see for example Markusen et al., 1995), free trade advocates recognise that some – the inefficient – will not do well under international trade but that, left unfettered, the 'invisible hand' of the market (i.e. price mechanisms) will lead to better living standards overall.

Trade liberalisation has been promoted with growing force since the post-World War II era. Managed through the then General Agreement on Tariffs and Trade (GATT) (now the World Trade Organization – WTO), free trade principles have become fully integrated within national government policies and programmes in the global South. Yet the 'benefits' of free trade have continued to elude most Southern economies. Since 1980, international trade has undergone its heaviest liberalisation but the number of people living in poverty has risen by nearly 50 per cent. During this period, the value of world trade in agricultural commodities, on which developing countries depend heavily, has declined from 15 to 10 per cent (UNDP, 2005: 115). Markets for agriculture also operate somewhat differently from others in that they depend on market regulation to ensure that commodity prices do not spiral into a 'race to the bottom' (Robbins, 2003). While international commodity agreements provided such support up until the 1980s (see Chapter 2), their dissolution since then, along with structural adjustment programmes and (some) rich-country governments' continued protection of their domestic farmers,[1] has left commodity-dependent countries in severe poverty. Moreover, while free trade theorists condemn rich-country subsidies for causing distortions to international commodity prices, they tend to overlook those caused by corporate power:[2]

> Classical purists have always had a difficult time understanding the value of almost any government functions. The ideal of an unregulated market . . . provides an intellectual basis for condemning all but a few government services. But this view failed to recognise the role of monopoly and economic power as a powerful force in the evolution of markets. Because of limited entry, advertising, research and development, and mergers and acquisitions, firms accumulate power and exercise it in ways that are not universally beneficial. In a world of monopoly power, laissez-faire loses its claims to be the most efficient economic system. (Karier, cited in Murphy, 1999: 15)

The unprecedented expansion and concentration of corporate 'economic power' in the modern era is particularly noteworthy in agricultural commodity markets (see Murphy, 1999, 2002; McMichael, 2000; Morissett, 1997; Vorley, 2003; Chapter 2). And in rural agriculture, where the world's poorest predominate, market conditions do not conform to free trade theoretical models and thus contribute to producers' disproportionate disadvantage (Osterhaus, 2006). Summarising these market failures, Nicholls and Opal (2005: 18–19) observe the challenge they pose to free trade's ability to eradicate rural poverty:

Lack of market access. An export market free from importing-country interference through subsidies and tariffs may be considered 'free' and can function well for exporters, but if primary commodity producers cannot access these functioning markets, due to their remoteness and lack of transport, the benefits of this free market cannot be realised for them. To access markets, small-scale producers often rely on middlemen, who can collude to ensure that there is no competition for producers' goods and thus no fair market price for them.

Imperfect information. A fundamental necessity for the functioning of any free market is 'perfect information', implying that producers and traders have access to knowledge about market prices. Remote producers with no access to radio, newspapers, or telephones cannot access information about prices, and are at the mercy of the middlemen who come to their often isolated farms.

Lack of access to financial markets. Producers in developing countries have no access to income-smoothing devices like futures markets. A cocoa farmer living in a remote mountain village in Peru cannot call the London Coffee and Cocoa Exchange to lock in a set price for next year's harvest, because of communications difficulties and a lack of significant volume to trade. Peru's international cocoa exporters and the US's chocolate ice cream companies can and do use futures markets to stabilise the cost of goods. Thus the cocoa farmer is left completely exposed to world price fluctuations, when a perfectly functioning futures market exists to protect him or her from these variations. Similarly, such a farmer has no access to insurance cover to protect his or her income from extreme weather conditions or political unrest.

Lack of access to credit. Rural banks are either non-existent or do not lend in the small amounts that family farmers require. Thus, credit for farm machines and fertilisers is often available only through exploitative middlemen at extremely high rates of interest. Much as farmers are not able to access fair markets for their crops, they cannot access fair markets for credit.

Inability to switch to other sources of income generation. In a perfectly functioning market, economic actors can switch easily from one income-generating activity to another in response to price information. This is clearly not the case for the world's poor. Even if isolated producers had access to price information, their ability to change their source of income is limited . . . For families with no slack in their income and little by way of savings, risk-taking is not an option. A lack of access to credit or education about other income sources contributes to this inability to diversify income sources.

Weak legal systems and enforcement of laws. Many developing countries have passed strict environmental and labour laws that are ignored by local authorities. Factory owners may bribe local officials to overlook pollution and labour violations. Countries that do enforce laws may see investments move to more lax régimes. Farmers with insecure land titles cannot use their land assets as collateral for loans to diversify into other areas of production, or to invest in technology improvements on their farms.

From a free trade perspective the 'fairness' of the outcomes that trade liberalisation produces is not at issue, but it has been the central concern of the fair trade movement which, since the end of World War II, has offered market access to the most disadvantaged producers in developing countries on terms that favour their interests. For a definition of fair trade see Box 3.1.

BOX 3.1   F.I.N.E. DEFINITION OF FAIR TRADE

October 2001

Fair Trade is a trading partnership based on dialogue, transparency and respect, that seeks greater equity in international trade. It contributes to sustainable development by offering better trading conditions to, and securing the rights of, marginalized producers and workers – especially in the South. Fair Trade organizations (backed by consumers) are actively engaged in awareness raising and in campaigning for changes in the rules and practices of conventional international trade.

In this way, the movement aims to prove that international trade can benefit everyone – especially the weak and marginalised – if the rules and terms that underpin international trade are changed. Fair Trade Organizations (FTOs) uphold these standards to enable disadvantaged producers to engage with markets on more equitable terms.

Ten Standards of Fair Trade Organizations

1. Creating opportunities for economically disadvantaged producers
Fair Trade is a strategy for poverty alleviation and sustainable development. Its purpose is to create opportunities for producers who have been economically disadvantaged or marginalized by the conventional trading system.

2. Transparency and accountability
Fair Trade involves transparent management and commercial relations to deal fairly and respectfully with trading partners.

3. Capacity building
Fair Trade is a means to develop producers' independence. Fair Trade relationships provide continuity, during which producers and their marketing

organizations can improve their management skills and their access to new markets.

4. Promoting Fair Trade

Fair Trade Organizations raise awareness of Fair Trade and the possibility of greater justice in world trade. They provide their customers with information about the organization, the products, and in what conditions they are made. They use honest advertising and marketing techniques and aim for the highest standards in product quality and packing.

5. Payment of a fair price

A fair price in the regional or local context is one that has been agreed through dialogue and participation. It covers not only the costs of production but enables production which is socially just and environmentally sound. It provides fair pay to the producers and takes into account the principle of equal pay for equal work by women and men. Fair Traders ensure prompt payment to their partners and, whenever possible, help producers with access to pre-harvest or pre-production financing.

6. Gender equity

Fair Trade means that women's work is properly valued and rewarded. Women are always paid for their contribution to the production process and are empowered in their organizations.

7. Working conditions

Fair Trade means a safe and healthy working environment for producers. The participation of children (if any) does not adversely affect their well-being, security, educational requirements and need for play and conforms to the UN Convention on the Rights of the Child as well as the law and norms in the local context.

8. Child labour

Fair Trade Organizations respect the UN Convention on the Rights of the Child, as well as local laws and social norms in order to ensure that the participation of children in production processes of fairly traded articles (if any) does not adversely affect their well-being, security, educational requirements and need for play. Organizations working directly with informally organized producers disclose the involvement of children in production.

9. The environment

Fair Trade actively encourages better environmental practices and the application of responsible methods of production.

10. Trade relations

Fair Trade Organizations trade with concern for the social, economic and
environmental well-being of marginalized small producers and do not
maximize profit at their expense. They maintain long-term relationships
based on solidarity, trust and mutual respect that contribute to the promotion and growth of Fair Trade. An interest-free pre-payment of at least 50
per cent is made if requested. (Adapted from IFAT, 2008)

Fairtrade product certification includes some of these principles, including
(1) direct purchasing from democratically organised producers, (2) transparent and long-term trading relationships, (3) agreed minimum prices,
and (4) a social premium for investment in capacity-building, technical
assistance and social development projects (see Barratt Brown, 1993).
Together FTOs and Fairtrade certification promote principles that shorten
the supply chain to re-link producers and consumers, and maximise producers' return (see Figure 3.1).

The cooperative structure enables producers to pool resources and gain
access to information on market prices, trends and requirements. Access to
markets and more stable market conditions also tend to exist for Fairtrade
cooperatives because of the long-term, transparent trading relationships
required of traders, plus the payment of a minimum price.[3] The Fairtrade
minimum price[4] is calculated on the basis of the cost of production, the cost
of living and the cost of compliance with Fairtrade standards:

$$\text{Fairtrade minimum price} = \text{cost of production} + \text{cost of living}^5$$
$$+ \text{cost of compliance with Fairtrade standards}^6$$

A social premium is added to the minimum price to enable producers to
build business capacities and to diversify to alternative and/or additional

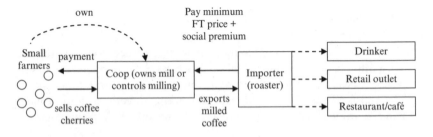

Source: Nicholls and Opal (2005).

Figure 3.1   Fairtrade in the coffee supply chain

sources of business income; and at a community level, to finance the construction of clean and proximate water facilities for domestic use and production, health facilities and access to medicines, community micro-credit schemes and community banks, housing and infrastructure such as roads, electricity, storage warehouses as well as schools and resources for educating children (see FLO, 2006a).

Whilst research on the impacts of fair trade remains in its infancy (Young and Utting, 2005: 140), it none the less paints a generally positive picture of the direct and indirect benefits for small-scale producers. Although fair trade does not solve all developing countries' economic problems relating to international trade, it does contribute important outcomes. In general, research on fair trade notes its capacity to reduce producers' market vulnerability, strengthen their bargaining position, increase organisational skills and value-adding capabilities, and build capacity in business, community and political terms (see Murray et al., 2003; Raynolds, 2000, 2002; Raynolds et al., 2004; Tallontire, 2002, 2000; Taylor, 2002; Pérez-Grovas and Cervantes, 2002; Mendez, 2002; Bacon, 2005). This body of research indicates that the greatest contribution of Fairtrade relates to its non-monetary contribution of organisational capacity-building and support (Tallontire, 2002; Murray et al., 2003: 11).

The Kagera Cooperative Union (KCU), for instance, is a coffee farmers' cooperative in north-western Tanzania comprising 90000 small-scale farmers in 124 village cooperatives. Since 1988 the KCU has been selling increasing amounts of its members' coffee to Fairtrade markets. During the 1960s, the Tanzanian coffee marketing body established an instant-coffee-powder production factory but it lay effectively dormant for many years. The factory, named 'Tanica', was later privatised, and the KCU was granted permission to buy a few shares in Tanica each year with the KCU's Fairtrade income. After 14 years of doing so, in 2004 the KCU gained a 51 per cent share of Tanica's ownership. Aiming to diversify income and reduce dependence on exports, the KCU's plan is now to multiply its instant-coffee sales by selling the product nationwide. KCU has also used its Fairtrade income to build three schools, hire more school teachers and provide healthy food for the children. Further investments in children's schoolbooks, blackboards and school-building reparations are currently being made (FLO, 2005b).

Another example is the Estwatini Kitchen, a jam and jelly factory in Swaziland, southern Africa.[7] Two hundred women and 20 handicapped villagers work in the business, and the ingredients are grown by Swazi farmers and processed by a women-only cooperative. In addition to jams and jellies, the Kitchen also sells woven baskets and wooden spoons carved by handicapped villagers who, being economically marginalised, have few other sources of income. The profits from the Estwatini Kitchen product range are invested in youth centres which house 200 AIDS orphans and street children. Estwatini Kitchen sells its goods in the retail outlets of its fair trade partners in Northern markets, namely AlterEco and SERRV International – Sales Exchange for Refugee Rehabilitation and Vocation (Nicholls and Opal, 2005: 144–5).

A third example is El Ceibo, a 700-member farmer cocoa cooperative in the Rio Beni region of Bolivia. Set up in 1978 by highland migrants, the El Ceibo cooperative is made up of 36 cooperatives and has received attention as a farmer-owned company trading internationally with a unique social organisational structure premised on equitable income earnings, reciprocity, solidarity and consensus-building assemblies (Tiffen and Zadek, 1998: 25; Organic Trader, 2006). All members spend time at the cocoa factory or in administration in the capital, La Paz, to ensure that they develop skills and training. Farmers reserve some of their revenue for social projects in order to ensure that community development and technical training are available, as well as to provide a safety fund for medical emergencies (Organic Trader, 2006). In 1995, El Ceibo embarked on the construction of a new factory with modern installations to improve product quality and value-added.

A final illustrative example is Kuapa Kokoo, a cocoa farmers' cooperative comprising some 48 000 small-scale cocoa growers located in Ghana. Established by Nana Frimpong Abebrese in 1993, with the assistance of the UK-based Third World Information Network Ltd (TWIN Ltd), Kuapa was intent on increasing its farmer members' power and presentation within the cocoa market. At its 1997 AGM, Kuapa decided to set up Divine Chocolate Ltd with the intention to increase their share of profits from the cocoa they produced, enhance their knowledge of the consumer chocolate market, and produce their own chocolate brand for sale in the UK market (Kuapa Kokoo, 2006; Divine Chocolate Ltd, 2006). The Kuapa Kokoo Farmers' Trust (KKFT), a unit of Kuapa Kokoo, was set up to receive the premiums gained from Fairtrade and oversee the use of these funds meant for the benefit of Kuapa farmer members. Their fair trade partnership in Divine Chocolate Ltd has ensured that the cocoa farmers have consistently received a better deal, enabling them to earn a living from their skills, and it has provided training and access to market information. Between 1995 and 2005, 100 projects have been financed by the KKFT, including the drilling of boreholes, income diversification and generation projects (such as women's soap production), a credit union for credit and banking services, schools and education (including the provision of educational resources), sanitary facilities and the purchase of three vehicles (Kuapa Kokoo, 2006).

In addition to the positive outcomes of fair trade for producers, researchers also note the positive impact on consumers (Levi and Linton, 2003; Murray and Raynolds, 2000: 67; Raynolds, 2000; Hudson and Hudson, 2003). As Murray and Raynolds (2000: 67) observe, through its awareness-raising activities, fair trade 'educate[s] consumers to move beyond their own self-interest in making purchasing choices'. For others, it 'unveils' (Hudson and Hudson, 2003: 1) and 'makes visible' the 'invisible hand of the market' (Raynolds, 2000: 306), serving to trigger the consumer's 'politically crucial leap from passive consumerism to active engagement' (Hudson and Hudson, 2003: 1) (see Chapter 4). At both the producer and consumer ends of international business and trade, then, the fair trade movement has attempted to challenge the corporate control of global supply and demand (see Chapter 2). Before we turn to investigate their attempts more closely in later chapters, it is instructive to ask: how did this movement begin? And how has it evolved since?

FAIR TRADE AS POLITICAL ACTIVISM AND 'ALTERNATIVE TRADE'

The earliest signs of fair trade trace back to the post-World War II context of 1946 with a US-based religious organisation now known as Ten Thousand Villages (Kocken, 2003; Wills, 2006: 9). Ten Thousand Villages traded directly with producers of needlework from Puerto Rico, joined soon after by SERRV International (also based in the USA), which began trading with producers in the South. By 1958, the first alternative trading organisation (ATO) was established to sell these goods to US consumers. In Europe, the goods of Chinese refugees were sold to consumers through Oxfam UK shop outlets. Simultaneously, groups in the Netherlands set up importing organisations for producers' goods under the name Fair Trade Organisatie (1967). Parallel to the emergence of these pioneering religious and charity organisations, the Generalized System of Preferences (GSP) was established at UNCTAD's Delhi conference (1968) as a means to create an equitable trading regime between North and South countries. The GSP was stimulated by developing countries' pressure for the creation of an equitable trading system from which they would receive the benefits of international trade to support their socio-economic development. Their advocacy of 'trade not aid' focused attention on Northern appropriation of value from the South for minimal return, delivered by way of (tied) international aid (Kocken, 2003; Low and Davenport, 2005: 145).

Within this political context and struggle for national economic liberation from Western countries' own interests, the ATOs' pioneering alternative approaches to trade played a vital role in consumer education and awareness-raising, and concomitantly in the spread of fair trade activism and support. The movement developed throughout the 1970s to 1990s among politically motivated individuals both in consumer countries and in Latin America, Africa and Asia (Low and Davenport, 2005). Through missionary contacts, export sales of handcrafts from producer groups provided valuable 'supplementary income' for households (largely run by women who were economically disadvantaged) (Kocken, 2003; see also Litrell and Dickson, 1999). Handcrafts were sold through world shops or ATO retail outlets (as remains the case today – see below). Many ATOs were established in these Southern regions with the help of development organisations with subsidiary branches. This support helped to organise producers into cooperatives and build capacity, establish social development initiatives, and enable producers to export their product.

Despite growing awareness in consumer markets about trade injustice through ATOs' campaigning efforts, the product range they offered was limited primarily to handcrafts[8] and the consumer market remained small. As Tallontire (2000: 168) writes, 'the producer focus of earlier periods was associated with the neglect of the consumer. As profits dropped and some ATOs faced bankruptcy, many ATOs began to look towards consumer needs and to balance these with those of producers.' By the 1990s, it became clear that the Northern ATO model – of religious or charitable origin – was proving to be an unsustainable and inadequate means of providing significant benefits to a significant number of producers. Losing their 'unique selling proposition' more generally to a rising international market in 'exotic' goods, ATOs were also receiving requests from their core consumer market for more guarantees and product information – ATOs' 'word' was insufficient (Low and Davenport, 2005: 146). To address the dwindling of an already small market, the 1990s saw new approaches adopted and structures emerge to incorporate a focus on consumer marketing, product development and product quality (Tallontire, 2000).

INSTITUTIONAL DEVELOPMENT (1990S)

Product Certification and the Fairtrade Labelling Organizations International (FLO)

A new – but not substitute – approach that emerged to address the problem of scale was the product certification system. At the end of the 1980s, a priest working with Mexican coffee producers and affiliated with a Dutch religious organisation, Solidaridad, developed the idea of a product label to create a new way to enable a broad consumer market to engage with fair trade. The idea was simple: goods that were bought, traded and sold on fair trade terms could be visually distinguished and recognised on any supermarket shelf by the product certification label; they would not need to be sold through ATO outlets to convey or ensure their unique production and trading value. This tool would enable a product to be sold in a wider number and range of outlets where the majority of consumers shopped. The certification and labelling system that was subsequently developed in the Netherlands was called 'Max Havelaar' – the name of a fictional Dutch literary character who exposed the exploitation of coffee farmers in Javanese colonies for the Dutch coffee market. ATOs throughout Europe instigated the establishment of labelling organisations in their countries – culminating in the establishment of the Fairtrade Labelling Organizations International (FLO) in 1997, an organisation representing the now 20 Labelling Initiatives (LIs) that exist in 21 countries.[9]

Today, FLO is the worldwide standard-setting and certification organisation for labelled Fairtrade. FLO's mission is to 'improve the position of the poor and disadvantaged producers in the developing world, by setting the Fairtrade standards and by creating a framework that enables trade to take place at conditions respecting their interest' (FLO, 2006a). Consisting of two organisations, FLO e.V. and FLO Cert. (see Figure 3.2), FLO has three responsibilities: setting the international Fairtrade standards; product certification and trade auditing; and producer support services.

FLO e.V. is a multi-stakeholder association involving FLO's 20 member organisations (Labelling Initiatives), producer organisations, traders and external experts. It develops and reviews standards, and assists producers in gaining and maintaining certification in order to capitalise on market opportunities.[10] Fairtrade standard development (for any product) involves developing producer organisational requirements (including generic product group standards – one for smallholder cooperatives and one for plantations), sustainable production requirements, and trade standards for requirements between producer, exporter and importer relations.[11] Once product standards have been developed and approved, producers are inspected for their compliance with the standards.

FLO Cert. works with more than 60 local inspectors to carry out this work, which involves the following steps. Once a producer group has registered for an inspection, an FLO inspector spends the requisite period of time for the size of the cooperative or plantation involved (e.g. around one or two weeks). Existing FLO-certified producer groups are re-inspected annually, and in addition, random inspection visits are conducted by FLO inspectors. Following the inspection of a producer group, the FLO inspector writes a compliance-assessment report on the group's adherence to the relevant product standards, which the Certification Committee[12] reviews to determine a group's compliance.[13]

Once the standard-setting, producer inspections and Certification Committee approvals are finalised, traders[14] can apply to the LI in their respective country to participate in FLO's system. Approved traders are audited on their Fairtrade transactions, submitting to FLO and/or the LI transparent reports of all sales and purchases of Fairtrade produce to the point of labelling the final product. Overseen by the Certification and Appeals Committee, FLO conducts trade audits of producers, exporters and importers. When an importer buys the product from the Fairtrade cooperative, the LI in the country in which that product is intended for sale tracks the supply chain, and the companies that buy the Fairtrade-labelled product from FLO registered traders require a licence from the LI in order to sell that product. Thus FLO Cert. ensures that producers and traders comply with the standards and that producers invest the benefits received through Fairtrade into development projects. It coordinates all tasks and processes all information related to the inspection of producers, trade auditing and certification.

In early 2004, FLO Cert. was legally separated from FLO e.V. as a subsidiary of FLO (see Figure 3.2). Until 2004, FLO was one organisation, and producer certification, standard-setting and producer organisations' involvement in FLO commingled. This was due to the developmental objectives of Fairtrade. Under this arrangement, FLO both set standards and monitored compliance, and producers were exempt from certification payments – these were subsidised by consumers (Tallontire, 2002). The separation of FLO into standard-setting and standard inspection/certification functions aims to mitigate the potential for conflict of interest and is in accordance with ISO Standards for certification bodies. It is also designed to help FLO cover the cost of inspection and trade-auditing functions for both producers and traders, which both groups now pay to FLO Cert. (Doppler and González Cabañas, 2006: 54–5).

The International Fair Trade Association (IFAT)

Parallel to the development of FLO and the LIs was the formal international organisation of Fair Trade Organizations (FTOs) (then alternative trading organisations).[15] In 1989, the International Federation for Fair Trade (IFAT) (now the International Fair Trade Association) was established.[16] IFAT is a global association for the fair trade industry of nearly 300 FTOs of producers and traders (of labelled and non-labelled products)

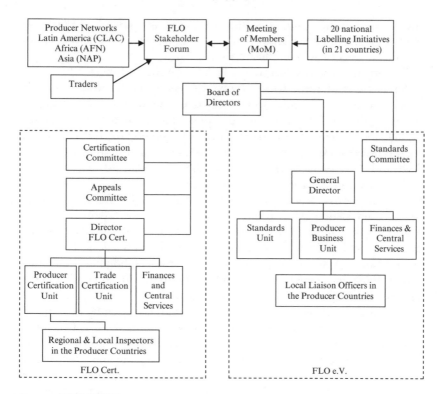

Source: FLO (2005b).

Figure 3.2 FLO organisational structure in 2004/05

situated in nearly 70 countries.[17] IFAT exists to 'improve the livelihoods and well being of disadvantaged producers by linking and promoting Fair Trade Organizations and speaking out for greater justice in world trade' (IFAT, 2006a). IFAT does this through three core organisational activities: (1) developing the market for fair trade (providing information on market opportunities to IFAT members, organising conferences and workshops and acting as an information centre); (2) building trust in fair trade (IFAT operates a three-levelled monitoring system including self-assessment, peer review and external verification, and for registering FTOs (distinguished by the Fair Trade Organizational Mark (FTO Mark)); (3) speaking out for fair trade (IFAT develops the voice of fair trade by building the IFAT network, building the capacity of its members, and through this, conducting advocacy campaigns more effectively). It also works through the F.I.N.E. Advocacy Office[18] to lobby political institutions and

coordinate international campaigns and advocacy (IFAT, 2006b). The
political achievements of the movement at regional and international levels
to date are documented in the Appendix.

The organisational structure for IFAT is shown in Figure 7.1 (p. 176).
IFAT consists of three main groups: its members, the Board, and the
IFAT Secretariat. Members are located in five different regions, each
region represented by one elected representative on the IFAT Board.
Today, more than two-thirds of IFAT's members are from Southern
regions (around 60 per cent of members are from the Middle East, Africa,
Asia and Latin America). IFAT members in Asia, Africa and Latin
America have established regional platforms: the Asia Fair Trade Forum
(2001), the Cooperative for Fair Trade in Africa (COFTA) (2005), the
Associacion Latino Americana de Commercio Justo (2006) and, soon,
Europe. National platforms are also being rapidly established within these
regions, including ECOTA Fair Trade Forum in Bangladesh, Fair Trade
Group Nepal, Associated Partners for Fair Trade Philippines, Fair Trade
Forum India and Kenya Federation for Alternative Trade (KEFAT) (see
Chapter 7 for further detail on IFAT's operations).

The Board is the second key group in IFAT. It is a voluntary committee
comprising five members elected by, and from among, the IFAT membership at the biennial Annual General Meeting (AGM). As of the 2007 IFAT
AGM, the Board has been expanded to include nine members, introducing three independendent Board Directors and an independent President
who are elected by the AGM. The Board develops and implements the
directive agreed by the IFAT membership at each biennial AGM, makes
policy, and decides on membership applications. IFAT's Secretariat is the
third group. The Secretariat is a contact point for members worldwide,
facilitating and coordinating members' initiatives and activities, and uses
its position at the centre of a global network to make links between, and
disseminate information to, individuals, groups and networks (IFAT,
2006c).

While the organisational development of Southern regional platforms
has been a more recent phenomenon (see Chapter 7), during the 1990s
IFAT's institutional development was predominantly Northern-centred,
with the establishment of the European Fair Trade Association (EFTA),
its US counterpart the Fair Trade Federation (FTF), and the Network of
European Worldshops (NEWS!). These strategic institutional arrangements (IFAT, EFTA, FTF, NEWS!) emerged to address not only issues of
networking and information exchange to link producers and traders, but
also macro-issues of fair trade market governance and development.

Established in 1990, EFTA is an association of 11 importing organisations located in nine countries across Europe (Austria, Belgium, France,

Germany, Italy, the Netherlands, Spain, Switzerland and the UK). Together they import from over 400 marginalised producer groups across Africa, Asia and Latin America. EFTA aims to support the work of its member organisations and to foster greater cooperation and coordination among them. It circulates information and organises member meetings in order to facilitate information exchanges and networking, divides overlapping functions between members for greater efficiency, and identifies and pursues joint initiatives (Krier, 2005: 25).

With its roots in the 1980s, the then North American Alternative Trade Organization (NAATO) held annual conferences for North American ATOs. This group incorporated in 1994 with an elected board, changing its name to the Fair Trade Federation in the following year (Novey, 5 June 2006, fieldwork notes). Today, the Fair Trade Federation (FTF) (USA) is an association of USA-based wholesalers, traders and producers whose members have fair trade principles at the core of their work. Specifically, members are committed to 'providing fair wages and good employment opportunities to economically disadvantaged artisans and farmers worldwide' (Fair Trade Federation, 2006). FTF also disseminates and exchanges information on resources and opportunities by producing a news journal for members about upcoming fair trade events. Furthermore, the FTF offers members access to its member directory and trading network to facilitate their work (Krier, 2005: 25).

NEWS! is a network of 15 national Worldshop associations, comprising roughly 2400 shops across 13 countries. The network was established in 1994 to facilitate networking and cooperation among members by providing information, to organise a bi-annual conference, and to develop and coordinate European-wide campaigns (including developing and disseminating the necessary campaign materials to its members).

MAINSTREAMING FAIR TRADE (2000–)

The rapid growth of Fairtrade markets in recent years can be largely attributed to the Fairtrade certification system (Raynolds, 2002; Caldwell and Bacon, 2005). The positive reception and success with 'mainstream' consumers during the 1990s enabled the movement to stake out a place in traditional mainstream outlets through conventional retailers and traders. With its emergence came the availability of a score of new product categories (beyond the tradition of textiles, giftware and handcrafts), including coffee, tea, rice, sugar, cocoa, fresh fruit, juices, honey, spices and nuts, sports balls, wine and flowers. With a wider product range available and rising consumer awareness through novel social marketing initiatives,[19] 'sympathetic' large retailers and health food stores were the first to begin offering Fairtrade products through mainstream distribution channels such as the UK health food store 'Fresh and Wild' and the Co-operative Group ('the Co-op'). For instance, the Co-op converted all of its own-label coffee and chocolate to Fairtrade in 2002 and 2003 respectively and it endeavours to work in long-term partnership with, and for the benefit of, the producer cooperatives with which it is associated (Barrientos and Smith, 2007: 111–12).

The uptake of Fairtrade products in more traditional commercial retail settings and by conventional multinational retailers and manufacturers is gathering strength, which has in turn immensely increased the volume, turnover and awareness of Fairtrade products.

During 2004, the global retail sale of roughly US$1 billion in Fairtrade-labelled products contributed roughly US$100 million in financial return to producers (FLO, 2005b). In 2005, global retail sales rose by 37 per cent to roughly US$1.5 billion, and a further 42 per cent in 2006 to €1.6 billion (over US$2.5 billion) (FLO, 2007a). The fair trade market is hence considered to be one of the fastest-growing markets in the world, with an annual growth rate of 40 per cent (Krier, 2005: 7; FLO, 2007a: 3). Conventional retailers have played a particularly significant role in fast-tracking the growth of Fairtrade-certified product markets through access to established retail channels.[20]

In Switzerland, for instance, the two national retailers, Migros and Coop, offer own-label Fairtrade products in ten and nine different own-label product groups respectively (Nicholls and Opal, 2005: 196). Migros's turnover of Fairtrade products accounted for 40 per cent of the total sales of Fairtrade in Switzerland in 2002 (ibid.). This kind of mainstream retail access has enabled Fairtrade bananas, for instance, to hold 55 per cent of the Swiss banana market (FLO, 2007a: 16). In the UK, in addition to the Co-op, Sainsbury's (2002) and Tesco (2004) offer own-label Fairtrade products and the other remaining retailers have begun stocking Fairtrade goods (Nicholls and Opal, 2005: 193). Albert Heijn (Holland), Monoprix (France) and Albertson's (USA) are other large retailers stocking Fairtrade goods. The year 2006 also saw Fairtrade teas and coffees expand further into the market, with Marks and Spencer converting its entire tea and coffee range to Fairtrade, one of Sweden's major hotels Scandic and Hilton serving only Fairtrade coffee to customers, and the Irish airline Ryanair and German Air Berlin offering Fairtrade coffee to passengers (FLO, 2007a: 19).

FTO importers and brand companies have also contributed to this growth. Krier (2005: 28) notes that the seven largest EFTA members (fair trade importers) have seen their sales figures increase by 80 per cent in five years, and altogether the 11 EFTA members sold more than US$250 million worth of labelled and non-labelled fair trade goods in 2004. Cafédirect is now the fourth-largest coffee brand in the UK market, and worth £8.4 million (Cafédirect, 2006; see Chapter 6). Equal Exchange in the USA saw its sales grow from US$10.4 million in 2002 to US$20.7 million by 2005 (Equal Exchange, 2005a). For its part, Divine Chocolate Ltd grew by 18 per cent in 2006 to reach US$18 million in sales and recorded a post-tax profit of over £450 000. After ten years of business, in 2007 the company made its first dividend of £500/share (Martyn, 2007) and, like AgroFair, has recently expanded into the US market (*The Economist*, 2007).

Notably, large-scale brand companies' move into the Fairtrade market – including those discussed in Chapter 2 from the coffee market – has been recalcitrant and largely superficial, a response that has gained increasing attention at a practical and academic level (see Chapters 5 and 7; Fridell et al., forthcoming; Raynolds et al., 2007; Low and Davenport, 2006). In practice, conventional brand companies have engaged in 'tokenism' – stocking minimal amounts of Fairtrade products under new niche brands (see Hood, 2007; see Chapters 5 and 7). A key example is Nestlé's 'Partner's Blend' (launched in the UK in 2004), which amounts to less than one-tenth of 1 per cent of Nestlé's total volume (North, 2006).

Corporate buyers' response has been met with severe criticism from within the fair trade movement (AGICES, 11 November 2005; Equal Exchange, 2005b; North, 2006; Ransom, 2005; see also Caldwell and Bacon, 2005; Wills, 2006: 13–14; Hood, 2007). The corporate-buyer model of Fairtrade market participation contrasts FTOs' model of fair trade. They are the 'first-movers' in fair trade markets who see conventional traders selling a few Fairtrade products – largely in response to consumer pressure – as falling well short of fair trade's broader principles (see Traidcraft, 2003, 2004). FTOs share a more expansive vision of fair trade encapsulated in the International Fair Trade Association's (IFAT) stand-ards for FTOs (see above, pp. 58–60). As part of the FTO movement's critique of traditional corporations' commitment to fair trade (or lack thereof), during the 1990s a number of 'new' FTOs emerged that pushed the traditional boundaries of FTOs' alternative-market status to compete with conventional firms on fair trade principles and practice in a commer-cial arena. A number of fair trade pioneers created for-profit, FTO brand companies to sell branded fair trade products to mainstream consumers. As well as having thrived commercially (see above), each company – such as Cafédirect, Divine Chocolate Ltd, Equal Exchange and AgroFair – is a unique experiment in producer co-ownership that attempts to shift the distribution and ownership of market value in favour of producers and to confer greater market control on them (see Chapter 6). On the whole, the

recent phase of 'mainstreaming' Fairtrade in consumer markets has produced a spectrum of commitment to fair trade principles (see Figure 3.3).

Research on 'mainstreaming' Fairtrade has begun to question the
capacity of the certification system to produce meaningful and sustainable developmental outcomes for small-scale producers (see Hutchens,
forthcoming; Raynolds et al., 2007; Tallontire, 2006; Barrientos and
Dolan, 2006; Doppler and González Cabañas, 2006; Low and Davenport,
2005: 151; Bezençon and Blili, 2006; Renard, 2003; Aranda and Morales,
2002: 20; VanderHoff Boersma, 2002; Chapters 5–7). Indeed, it is between
the two approaches to fair trade – as an organisational model and as a
product certification and labelling system – that empirical discrepancies
have emerged. Bezençon and Blili (2006), for instance, draw attention to
the different supply chain configurations between the 'alternative' (FTO)
model and 'mainstream' (product certification) model and note that key
fair trade principles are relaxed, if not absent, in the latter. The affected
principles include direct partnerships, long-term trading relations, minimal
social distance between producers and consumers, a prioritisation of marginalised producers, cooperation between traders to expand the fair trade
market, and political lobbying and campaigning for trade justice.

In the absence of these principles, Shreck (2005) observes that the power
relationship in conventional supply chains – indeed the supply chain configurations themselves (see Chapter 2) – as well as the market realities that
small-scale producers face, remain unchanged in the certification system.
At one with this view, researchers Low and Davenport (2005: 151–2)
contend that whilst delivering meaningful development and empowerment
for producers in the future does not preclude 'mainstreaming', it will presuppose a more 'radical mainstreaming' approach pioneered by FTOs (see
Chapter 6; Hutchens, forthcoming).

In the context of corporate buyers entering Fairtrade markets, the principal concern for FTOs is that consumers will perceive conventional brand
companies and FTOs as alike; that corporations have 'reformed' their business practices and policies when little about them has changed – and instead
the Fairtrade system changes to accommodate *them*. In other words, this
new context will blur the perceptual differences between a Fairtrade-
labelled product and a fair trade company (Equal Exchange, 2005b; North,
2006). The risk is to consumers' understanding of the FTO 'gold standard'
and the value they place on it, and indeed to the loss of the movement's
core constituents who in the meantime perceive fair trade to be 'selling out'
(see Chapters 5–7; Renard, 2003; Murray et al., 2003; Tallontire, 2002;
Caldwell and Bacon, 2005; Nicholls and Opal, 2005: 246; Sweney, 2001;
Low and Davenport, 2005: 148).[21] As a voluntary market-based system, the
movement relies on its fair trade supporters, consumers and FTOs at the

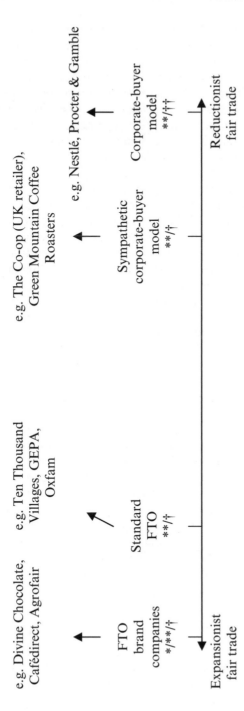

e.g. Divine Chocolate, Cafédirect, Agrofair

e.g. Ten Thousand Villages, GEPA, Oxfam

e.g. The Co-op (UK retailer), Green Mountain Coffee Roasters

e.g. Nestlé, Procter & Gamble

FTO brand companies
*/**/†

Standard FTO
**/†

Sympathetic corporate-buyer model
**/†

Corporate-buyer model
**/††

Expansionist fair trade

Reductionist fair trade

Notes:
* Producer brand co-ownership in specialised product.
** FLO Label.
† FTO Mark/meet FTO standards.
†† Corporate buyer-owned brand.

Source: Hutchens (forthcoming).

Figure 3.3 Typology of trader participation in fair trade/Fairtrade markets

community level who have been and continue to be the engine of the fair trade market's growth (see Nicholls and Opal, 2005: 163–78; see Chapter 4). Hence, in a market where certified Fairtrade goods are widely available, yet essential 'fair trade' principles are being poorly applied by mainstream traders (i.e. non-FTOs), IFAT developed a monitoring system for 100 per cent FTOs in 2004. The FTO Mark is of special importance to FTOs selling a range of fair trade products in the market (many of which do not carry a Fairtrade Mark, such as handcrafts[22]): it strengthens the credibility and value of their shops and products among consumers (see Chapter 7).

This development makes explicit a fundamental philosophical difference between those overseeing and administering the Fairtrade-labelling system under the auspices of FLO and the LIs, and those promoting FTO principles under the auspices of IFAT and FTO networks. While not mutually exclusive, and though sharing a broadly defined mission, the two constituencies use different models that reflect their different visions for fair trade. The former views fair trade as a means of corporate reform, but one that continues to recognise the prevailing market system. The latter sees fair trade as a means for transforming the institutions and values of the existing market on the basis of fair trade principles (Wilkinson and Mascarenhas, 2007a, 2007b; Renard and Pérez-Grovas, 2007; Chapters 5–7).

The future of fair trade depends largely on the capacity and willingness of IFAT and FLO – with the different visions and approaches they represent – to achieve institutional coordination and cohesion (see Raynolds et al., 2007; Jaffee, 2007; Wilkinson and Mascarenhas, 2007a; Renard and Pérez-Grovas, 2007; Murray et al., 2005; Nicholls and Opal, 2005). The controversy and significance of this issue – and many more – is brought to life in the accounts of practitioners, policy-makers and industry players contained in the chapters that follow. This is particularly the case with the controversial decisions that have flowed from FLO's determination of issues such as MNC participation in the Fairtrade system, certification of plantations and producer certification costs (see Chapter 5). On the other hand is a broader challenge of how to govern markets in ways that uphold the movement's 'gold standard' to progress the movement's mission while simultaneously influencing conventional market actors to move towards a fair trade paradigm rather than undermine it. These issues and more are the subject of the following chapters.

CONCLUSION

While the fair trade movement spans more than 40 years of offering market access to small-scale producers in developing countries on beneficial terms, today it is being driven forward by a diverse set of actors with different roles and objectives. The need to reconcile the tensions that have emerged between them is made all the more pressing by its continued and rapid market growth worldwide. As fair trade has evolved into a mainstream phenomenon, principally via the Fairtrade certification system led by FLO and the LIs, challenges to fair trade's capacity to deliver developmental gains have begun to emerge in greater numbers (see Chapters 5 and 7). In light of the tensions and inconsistencies that have emerged in the present-day era of 'mainstreaming' fair trade, the following chapters empirically examine the two models of fair trade – as an organisational model and as a product certification model – and the institutions (IFAT and FLO) and the actors that have guided their development thus far.

The story of fair trade that follows derives directly from the author's own travels and conversations over a period of four months in 2005 with a diverse group of actors involved in fair trade located in Europe, the USA, and in Latin America.[23] It covers the mechanics of fair trade's grassroots-based expansion and its complex political and organisational trends and dynamics. In addition to interviews, several respondents offered documents, leaflets, annual reports, draft policy documents and minutes of meetings to aid the research project and to assist in building a picture of the historical context of particular issues and debates. These documents have been important for staying abreast of organisational and policy developments during the writing process. This was significant in the case of Chapter 7, which was being written at a time when parts of its story were unfolding and key institutional decisions within the fair trade community were being made. Without the thoughtfulness and goodwill of these respondents, the in-depth story of the movement, and the theoretical insights about the process of social change that it offers, could not have been documented and conceived.

NOTES

1. According to the UNDP's Human Development Report (2005: 129), the agricultural subsidies paid by the USA and EU to agricultural industry lobbies are *the* root cause of the failure of the Doha Development Round of the WTO to deliver concrete change – a round of negotiations designed to make international trade 'work' for the developmental needs of developing countries. Per year, the US and EU pay US$350 billion to the most politically influential agricultural farming groups – corporate agribusiness entities and landowners, and large-scale farmers.
2. Heffernan et al. (1999) and others highlight that the growing vertical integration of global firms' production – from 'gene to supermarket shelf' – is removing any point of sale from which 'price discovery' will be realised (see also Murphy, 1999, 2002).
3. Long-term transparent relations are less common among conventional traders engaging

with Fairtrade (see below; see Bezençon and Blili, 2006; Tallontire, 2006; Barrientos and Smith, 2007; Traidcraft, 2003, 2004).

4. While the minimum price is a sticking point of fair trade for free trade proponents (who see it as an inefficient subsidy that encourages overproduction of low-quality coffee) (see Lindsey, 2004), the notion of a minimum wage is not unfamiliar to economists, Keynes being a notable example. For a counterargument to the 'inefficiency' thesis see Hayes (2006).

5. Production and living costs are calculated per country or region, determined through consultation with producers. Production costs include land, labour and capital outlays, and living costs are determined on the basis of national minimum wages and interest rate estimates. Further costs for organic certification are also built into the minimum price where applicable (Nicholls and Opal, 2005: 41).

6. Compliance costs include organisation of producer meetings, inspection and reporting administration, regional and international FLO meetings (Nicholls and Opal, 2005: 41).

7. A British volunteer helped to set up the Estwatini Kitchen to enable marginalised women and the handicapped to earn an income and be empowered by the social organisation of the business.

8. Trading in coffee between coffee producers in Guatemala and Fair Trade Organisatie in the Netherlands began only in 1973.

9. There are 20 LIs in 21 countries: Austria, Belgium, Canada, Denmark, France, Germany, the UK, Italy, Ireland, Japan, Luxemburg, the Netherlands, Norway, Finland, Sweden, Switzerland, the USA, Australia, New Zealand and Spain. Mexico and South Africa are 'Associate' LIs.

10. FLO's standards for coffee were developed on the basis of the pre-existing LIs' coffee standards, which have served as a template for subsequent product standards. Comprising two FLO staff, three LI representatives, one ATO, producer group, commercial trader and independent actor, the Standards & Policy Committee meets five to six times per year (Nicholls and Opal, 2005).

11. The Committee approves new – and amendments to existing – Fairtrade product standards, and addresses proposals to draft new ones, changes to minimum prices attached to existing Fairtrade products and changes to particular aspects of existing Fairtrade standards (whether in relation to trade standards, producer or sustainability requirements). Given the relationship between Fairtrade standards and its strategic objectives, the Standards & Policy Committee can seek FLO board guidance and clarification over certain issues.

12. Similar to the Standards & Policy Committee, the Certification Committee meets five to six times per year, and comprises the same number of specific actors (two FLO staff, three LI representatives, one ATO, producer group, commercial trader and independent body).

13. Producer groups that are judged as unsuccessful in fulfilling the requirements can appeal the decision to the Appeals Committee (comprising of FLO board members and experts appointed for the specific case in question), whose decision on producer compliance is conclusive.

14. Traders can include product exporters, importers and manufacturers, but are limited to those involved in the labelling and packaging of the product (which excludes supermarket retailers from contractual commitments) (see Barrientos and Smith, 2007).

15. For the purposes of the book, the section on IFAT in this chapter deals only with IFAT's emergence. Its operation, system of governance and evolution are elaborated and examined in Chapter 7.

16. At the time of publication IFAT was changing its name to the World Fair Trade Organization (WFTO). The term 'IFAT' is used in this book as being correct during the research period.

17. FTOs have 'Fair Trade' principles at the core of their business model (IFAT, 2006j).

18. The F.I.N.E. Advocacy Office in Brussels, Belgium, was set up with the purpose of influencing European policy-makers. The acronym 'F.I.N.E.' represents the four networks

that support, manage and fund this organisation, FLO, IFAT, NEWS! and EFTA. F.I.N.E. exists to facilitate cooperation between these members and their networks on issues of advocacy/campaigning and 'Fair Trade' standards and monitoring (IFAT, 2006b).

19. The movement has initiated and exploited novel forms of social marketing and consumer education to continue to expand fair trade markets including phenomena such as 'Fair Trade Fortnight', 'Fair Trade Towns', 'Fair Trade Churches' and 'Fair Trade Universities/Schools'. These grassroots community initiatives bring together members and organisations in a town, university campus or school for the purpose of promoting Fairtrade and have spread quickly from the UK to Canada and Australia. Active student networks and movements have likewise spread, with annual or biennial conferences organised in the USA, Canada, Europe, the UK, Australia/New Zealand as well as at international fora such as WTO's Ministerial Meetings.

20. According to IFAT (2006j), more than two-thirds of Fairtrade products are sold in catering and retail outlets. Fairtrade-certified products are now being offered to consumers by global brand companies, movie theatre complexes, global retailers and catering services.

21. Global brand companies engaging with Fairtrade such as Nestlé, Chiquita, Starbucks or Procter & Gamble are long-standing targets of political campaigning and activism, with dubious reputations for their social and environmental practices abroad. Nestlé is the world's most boycotted company and 'the largest single source of violations of the World Health Organization and UNICEF's International Code on Marketing Breast-Milk Substitutes' (cited in Ransom, 2005). Given Nestlé's history (see *New Internationalist*, 1973), anti-Nestlé campaign organisations have encouraged UK consumers to boycott the Partner's Blend brand because it 'makes an absolute mockery of what the public believes the Fairtrade Mark stands for' (Randall, cited in Ransom, 2005).

22. FLO's system is more amenable to food product certification than for textile and handcraft production. The variation in the techniques and logistics of production for craft products is highly problematic as far as developing across-the-board standard specifications is concerned (Nicholls and Opal, 2005: 24). Yet many Southern FTOs produce handcrafts, for which FLO does not have standards. These producers have been ultimately excluded from the benefits which food-producing farmers receive in the Fairtrade certification system, and the market for fair trade handcrafts has languished (ibid.: 24–5). Despite the logistical and political difficulties, IFAT is presently working with FLO to develop an 'on product' mark for all 'Fair Trade' products in order to incorporate handcrafts into 'mainstream' Fairtrade product markets (see Chapter 7). The commercial market potential for handcrafts is significant. As Nicholls and Opal (ibid.: 236) observe, by contrast to the US$107 million worth of sales in fair trade handcrafts made in Europe in 2003, the European 'exotic gifts' market – comprising principally private sector enterprises – amounts to an estimated US$6.3 billion.

23. For further detail on the research methodology used for this research, see Hutchens (2007).

4.   Networking networks for scale

In the overview of power theories offered in Chapter 1, 'power over' was identified as the traditional way of scaling up, such as by building a geo-political empire through conquest or a business empire through takeovers. The example of the global coffee market in Chapter 2 provided a vivid example of the exercise of modern 'power over'. Yet in this context, the fair trade movement has also risen to challenge corporate hegemony (Chapter 3). It is here that theories of empowerment become relevant. In a corporate-dominated market and culture, fair trade's growth gives us a glimpse of the incipient possibility of scaling up by means of 'power beyond' as an emergent property of the interaction among 'power with', 'power to' and 'power within': the 'power to' enrol networks of networks comes from the 'power within' fair trade's pioneers, which in turn is constituted through 'power with' their supporters. In other words, an alternative theory of power allows an alternative theory of the micro–macro mechanisms of networked transformation of regulatory capitalism.

NETWORKS' CONTEMPORARY RELEVANCE TO SOCIAL ACTION AND POWER

Network theory explores a large number of forms of social organisation, from families to organisations to nation-states.[1] The term 'network' refers to a set of actors or entities ('nodes') situated in a network, and network analysis involves mapping the relationships between these nodes ('ties'). Focusing on these nodal relationships, (social) network theory seeks to understand the way in which these relationships, and their nature, determine the behaviour, beliefs, social capital[2] and capacities of an entity.

Networks are thought to serve individuals by coordinating diffuse information, knowledge and capacities to facilitate action (Hayek, 1960).[3] Socially, networks are of especial value to human and societal well-being (Putnam, 2000; Lin, 2001; Portes, 1998), providing access to social resources derived from the networked relationships such as information, influence, social credentials, and social identity and recognition (Lin, 2001: 3). These endowments, often described loosely as 'social capital', are relational and thus unable to be 'owned' by, or attributed to, any one individual (Szreter, 2001: 291). Given their importance to individuals in society, exclusion from social networks is considered both a factor in, and a form of, social disadvantage (see Putnam, 2000; Portes, 1998).

Castells (1996) has been a seminal figure in stressing the significance of networks for our understanding of (power in) a knowledge society, describing networks as the 'new social morphology of our societies'. Information technology has recast traditional social networks as 'information' networks in one form or another, and as organisationally superior for operating in information-rich environments (Castells, 1996; Achrol and Kotler, 1999). As Dupont (2006: 35) argues, networks 'promise to absorb, recombine, and merge the two dominant and competing forms of social organisation (the bureaucratic hierarchy and the market) . . . [n]etworked governance seems to transcend the proclaimed obsolescence of bureaucracies . . . and the unsavoury smell of the market'. So influential are networks that 'the power of flows takes precedence over the flows of power' (Castells, 1996: 500). Strategic networking becomes a powerful weapon for rich or poor, weak or strong (see for example Burris et al., 2005; Braithwaite and Drahos, 2000).

Granovetter (1973, 1983) made early observations of the importance of networks to individuals, relative to the type of network relationship in question. Specifically, Granovetter (1973) suggested that new ideas, contacts, opportunities and access to resources flow abundantly in networked relationships that are of loose and/or informal affiliation, which he termed 'weak ties'. If the strength of a tie is constituted roughly by high levels of time, emotional intensity, reciprocal service and intimacy, weak ties have greater cohesive power in macro-social terms because 'weak ties are more likely to link members of different small groups than are strong [ties]' (ibid.: 1376). More than just linking them, 'ideas and information different from one's own' can reach out to benefit other individuals and groups by providing 'access to information and resources beyond those available in their own social circle' (Granovetter, 1983: 208–9). Weak ties, then, are highly suited to the knowledge society in which an abundance of information exists. Conversely, the qualities attributed to weak ties are scarce in networked relationships whose ties are 'strong', or proximate and insular in nature. Examples include those belonging to one's immediate social circle and family, or those premised on inequitable authority relationships. Hierarchical and bureaucratic organisations in particular are thought more readily to foster the insular, self-referential type of relationships described as 'strong ties' (Achrol and Kotler, 1999; see also Putnam, 1993),[4] which inhibit the free flow of information, ideas and knowledge. Put simply, individuals and groups have greater influence and access to available resources to the extent that they are networked with many others, and those many others likewise enjoy numerous dispersed relationships.

From a Latourian perspective, the reason why horizontal, broad-based network relationships have greater potential to exercise influence is that 'the amount of power exercised [by a person or group] varies not according to the power someone has, but to the number of other people who enter the composition' (Latour, 1986: 265). For Latour (1986), the real value of networks derives from the number of actors that constitutes a network. To the extent that 'weak', decentralised networks linking distant parts of the social system offer potential access to a greater number of networks than do 'strong ties', power rests with the cumulative effect of many agents who each 'translate' the project according to their worldview and contribute to the project's realisation. This account of power leads to the conclusion that, in a networked world, effecting power necessitates enrolment competence rather than the possession of military, technological or financial muscle (see Braithwaite and Drahos, 2000: 482; see also Allen, 2003).[5] This perspective offers the hopeful suggestion that resource-deficient groups can exert power in a knowledge economy through strategic networking – a type of networking that engages those necessary – and the numbers necessary – to trigger change.

NODALLY COORDINATED NETWORKS: FROM INFORMATION TO ACTION

While networks are crucial for enabling actors to better comprehend and influence the complexity of their social environment, little is understood about the means by which networks actually translate information into action (Burris et al., 2005). Aiming to further our understanding of the superiority of networks for producing outcomes, Burris et al. (2005: 37) draw attention to the 'nodes'[6] within networked arrangements that give the 'marching orders' to produce action in those networks. The authors posit the concept of nodally coordinated networks in order to develop a more nuanced and inductive account of governance through networks. This account accommodates the responsibility of particular nodes in a network for producing outcomes – and thus their conceptual priority for any accurate explanation of governance.

While theories of networks and networked and nodal governance aid a conceptualisation of why and how networks facilitate action and enable coordination, the fair trade movement's experience in scaling-up fair trade among a decentralised pool of consumers and supporters shows the networked mechanics of bringing about regulatory transformation in markets. The alternative theory of power on which this is based helps to reveal that actors tie existing networks together to catalyse a sequence of

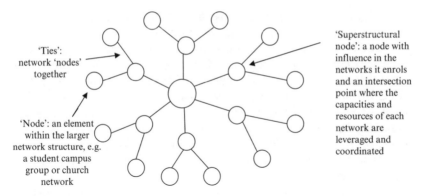

Figure 4.1   Networking networks to mobilise the resident resources, knowledge and capacity of network members

expanding circles of enrolment, thereby capitalising on the resources of many other networks.[7] In other words, scale is precipitated by tying existing networks together.

Figure 4.1 magnifies the expansionary effect of networking networks. A brief illustration of the process here sets up where the chapter is headed. This figure will be broken down into smaller segments shortly to provide a more nuanced explanation of the micro-activity of nodes.

In Figure 4.1 a 'node' refers to a cluster of people or organisations of varying size, whether dense networked relationships (such as a family unit) or dispersed and informal ones (such as a gym club). Nodes can include organisations, families, a shop, a swimming club, entire networks (such as a women's network) or office. The 'ties' refer to a networked relationship between two nodes initiated by one of them. Families enlist their children's schools, or a swimmers' club enrols the organisations for which each member works. Networking networks does not result in the conflation of the two networks. The first node simply mobilises the diffuse resources that reside in the second node and those that can be accessed beyond it. As will be shown below, networking networks is dialogic: networkers enlist networks in which they have established trust and credibility, using their contacts as 'bridges' to spread their mission among wider social circles. Networkers enlist networks in which they have established trust and credibility. Once enrolled, new networks open doors into a labyrinth of endless other networks.

Networks that tie several other networks to themselves can be conceptualised as 'superstructural' nodes (see Burris et al., 2005). A 'superstructural' node 'brings together representatives of different nodal organisations in a "superstructural" node to concentrate the members' resources and technologies for a common purpose but without integrating the various networks' (ibid.: 38). This chapter draws on the idea that a superstructural node ties but does not merge networks together; it is an intersection point that links different networks. It has influence and authority in the networks it ties to itself and is capable of effectively enrolling those networks to support the project. Those networks themselves become active agents or advocates of the project and are, in fact, the only way to generate increasing scale. The evolution of superstructural nodes begins by being activated themselves by other superstructural nodes. This is a feature of superstructural nodes not explored in Burris et al. (2005) but to which the chapter returns.

The analysis of the fair trade movement's experience of scaling up contributes to a growing body of research on fair trade to which the application of network theory is not without precedent.[8] While these studies focus on relatively contained networks and those tied to the structure of production and consumption relationships – whether directly between producer-and-consumer or producer-and-ATO, or a consumer community and producer community – they have not explored less contained or amorphous social networks or conceptualised their dynamic process of expansion.

NETWORKING NETWORKS: ACHIEVING SCALE WITH FAIRTRADE

According to Rosemary Byrde, Global Adviser on Fairtrade/Fair Trade for Oxfam GB, having 'reach' beyond activist circles was of strategic importance in the early days of the movement. Until the certification system emerged, consumers had not been effectively enrolled and were undervalued and unrecognised as a 'huge force' for social change (Byrde, 29 April 2005, fieldwork notes). Fair trade pioneers set up the Max Havelaar system (the initial model for Fairtrade certification and labelling) to remedy their lack of mainstream market access in that it 'addressed the everyday person in the street', not just activists, and has enabled everyone to participate in changing trade relations. Yet mainstream market access was no guarantee of mainstream market demand. The solution to this problem was found in the 'grassroots'. Recollecting the early days of the Max Havelaar system, Jeroen Douglas, Director of Fairtrade tropical fruit and cotton programmes at Solidaridad in the Netherlands, highlighted the key role of the 'grassroots' in solving this problem:

> the introduction of the Max Havelaar label was really a joint effort between the NGO movement and, in particular, the grassroots groups. It was not with love

that the product label entered the supermarket shelves . . . we really had to fight and *force* supermarkets to open market space, and the only way to do that was to mobilise grassroots campaigns. And *that* is really the clue to [our] success. We have managed through our campaign leaflets, through all the churches, the schools, the women's movements, the agricultural movements, to raise a lot of anger or *anxiety* from the grassroots groups who have been informed on the exploitative situations in the third world and they wanted to do something about it. So we said to them, 'we can offer you *fair* [trade] coffee' which you can buy with a fair conscience, which is promoting sustainable growth for the farmers involved. They all said 'where, where, where?', so we got to the problem: 'we don't have the distribution *yet*, and you have to bring it to us'. 'How then?' 'Well, let's organise actions, entering massively the supermarkets and obliging the managers of the supermarkets to incorporate fair [trade] coffee onto their shelves . . . if [the managers did] not?' – that was the threat – ' . . . we'll all move to your neighbour [competing retailer], who does have Max Havelaar coffee'. Within one week, all of the supermarkets turned to take the [fair trade] product on board . . . (12 April 2005, fieldwork notes)

This excerpt describes how fair trade rapidly achieved scale by networking social networks to spread the fair trade message. The movement did not build new networks, but tied established networks together. Solidaridad's experience brings Figure 4.1 (above) to life: Solidaridad is a superstructural node that networked powerful social networks – churches, schools, the agricultural, sympathetic businesses and women's movements – to its project. Figure 4.2 illustrates this arrangement.

The movement's successful enrolment of many networks reveals the rapidity with which this strategy achieves scale. Rather than spend years and significant resources building completely new networks, Solidaridad leveraged the 'ready-made' or well-established social capital embedded in other networks (Lin, 2001). Social network analysis tends to focus on how building or becoming part of a network benefits members (particularly marginal or disaffected members of society) (see Putnam, 2000; Granovetter, 1973). The micro-level activity occurring within and between networks in this case departs from this trend to show actors interpreting, perceiving and exploiting networks – their own and others – in highly advanced, entrepreneurial ways to achieve their ends. This points not

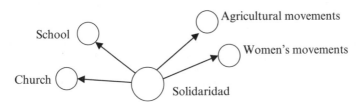

Figure 4.2 A superstructural node networking networks to itself for scale

only to social actors' awareness of networks as valuable and enabling in the process of social change, but also to their exploitation of networks to produce rapid outcomes.

The fair trade movement's story of success with the grassroots (its 'clue' to success) resonates with a Latourian (1986) conception of power as 'enrolment', where power is 'the consequence, not the cause, of collective action' and the amount of power produced is relative to 'the number of actors enrolled in the composition'. The fair trade movement's strategy of networking networks gives practical expression to the idea that only multiple networks acting in concert have the power to create scale. By linking more and more groups or networks of actors to support the certification system, the movement has realised power and scale in the marketplace. This process of building new structural patterns and outcomes through collective action is akin to Young's (2004) notion that new forms of 'social connections' can achieve structural change (see Chapter 1). Figure 1.1 (p. 21) depicts the process by which macro-scale and influence are generated: innovating in the first step triggers the process of scale at the second step (the collective level) by enrolling social networks. Collective action produces power at the local level and these pockets of power are linked at the transnational level by the regulatory model. 'Superstructural' nodes such as Solidaridad network networks together, weaving and activating new pockets of support that contribute new sources of power. The point is that the process of enrolment picks up speed and triggers large-scale change once networks start networking the idea across their own networks in organically expanding circles of enrolment (see Figure 4.5). As respondents from 'superstructural' nodes in the fair trade movement explained:

> The campaign I'm working on right now is to connect consumers of World's Finest Chocolate – the company that makes the fundraising bars for schools and churches and faith groups, and other charitable causes. We're [Global Exchange] trying to pressure them [World's Finest Chocolate] to carry Fairtrade, or to source some amount of Fairtrade for all their chocolate bars, and in *that* [campaign] action, it's *really* important that we bring together the actual customers that are organisations . . . here in San Francisco we work with the Archdiocese to support Fairtrade. We bring together these blocks of customers to support Fairtrade. (Guzzi, Fair Trade Chocolate Campaign Coordinator, Global Exchange, 10 May 2005, fieldwork notes)

> our [Lutheran World Relief] [LWR] whole goal is to get a greater number of congregations and individuals participating. . . . in 2002–2003, we looked at our records and saw that through the Lutheran World Relief coffee project we had sold 45 tonnes of Fairtrade coffee. [That figure] still put us at the highest percentage of faith groups at that time, but what we did was partner with the ELCA with the women's group and the women's *magazine* of the church. We did a one year project for the 2003–2004 year to run a project called 'Pour

Justice to the Brim: The 90-Tonne Challenge'. We challenged Lutheran congregations to double the amount of Fairtrade coffee that they purchased in a
year – to go from 45 to 90 tonnes. By October 2004, Lutheran affiliates, individuals, congregations and businesses – people who called and bought coffee
and identified themselves as Lutherans for this project – bought 99.4 tonnes of
coffee. So . . . we feel there's *real value* in putting this information out, maybe
it's not in the big world of coffee, but it's a lot for a single identified group to
buy. (Ford, former Policy Director, Public Policy, Lutheran World Relief, 14
July 2005, fieldwork notes)

The first comment illustrates the central point of this chapter: rather than
create a new network to expand the fair trade chocolate market, Global
Exchange mobilises other communities that have their own established
constituencies and resources. Guzzi's reasoning for this strategy is that the
'accumulation of all these small community initiatives adds up'. Global
Exchange is the intersection point between disparate initiatives. To make
linkages, superstructural nodes amidst larger fair trade structures appear
to work through communities in which they have influence. Individual
connections and contacts in other arenas have been vital for achieving
scale because they trigger new circles of enrolment in completely different
or inaccessible worlds. As one respondent put it:

the way we've organised ourselves has been as simple as saying . . . 'who do you
know?' Then we've built up a list. Everybody will know somebody who knows
somebody . . . and gradually you build up support . . . now, for example, we have
a cross Parliamentary working group on fair trade . . .

Important to note here is the evidently Latourian (1986) operation of, and
presumption about, power: no one particular organisational network or
institutional community is engaged but as many as possible in order to
weave a thicker social fabric with the many social threads that feed out
into broader society.

The second example of Lutheran World Relief's outreach initiative
illustrates how a superstructural node such as LWR (depicted in Figure
4.3) can itself be considered as 'a single identified group' within a much
larger fair trade network (Ford, 14 July 2005, fieldwork notes) (Figure
4.4). So while superstructural nodes are significant for initiating multiple
ties between many networks, they are not more 'special' or 'powerful' than
others. Within the larger networked structure of the movement they too
are activated by superstructural nodes (node 'x') that have enrolled them;
they are but one of a cluster of nodes that another superstructural node
has tied to itself.

The examples of Solidaridad, Global Exchange and LWR above demonstrate the scale that has been achieved by this unique nodal strategy

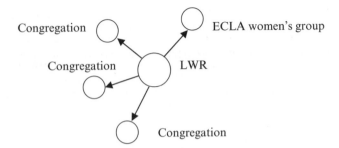

Figure 4.3   Lutheran World Relief as a superstructural node

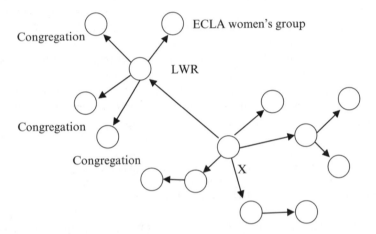

Figure 4.4   Lutheran World Relief as both a superstructural node and a nondescript node within the larger networked structure

for broad-based enrolment: micro-level networking translates into scale through an ongoing process of enrolment. As Joe Curnow, a former member of the United Students for Fair Trade (USFT), put it:

> we have a lot of power in terms of *numbers* – our potential outreach is every college campus, and the communities they affect. So once we have affiliates on each of these campuses, we are able to foster education and empowerment and grassroots organising in each of those cities and campus communities. I think that is pretty unique. Because we have this [attribute] – [of] students in a block – we are especially suited or uniquely suited to organise a group of students . . . and they're eager to get involved. . . . (25 June 2005, fieldwork notes)

Curnow's observation makes clear that the power of USFT is realised through numbers. Figure 4.5 brings together the examples of Solidaridad,

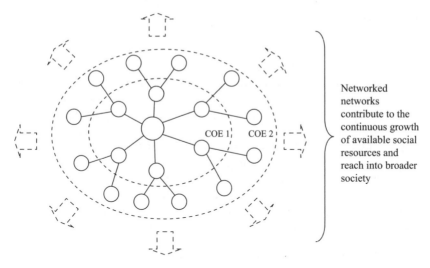

Note: COE: circle of enrolment.

Figure 4.5   The cumulative and continuous nature of the process of networking networks

Global Exchange and LWR to show how their micro-level networking has translated into a macro-phenomenon. It reveals the explosive pattern that lies behind the spread of fair trade. Figure 4.5 demonstrates the ongoing circle of enrolment (COE) achieved by networking networks (each network is pictured as an individual node) and the cumulative influence this process generates (depicted by the dotted arrows). The networks enrolled and energised in COE1 spread the message among their networks, triggering momentum in COE2.

This conception of growth sits oddly with a 'power over' approach to scaling up (see Chapter 1). The fair trade movement's scale has been achieved by many people at an individual level collaborating to build the market. Its scale is constituted by small-scale yet interconnected nodes of action. This stands in stark contrast to Chandlerian corporations' methods of accumulating and exploiting enormous financial resources to monopolise the construction of global hegemonic discourses (see Chapter 2). The power of the fair trade movement to build a collective discourse has been generated among, and is dependent on, many decentralised groups acting 'in concert' (Arendt, 1958). This notion of power maps on to a Latourian topography in which the continuation of individual and group action is required to sustain power (Latour, 1986). It adds an evolutionary dimension to understanding nodes and offers insight into how power operates in the process of expansion: creating more and more 'social connections' between networks generates 'power with'.

Their approach has not been haphazard or 'spontaneous' in a Hayekian sense. Not least, this unique process of expansion through ongoing group enrolment appears the most efficient means of creating scale by overcoming several barriers: the time-cost associated with network-building; the social psychology of belief in new messages/ideas; and the challenge of maintaining momentum.

First, network theory tells us that an existing network has an organised constituency and established set of relationships, information channels and social capital (see Lin, 2001). Tapping these capacities via networking networks, rather than fostering these capacities from scratch in the form of network-building, suggests why fair trade has spread so rapidly. Fair trade actors have made themselves an intersection point where the capital embedded in existing social networks coalesces and can be coordinated. While network theory conceptualises how networks – and their composition – benefit (or disadvantage) members (see for example Putnam, 1993; Granovetter, 1973), the fair trade movement's experience offers new insight into how social movement actors capitalise on the resources, capacities and knowledge embedded in other networks for scale. The implication is not only social actors' awareness of networks as sources of value and enabling pathways for social change, but also their exploitation of the potential of networks in highly creative and efficient ways.

Networking networks appears to have also overcome individual barriers to supporting new ideas. The source or 'messenger' of new information plays an important role in motivating an individual to support an idea and take action (Granovetter, 1973).[9] An individual is more likely to believe or be persuaded by a friend or family member about the worth or credibility of something than by a stranger or random advertisement. Fair trade 'nodes' work through communities and contacts with whom they have influence, giving entrée into completely new networks.

Activating power (a consequence of enrolment) can thus be seen to depend on 'weak ties' (Granovetter, 1973) which lie beyond more intimate networked relationships but offer access to 'ready-made' constituencies with their own resources, information and reach. The seemingly disordered and highly dispersed nature of fair trade's scaling up has none the less proved to be comparable to hierarchical and bureaucratic models (see Putnam, 1993; see also Achrol and Kotler, 1999; Schaper and Volery, 2002: 271). The horizontal topography of the fair trade movement's organisation offers insight into the micro-foundations of new market structures that are premised on an alternative understanding of power and thus social change.

Networking networks also provides a mechanism for maintaining momentum to the spread of fair trade. Latour (1986) suggests that, since collective action is dependent on continued individual action, those who enrol others in a project are no more important for breathing new life into the project than any other subsequent agent in the chain. So while a superstructural node might enrol several other networks in its project, it is no more important than those individual communities – and those that stretch out beyond them – for generating power. As we saw above, fair trade supporters utilise their contacts within other social networks and communities to enrol these groups – and those beyond them – to support fair trade. This networked process of generating support is rapid because the networks operate organically. Speaking about the UK context, Byrde observed that grassroots support for fair trade had 'generated a life of its own'. The empirical observation that superstructural nodes are, in the context of the broader networked structure, simultaneously nondescript nodes not only illustrates the utility of Latour's point about sustaining power, but also furthers our understanding of nodal governance by adding greater characterisation to the activity of superstructural nodes in networked structures.

GAME-PLAYERS' INNOVATIONS IN LIBERATING INDIVIDUAL AND COLLECTIVE POWER

Networking networks thus appears to be a very powerful – in an unconventional sense of power – and efficient way of creating scale by channelling the power produced by multiple social connections (see Chapter 1). This 'channel' has been constructed by the fair trade pioneers who innovated in the act of social protest. To put it another way, game-players' innovations have enabled new social connections for power (see Chapter 6 for further analysis). For its time, the certification and labelling system was an important innovation for the fair trade movement (Douglas, 12 April 2005, fieldwork notes) (see Chapter 6). Until it emerged, so-called 'alternative trade' products – primarily handcrafts – had been sold in 'alternative trade' shops and were not 'accessible' to a wide population (Eshuis, 11 April 2005, fieldwork notes). These outlets catered for a minor market – 'activists' (Byrde, 29 April 2005, fieldwork notes) – and created a perception that fair trade was too 'weird' and 'fringy', and presupposed that people would 'buy into a whole set of political beliefs that they [did not] necessarily believe in' (Gorman, 12 July 2005, fieldwork notes).

So, fair trade pioneers revolutionised the idea of protest, making protestors matter in the economistic sense of attaching a 'price' both to

conventional firms' support of, or opposition to, Fairtrade. The certification system made Fairtrade accessible to 'mainstream' markets such
as supermarkets by turning fair trade's 'philosophy' into a mainstream
'reality'. As Jeroen Douglas of Solidaridad suggested:

> how come mainstream business and business leaders take notice of these [fair
> trade] standards? It is because they know that [fair trade] is a real thing. And
> they know that by getting into the marketplace and by really competing –
> *playing their ball game* – that we are a player to be taken seriously, because we
> can do their trick, and even better . . . We play their ball game and that gives
> you a license to speak. . . . In the 70s we were very much linked to what we call
> the protest movement – we were against this and against that – and the Spanish
> would say we went from *protesta* to *propuesta*. Instead of being a protest move-
> ment we went to an alternative, by showing that it can be done in our way,
> and by offering a tool to the end consumer to act. This creates a rather unique
> . . . campaign model [and] a certain *authority* to the fair trade movement. If
> you come with realistic alternatives [as we do] . . . you get a license to speak,
> a license to operate. There I think the fair trade movement has been able to
> create a niche for itself in the political debate and in industry. (12 April 2005,
> fieldwork notes)

Douglas emphasises here how the fair trade movement reinvented the
traditional 'protest' model of social change to enable a wider consumer
market to 'protest' through the market by supporting fair trade. On the
one hand, it created new spaces for expressing alternative social values and
discourses in new ways. On the other hand, it assigned a dollar value to
consumers' values in the market, enabling them to institutionalise protest.
Thus while it was a social protest, the fair trade pioneers' reinvention of
the concept of protest was also capitalistic to create traction for the fair
trade idea. From an economic perspective, the fair trade pioneers' innovation in Fairtrade product certification exploited a 'competitive advantage'
(Porter, 1980), a new opportunity to 'reconfigure markets'.[10] Reconfiguring
markets enables market actors to materialise new business models which
are otherwise hampered by existing barriers (organisational, regulatory or
technological) (McGrath and MacMillan, 2000: 89). Strategic innovation
is a deliberate attempt to use innovation to disrupt existing market power
structures to enable the possibility of new ones. In the fair trade movement's case, the pioneers have strategically reconfigured the market on
political grounds as opposed to the conventional profit-maximising drivers
of entrepreneurship posited in market theory. The pioneers radically reconfigured the established market structure – a social power structure – with
a new model that embedded values of social justice in markets to meet a
rising, albeit political, 'need' for their market expression. An observation
from Ian Bretman, Deputy Director of the UK's Fairtrade Foundation,

indicates well the (monetary) value the Fairtrade system has given its new type of protestor:

> [our marketing approach is] really working with this sense of consumer empowerment. I think that that's really important, an issue like international development is so huge, and although everybody *cares* about it – and the issue of poverty – and that it's a bad thing and that something should be done about it, people don't actually feel *empowered* to do it, so when they're presented with a situation like that, they just sort of switch off from it, because it's uncomfortable . . . [ours] is a tried and tested strategy of saying 'there is this huge problem, but you can do something about it, you can be part of the solution not part of the problem'. I think that that's something that excites people, and we've been plugging away at this message for several years now. . . . (3 May 2005, fieldwork notes)

This comment offers a window on how the Fairtrade product certification system liberates or 'empowers' consumers – by offering them a tool to act in the market in a way that delivers tangible impact and that expresses different values ('they don't actually feel empowered to do it'). Fairtrade products enable consumers to reveal their preferences via the market. This creates competition for established businesses, competition that on cost grounds alone they cannot ignore. The deeper insight raised in the above excerpt is that innovation unlocks new flows of human power: being given a tool to act in line with normative values, a tool that activates alternative structures and has a tangible or demonstrable impact, generates 'empowerment' among consumers. While a small change in a single consumer's purchasing habits/ choices ('power to') seems insignificant in a macro-system, a small change made by *many* consumers has definitely proved significant.[11] As respondents explained:

> For me [the fair trade movement] is much stronger than initiatives like the anti-apartheid movement . . . It [fair trade] is felt much more strongly than other initiatives because it does not simply oppose an existing [trading] system but demonstrates that an alternative one is there and is workable. So, if the fair trade movement were to react negatively to companies or products on the market [as the anti-apartheid movement did], it would have been simply disastrous for the company because the fair trade movement has this available and workable alternative trading system. This is the basis of the [fair trade] movement's power. (Paulsen, 14 April 2005, fieldwork notes)

> [the alternative trade system] is an *extremely* important part [of fair trade] . . . [because] making a criticism is very easy, but people are very quickly bored. But just to say 'okay I don't like the existing trading system, it needs to be changed', that's all well and fine. Okay – *so what? How do I do that?* And in the fair trade context we can say 'well if you don't like the existing trading system, then you can go and buy Fairtrade products! We can give you an alternative.' Then we can demonstrate that it *can* work *differently*, and you can show the world by growing the fair trade percentage in the market that *people* actually *want* this to change. (Ibid.)

consumers are *voters*, I really think it comes to this. Politicians are practical, pragmatic people, and they need those votes, and if they see that this is something that consumers care about, then they really have to take notice, or they'll get voted out. So that's it at base . . . *ordinary* people across Europe are expressing a concern and care for people across the rest of the world. And so of course that now has to be taken into account [by politicians]. (Wills, 29 April 2005, fieldwork notes)

Brought into sharp relief by these comments is that enabling individual 'power to' practise new market behaviours, multiplied or replicated many times over, produces 'power with'. 'Power with' accumulates from the individual – and group – exercise of 'power to', and brings about structural change the more others enact the same new behavioural patterns. By offering people a small, everyday and practical way to make trade exchanges a positive force for change in *status quo* trade and business practices, via the activities that make up their own lives, the fair trade movement has operated outside of formal political processes – through trade – to further its project of bringing about social justice in the market. In conceptual terms, by innovating and networking networks to support it, the fair trade movement has mobilised a widening circle of activists and consumers to create new market patterns. In this light, networking networks is a conceptual model of a decentralised political process through which social change is realised and 'social epidemics' (Gladwell, 2000) take hold. The deeper insight signposted earlier is that liberating individual power to unleash this potentiality hinges on game-playing. Game-playing is analysed in depth in Chapter 6.

Given the political and economic implications of networking networks, the actors responsible for networking new connections between unrelated social networks are key players (see Steinberg, cited in Granovetter, 1983; see also Braithwaite, 2004; Drahos with Braithwaite, 2002). It is because of them that fair trade continues to spread through an ever-growing number of networks. These network entrepreneurs are considered in more detail below.

NETWORK 'NETWORKERS': FAIR TRADE MISSIONARIES IN THE CULTURAL ECONOMY

A seeming irony in fair trade's contemporary scale is that the fair trade pioneers and activists have always been of small means and resources.[12] In their attempt to further their mission in the market, fair trade pioneers have been forced to enrol the grassroots (to whom they have access and affiliation and wherein lie established constituencies and social resources), persuading these communities to support fair trade and to spread the message further.

The subsequent irony of their makeshift approach was summed up by one respondent who made the observation that 'what today we call "strategy" was once a necessity' (Bretman, 3 May 2005, fieldwork notes). Though driven by 'necessity' at the time, gaining support through grass-roots networks has indeed been recast and valued as a 'strategy' because it works. It has sent thousands of fair trade activists and consumers running with the fair trade mission and message, a modern-day evangelism reminiscent of the work of (most commonly Christian) missionaries.[13] The success of the strategy for enrolment purposes reveals – from a business perspective – the power of 'guerrilla campaigning', a Mao Tse Dung-inspired strategy that exploits unconventional means of achieving victory over an opponent when they are better financed or have well-established strengths or competencies (see McGrath and MacMillan, 2000: 207–9). One respondent described fair trade's success at scaling-up in terms of its unconventional tactics:

> I was recently having a conversation with the woman who's in a parish in Seattle. First of all, in the coffee world, Seattle is kind of ground zero. She was saying that [the parish] did coffee sales of Equal Exchange coffee and one of her parishioners decided not to just drink it after Mass, but in his home and *then* he also took it into his office at *Boeing* . . . he began serving fair trade coffee at Boeing, so all of those people would be exposed to fair trade and learn about it . . . In my mind, that kind of tipping point effect . . . guerrilla marketing . . . has a lot of power. Like when students go home for the holidays and they've shopped on campus at a fair trade sale, and their parents and siblings are opening these really beautiful and precious items and saying 'well, where did you get this?', and then they tell the story. . . . (DeCarlo, author, *Fair Trade: A Beginner's Guide*, and former Executive Director, Fair Trade Resource Network, 30 June 2005, fieldwork notes)

This comment shows that fair trade 'missionaries' have played a critical role in continuing the process of expansion of fair trade. Rather than being a handicap, the small-scale and diffuse nature of networking social networks together at the grassroots has been the movement's key weapon against the structured commercial mechanisms and routes of global corporate brand advertising (see below). Braithwaite and Drahos (2000: 31) suggest that networking can be a powerful weapon in their observation that persuading others to join one's project to influence outcomes is more important than commanding organisational power or possessing resources. This gives processual dimension to, and explicates the operation of power in, Drahos's (2004) idea that enrolling more and more actors is a tactic that weak actors can exploit to amplify what power they do have to topple the stronghold of more powerful actors. The modest social means and resources from which fair trade has gained scale is testament to the influence that 'weak ties' linking distant parts of the system can exert on the social environment (see Granovetter, 1973, 1983; Gladwell, 2000: 54), and the social capacities and resources these ties shore up.

In building these bridges, dialogue – persuasion – rather than physical and financial resources, is the essence of power. The potency of this dialogic approach is exemplified in the fair trade case in the sense that it describes the fair trade movement's approach to scaling-up. As Carol Wills, the former Executive Director of IFAT, and Erin Gorman, CEO Divine Chocolate Ltd in the USA, explain:

> what the fair trade movement hasn't ever had is the advertising budgets of the big corporations and so they [fair trade movement supporters] have to be *very very* good at public relations and getting free PR through articles in the press, and *any other* way they possibly can. . . . (Wills, 29 April 2005, fieldwork notes)

> it's just amazing, there aren't *that* many national organisations [in the USA] – like large-scale organisations – that actually do fair trade work. It's really being fuelled by individual churches and individual schools and community groups and women's organisations and citizens' groups that are really committed to this issue [fair trade] and are taking action in their own community to make it possible. So one of the things we [Co-op America] do is run something that's called the Fair Trade Alliance which is a network of about 350 grassroots organisations all across the country that work on all kinds of things – forestry organisations, hunger relief organisations, housing co-ops – that all have a commitment to do something on fair trade, and it's actually one of the more *powerful* things that I've seen [for spreading the message about fair trade] because what it does is to really get people out there and say 'this is what it [fair trade] means to me and this is why fair trade is important, and that's why I think you should buy fair trade too, and *you* live in my community and I *know* you. . . . (Gorman, 12 July 2005, fieldwork notes)

These observations illustrate empirically the 'intense activity of enrolling, convincing and enlisting' that is constitutive of power (Latour, 1986) and the 'webs of dialogue and persuasion' through which actors must work to convince others of their idea (Braithwaite and Drahos, 2000), such as an idea for an alternative trade. Gorman's comment captures the potency of missionaries' dialogic activity given its role in building cultural consensus around the value of fair trade. As Gorman states, those who initiate conversations to persuade those they know about the genuine value of fair trade are, in her terms, the 'marketing department' for fair trade in the USA. Indeed, this amorphous group can be seen to imbue fair trade with cultural meaning and value, indicating an alternative means of 'advertising' to create markets (see below).

For cultural economists, the market has always played a discursive function of exchanging competing ideas and 'meanings' rather than a purely utilitarian one of exchanging functional goods (Fiske, 2000: 283; see also Featherstone, 2000). From this view, economic activity is embedded in cultural meaning and perceptions of culture itself are 'created and preserved mainly by communication' (Holt et al., 2004). As Douglas and Isherwood (2000: 74) write, 'consumption is the very arena in which culture is fought over and licked into shape'. Harper (1996: 5), for instance, portrays the marketplace as an 'intersubjective and pluralistic process for generating conjectures, exchanging and promoting ideas and attempting to refute them'. Viewed as such, a business model, product or brand each becomes a 'text . . . a discursive structure of potential meanings . . . that constitutes a major resource of popular culture' (Fiske, 2000: 283).

The commercial advertising and marketing communications used by brand companies to imbue their brands with the aura of premium cultural value and meaning represents but one of the multiple forms of communication in society that influence the individual. Other forms of communication are those social informational channels that have grown cultural consensus around the value of fair trade, such as word-of-mouth (Coates, 13 June 2005, fieldwork notes), website discussions, press releases, newspaper articles, community radio interviews, social group events, community meetings, local market stalls, conferences, promotional events or campaigns and through physical and virtual networking between organisations and networks dispersed across cities, countries and regions (Curnow, 25 June 2005, fieldwork notes; Ford, 14 July 2005, fieldwork notes; Byrde, 29 April 2005, fieldwork notes). These are some of the many paths of communication that contribute to enabling individuals to construct, contest and perceive culture (see Holt et al., 2004). Through these routes and multiple sites of shared conversation, cultural value in fair trade has been and is being constructed. This was reflected in the following observations:

> the *faith* movement [in the USA] . . . has been focused on doing general education . . . at the level of the congregation, hoping to influence congregations as institutions, and their congregants as individual *consumers*, to look at fair trade within the context of their faith, to say that – say within the Christian tradition, similar arguments obviously are in the Jewish tradition based on the Hebrew bible – the *teachings* of their faith tell them, whether Lutheran, Presbyterian, Catholic . . . that their economic life should not be based on the exploitation of others, that the scripture calls people to live a life in line with their values, and that their values call them to make choices – and the scripture calls them to make

choices – that places human life and human dignity above economic concerns
... fair trade makes such *intuitive* sense for the people we talk to. (Ford, 14 July
2005, fieldwork notes)

[NGOs supporting fair trade and doing consumer education work] have truly
inspired the consumer at the grassroots level by promoting the [Fairtrade] mark
itself so that people recognise it, but also by building the fantastic motivated
consumer movement by these other various activities, like Fairtrade towns, like
Fairtrade universities, building a grassroots movement from the bottom up.
And Oxfam supporter groups, who work with Fairtrade . . . two very dynamic
and driven [Oxfam volunteers] who were just *determined* to make [Fair Trade
universities and Fair Trade towns] start. And once they got the ball rolling,
because in both cases it was a fantastic idea, it generated a life of its own (Byrde,
29 April 2005, fieldwork notes).

The above excerpts capture the dialogic process of meaning creation
around fair trade in the context of different communities.[14] One respondent described how, for instance, in enrolling widespread support from
different communities, each with its own shared worldview, 'fair trade
means different things for different people, and effectively communicating
the essence of fair trade needs different messaging for different audiences'
(Coates, 13 June 2005, fieldwork notes). Skilled in the art of persuasion,
the fair trade missionaries have exploited the discursive roots of economic
activity to set off large-scale, politically consequential effects without
recourse – or access – to traditional resources of market power, such as
money, legal authority or economies of scale.[15] They are instead 'masters of
the weak tie' (Gladwell, 2000: 54) and theirs is a cultural power, a capacity
to exploit grassroots connections to influence the evolution of social ideas
and values.

Given its direct role in expanding the fair trade market, fair trade
missionaries' networking activity can be seen to challenge conventional
commercial advertising as a method of market-building. Thousands of fair
trade activists and consumers are continuing to mobilise millions of 'everyday' people worldwide through existing social channels to buy fair trade
products and spread the message about their availability and value. This
message is conveyed largely through established social networks and in
the many conversations and ongoing dialogue/discourse about fair trade.
This is a many-to-many model of advertising: fair trade activists are in the
many thousands worldwide and have capitalised on the potential of broad-
based social networks ('weak ties') to deliver mass enrolment (see Figure
4.5). The fair trade movement's capitalisation on its competences (in social
networks and network resources) rather than its attempt to match the competences of commercial brand firms is exemplary 'guerrilla campaigning'
(see McGrath and MacMillan, 2000: 207–9).

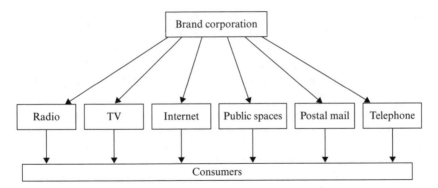

Figure 4.6   One-to-many model of gaining market share

It also suggests that the movement's counter-narrative is subject in its construction to the participation and deliberation of many individuals who translate Fairtrade in their social/communal contexts (see Chapter 7). In conventional markets, corporate-dominated discourses are constructed exclusively by firms to serve corporate ends. These subjectivities are expounded through commercial avenues that are not subject to collective governance. For instance, and by comparison, unlike the many-to-many process that has led to the expansion of fair trade, one corporation works to spread an image to millions of consumers (a one-to-many model of communication), spending perhaps billions of dollars each year on commercial advertising to have a Pavlovian-like influence on consumer behaviour in response to its brands (see Chapter 2).

This corporate approach can be seen to construct value by deception: consumers are largely unaware of the consequences of acting on the 'brand' preferences they are being subconsciously influenced to make (see Chapter 2). To put it in terms analogous to the market as a cultural forum for competing ideas (see Harper, 1996; Fiske, 2000), the one-to-many model of market-building is one in which brand companies monopolise the podium and keep other voices from reaching the microphone. Figure 4.6 offers a simplified depiction of this one-to-many approach to gaining market share.

Tying together networks in a dialogic fashion to widen the circle of enrolment can be seen as a powerful 'bottom-up' antidote to corporations' mass advertising of brands. Given the ultimate effectiveness of the fair trade missionaries' approach to building cultural value around, and support for, fair trade, particular emphasis must be placed on fair trade missionaries – the network networkers – who spread fair trade's discourse. To the extent that the fair trade activists' mobilisation of many actors has created scale and increasing awareness, and that corporations' power relies ultimately on consumers buying their brands, the fair trade activists' strategy of networking networks to send forth further grassroots marketers is a potentially potent (and arguably comparable) source of power to corporations' command of organisational power and possession of vast resources. The fair trade 'missionaries' are themselves of simple means but have enrolled the large and established grassroots constituencies belonging to other networks. Indeed, the scale of fair trade far outweighs the initiators' and pioneers' own organisational capacities and resources. Network networkers step into the cultural market brandishing innovative business models that challenge the prevailing discourse of conventional commerce.

CONCLUDING COMMENTS

This chapter has examined the way in which the fair trade movement has approached the problem of expanding fair trade. It has illuminated a key finding: to create scale, fair trade networks tie other networks to themselves to activate those networks, and through their support, further networks. This is not a strategy of building networks from the ground up, but rather an assumption that multiple, overlapping social networks exist and represent superior channels of communication, information acquisition and sources of latent collective power. These channels have become tied to fair trade. Game-players' innovations free up capacities and relationships that are inhibited or obstructed by existing structures; they exploit a 'competitive advantage' (McGrath and MacMillan, 2000) by spotting a perceived need for, and existing restraint on, human freedom in the values underpinning conventional business and market practice. As such, they create new structural avenues that offer and rely on these communities to exercise 'power to' (see Chapter 6). This innovation in market segmentation alone is a significant achievement: fair trade pioneers have made it possible to institutionalise group protest in an innately atomising social environment – the capitalist marketplace.

The political relevance and influence of this economistic innovation has been exploited by fair trade pioneers and activists, who have encouraged group-oriented or group-related action. Because fair trade activists, resource-deficient as they are, have never been in a position to 'command' organisational power, they have had to capitalise on their social networks and actively enrol others through persuasion (see Braithwaite and Drahos, 2000). The movement's apparent weakness – its lack of financial capital and diffuse or decentralised social organisation – has been its greatest – and paradoxical – strength, a guerrilla-like move that has served as an antidote to corporate power and central organisation. The above account of fair trade's experience of scaling up indicates instead the importance of widely dispersed social networks and the utility of a Latourian vision of power in a networked world. In this world, the possibility for the weak, or under-resourced, to trump the strong by intense 'enrolling, convincing and enlisting' (Latour, 1986) is very real (see Braithwaite and Drahos, 2000; Burris et al., 2005). In fact, whilst viewed in traditional terms as 'weak', social actors who are rich in social resources are strong in a networked world.

The surprising scale that the fair trade missionaries' *praxis* has produced points to the significance of the actors who weave unrelated networks together to widen the circle of enrolment. These actors ensure that the circle of enrolment expands and continues by starting the conversations and dialogue in different arenas that are construction sites for building shared perceptions about, and understanding of, the cultural value of economic activity. The strategy of networking networks highlights the sophistication of fair trade activists' utilisation of opportunities afforded by a networked landscape. It also brings into sharp relief the importance of networks as an enabling pathway for social actors dealing with the constraints posed by existing institutions and structures.

The effect of the detailed networked and nodal activity analysed in this chapter demonstrates the (political) importance of weak ties – or horizontal networks – for extending beyond more intimate social circles to facilitate widespread enrolment and achieve macro-social aims (Granovetter, 1983; Putnam, 1983; Steinberg, cited in Granovetter, 1983). In this way, the analysis of power in the process of networking networks enables a view of the nodal life of larger, more complex network structures (Burris et al., 2005) and their role in market evolutionary processes. This adds greater complexity to the micro- and macro-role of superstructural nodes for producing large-scale outcomes and a framework for understanding the social mechanics behind seemingly naturally occurring outcomes and the market's cyclical processes (see Schumpeter, 1934; Hayek, 1960; Nelson and Winter, 1982).

The attempt to institutionalise or 'consolidate' the Fairtrade certification system has, over time, brought its own challenges. These challenges, which are features of what is known generally as the 'cycle theory of innovation', is not new to theorists of economic evolution (see for example Nooteboom, 2001; see also Schaper and Volery, 2002: 261), but the networked way in which consolidation has occurred in fair trade and the implications of this process for theorising power, knowledge and social change do provide new insights. We now turn to look more closely at the evolution of the FLO system of product certification and governance of Fairtrade product markets.

NOTES

1. The concept of social networks emerged over 50 years ago with Barnes's (1954) study of a Norwegian island parish. Since then, Mark Granovetter (1973) has been a key proponent of social network theory in the social sciences and today it is used widely in the fields of politics, globalisation studies, anthropology, social psychology, sociology, organisational studies, mathematics, communications, marketing and mental health.
2. Social capital broadly refers to the benefits and resources that are available to and used by both individuals and groups as a result of their social/community connectedness (see Lin, 2001; Coleman, 1988). Social capital is thought to be 'captured from embedded resources in social networks' (Lin, 2001: 3).
3. Hayek (1960) developed a theory of spontaneous ordering to describe the way in which diffuse resources, capacity and knowledge are coordinated within complex networked arrangements (specifically markets) to produce order.
4. The benefits that flow from networks are thought to predominate in, and be an asset to, organisations with porous structures (meaning that staff are well connected outside the firm) and egalitarian management. By contrast, these benefits appear to be stifled in hierarchical and closed bureaucracies. These differences in organisational structure are increasingly relevant for understanding optimal organisational and managerial models for competitiveness in a knowledge economy (see Achrol and Kotler, 1999; see also Schaper and Volery, 2002: 271). Putnam's (1993) research on the Mafia in Italy led him to conceptualise networks in a way similar to Granovetter's 'weak ties' and 'strong ties' categories, namely 'horizontal networks' – those that link decentralised, loosely connected and equal members of a network – and 'vertical networks' – those that display strong inequalities in authority and power and are insular or 'closed' to outside sources.
5. Developing this line of thinking are Braithwaite and Drahos (2000: 482), who, in the context of global business regulation, find that those who exercise the greatest power in global regulatory regimes are not those who possess the most resources (money, knowledge, technology) but rather those who enrol others with more resources and authority than themselves, and/or those who can enrol others with more effective enrolment capacity. Corporations, for instance, frequently enrol states to do their enrolment work for them.
6. A node is a site of governance that mobilises diffuse knowledge, capacity and resources residing within networked arrangements (see Burris et al., 2005: 37).
7. Burris et al. (2005) have conceived of the idea of 'tying' networks together through 'superstructural' nodes (see below). Yet this idea relates to the process of creating 'superstructural' nodes, not utilising existing nodes in strategic ways. Also, they use the idea of superstructural nodes to examine issues of governance and influencing outcomes rather than achieving scale *per se*.
8. Researchers of fair trade have drawn on social network theory, actor network theory and commodity network theory to understand the operation of information flows, marketing and the interpretation of the meaning of fair trade (Nicholls and Opal, 2005; Raynolds, 2002; Renard, 2003; Murdoch et al., 2000; Leslie and Reimer, 1999; Whatmore and Thorne, 1997).
9. Granovetter (1973: 1374) emphasises that 'people rarely *act* on mass-media information unless it is also transmitted through personal ties . . . otherwise one has no particular reason to think that an advertised product or an organization should be taken seriously' (author's italics).
10. Markets can be reconfigured in relation to the attributes that can be offered, or in the organisation of consumption and value chains (McGrath and MacMillan, 2000).
11. These seemingly insignificant inputs or catalysts tend to appear disproportionately small compared with the large effects they cause if we assume that causes are generally directly proportional to their effects (Gladwell, 2000: 11).

12. The fair trade movement relies heavily on the personal commitment of a small number of highly committed and dynamic (underpaid) staff, and more significantly, on the unpaid work of dedicated volunteers.
13. The term 'missionary' need not carry a religious connotation but can instead describe in broad terms a person who seeks to convert others to embrace a particular regime, belief system or programme. By this definition, Braithwaite and Drahos's (2000) 'entrepreneurs' in global regulatory agendas – who work to 'convert' and 'enrol' other actors in their project – can be thought of as examples of (non-religious) missionaries.
14. To the extent that cultural values and identity inform who we are and desire to be, this dialogic process is relevant to politics itself (Bowles & Gintis, 1986).
15. Drahos's (2002) study of how the WTO's Agreement on TRIPs came to be shows that even strong actors depend on enrolment to achieve large-scale effects.

5. Fairtrade as resistance

Chapter 4 detailed the rapid growth of the fair trade pioneers' innovation in the Fairtrade certification system. Those who now administer and govern the expansion of FLO, the Labelling Initiatives (LIs) (formerly National Initiatives – NIs), have an organisational mission to consolidate the Fairtrade system within the wider conventional marketplace. This chapter provides an empirical account and analysis of the distinctive market-oriented path along which these actors have expanded the Fairtrade system. This is also a story about the evolution of 'resistance' and how its organisational and political trajectory invites real threats to the prospect of genuine market evolution.

The starting point for the conceptual story in this chapter is that within evolutionary economics it is an accepted proposition that innovation has a cyclical or temporary nature (see Nooteboom, 2001). As a new business venture moves towards consolidation, it becomes a more bureaucratic and rigid structure. In this phase, it becomes increasingly challenging for the organisation to exploit new opportunities to 'capitalise on new ideas' or adapt effectively to a dynamically changing environment (see Schaper and Volery, 2002; Foster and Metcalfe, 2001; Nooteboom, 2001; Achrol and Kotler, 1999; Robert and Weiss, 1988).[1] This is because bureaucratic, hierarchically structured organisations are poor receptors and exploiters of new information. As Achrol and Kotler (1999: 147) suggest, 'large, vertically integrated hierarchies are inefficient means of governance in knowledge-rich and turbulent environments . . . [a]daption is slow and costly because of entrenched interests eager to preserve their power and prerogatives'. Intent on survival, traditional organisational forms maintain *status quo* bodies of knowledge (Ramazzotti, 2001: 76). This inhibits the generation and spread of new knowledge – not least because new ideas and knowledge pose inconsistencies with the dominant belief system (Schaper and Volery, 2002: 271; Achrol and Kotler, 1999: 146; see also Granovetter, 1973, 1983). As Popper (cited in Loasby, 1999: 27) observed, 'orthodoxy is the death of knowledge, since the growth of knowledge depends entirely on the existence of disagreement'.

While the new knowledge that emerges from disagreement and debate feeds new cycles of innovation (see Harper, 1996), what is accepted as 'valid' knowledge is highly political: 'contests for knowledge are contests for power'

(Pimbert, 2001: 81; see also Pimbert and Wakeford, 2001; Elster, 1998; Bohman and Rehg, 1997; Gaventa, 1993). For this reason, the organisation of knowledge is not value-free (Hayward, 1998; Lefebvre, 1991; Gaventa, 2006a; see also Chapter 7). The organisational form suited to exploiting new information, especially in a knowledge-rich environment, differs from that which supports the process of consolidation (see Abernathy, 1978; Nooteboom, 2001; Achrol and Kotler, 1999). The latter is in fact averse to the discovery of new knowledge and information. To the extent that innovation drives the evolution of the economy (Schumpeter, 1934) and is dependent on new knowledge, evolution itself depends on the evolution of knowledge (see Loasby, 1999: 25–8). Requisite for evolution, then, are organisational structures – built on alternative power relations – that enable and value new discourses, ideas and information (see Achrol and Kotler, 1999; Doherty and Meehan, 2004). In an investigation of FLO's consolidation – and the hierarchical organisational form it has taken – this chapter shows how FLO's institutional preservation of 'orthodoxy' (Dewey, cited in Pimbert and Wakeford, 2001: 26) stymies a much-needed evolution in the Fairtrade system and jeopardises the movement's mission.

CONSOLIDATING INNOVATION AND THE POLITICS OF KNOWLEDGE

After a group of fair trade pioneers and Mexican producers set up the Max Havelaar labelling system in 1989 in the Netherlands, a group of Max Havelaar labelling initiatives began to emerge in other European countries, including Belgium, Luxembourg and Switzerland. In 1992 a fair trade labelling organisation in Germany adopted the name 'Transfair', pushing for a 'Transfair' certification mark to be recognised among the Max Havelaar community. Transfair Germany did not wish to adopt the Max Havelaar organisational title, which carried the historical 'baggage' unique to the Netherlands' socio-political background (Douglas, 12 April 2005, fieldwork notes). Transfair Germany brought an approach and attitude very different from those of the Benelux countries (VanderHoff Boersma, 7 January 2006, fieldwork notes; de Clerck, 28 April 2005, fieldwork notes). Until Transfair Germany arrived on the scene, a democratic 'mixed board' oversaw the Max Havelaar organisational initiatives, including producers, the certification organisations and consumers (VanderHoff Boersma, 7 January 2006, fieldwork notes). This mixed board is depicted in Figure 5.1.

Each labelling organisation was not only working with similar (though not uniform) standards, but also carrying out similar functions. At the

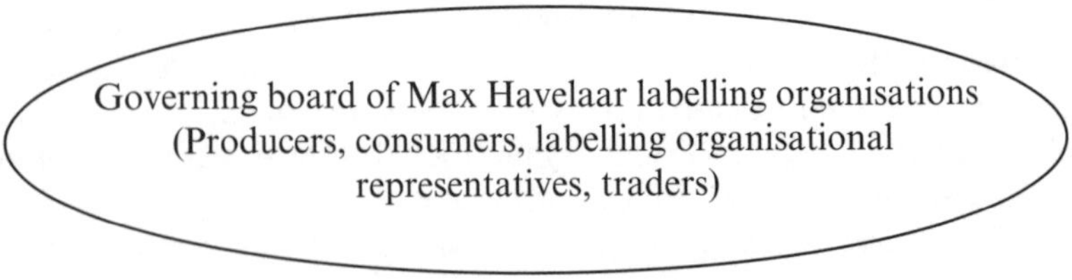

Governing board of Max Havelaar labelling organisations
(Producers, consumers, labelling organisational
representatives, traders)

*Figure 5.1   Mixed democratically elected board of Max Havelaar
initiatives before 1992 (i.e. pre-FLO, pre-Transfair)*

same time as sharing overlapping tasks, each LI was set up by different
individuals and at different times (albeit in general they were founded by
ATOs or non-profit organisations). As a result, no two LIs have the same
structure or character. The social, cultural and intellectual characteristics of each LI are different, their legal structure and national non-profit
organisational laws differ; their marketing strategies are diverse, as is each
organisation's governance structure. Another distinguishing feature of the
LIs is their ideological outlook and strategy for expanding Fairtrade (see
below). Describing the diversity of organisational characters found among
the LIs, one respondent referred to the LIs as a 'can of worms' (Tiffen, 25
October 2005, fieldwork notes).

Despite these organisational differences, as the Fairtrade market
demands grew, a new organisation was deemed necessary not only to
help realise economies of scale by cooperating with one another, but also
to administer the overlapping functions of the LIs – standard-setting,
producer relations and verification activities. The Fairtrade Labelling
Organizations International (FLO) was established by and for the LIs
to serve these members' interests and take direction from them. The LIs
became FLO's legal owners, and their organisational prerogative has been
to expand the Fairtrade product market in their own countries.[2]

As part of FLO's establishment, a new label was created as the international mark for Fairtrade products, for use as a symbol across consumer
countries. To this day, however, in countries where the respective LI
preceded the establishment of FLO and the international Fairtrade Mark
(1997), the Max Havelaar and Transfair labels can still be found alongside
the FLO product mark.

With FLO's establishment came a new governance structure. The governance structure that had overseen the fair trade certification organisations before FLO's establishment was made redundant and was succeeded
by FLO's new governing body, mostly composed of LIs (see Figure 5.2).
Producer representation was reduced in the new governing board in
order to create impartiality between the certification body and producer

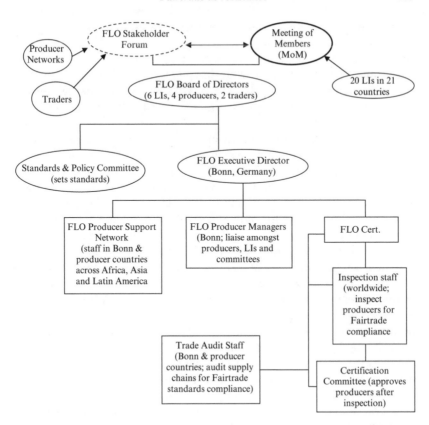

Note: The circle in bold around the Meeting of Members (MoM) alludes to the most powerful decision-making body within this complex structure and system of governance.

Source: FLO (2005b).

Figure 5.2 FLO governance structure at 2004

organisations (which were being monitored and certified by this body). An informal biennial meeting was set up as an alternative forum for producers and other non-LI members of FLO (e.g. traders) to deliberate FLO's affairs. Forming a minority in the governance structure from then on, producers have struggled to exercise influence over the LIs' decision-making forum in the development of FLO's Fairtrade policies and practices (VanderHoff Boersma, 23 December 2005, fieldwork notes).

This description of the emergence of the international network of LIs shows the evolution of networked governance structures built for the task of consolidating the certification and labelling system. The LIs' institutionalisation can be seen as a strategy of 'resistance' to drive a phase of Fairtrade product consolidation. The evolution towards organisational centralisation, efficiency and bureaucratic routinisation for scale (see Abernathy, 1978; Nooteboom, 2001) has involved shedding the democratically elected mixed board model in favour of a hierarchical and centralised organisation in which a superstructural node for LIs has decision-making power.

This coordinated network approach to evolution nevertheless stands in contrast to MNCs' evolution – which was a product of corporate mergers and takeovers (see Chapter 2; Chandler, 1964). Even so, while FLO was not formally established until 1997, since 1992 the 'socio-political thrust' and mission of the first Max Havelaar organisation in the Netherlands have diminished relative to, and because of, the more pragmatic 'market-driven' LIs that subsequently emerged and became part of the nodal community of LIs (VanderHoff Boersma, 7 January 2006, fieldwork notes). This has seen the emergence of hierarchy between nodes within networked structures. Indeed, the reference to the 'socio-political thrust' of the certification system and the distinction of pragmatic 'market-driven' LIs draws attention to an intricately entwined political and practical dynamic in the networked governance of fair trade that operates at two levels. FLO's nodal hierarchy is central in this dynamic.

First, at an international level, FLO's pragmatic market-driven approach agitates IFAT, the main fair trade association that represents the international fair trade movement of FTOs; IFAT's majority membership is comprised of Southern producer organisations (see Chapter 7). As mentioned in Chapter 3, this deep conflict internal to the fair trade movement pivots on two competing worldviews of fair trade: market reform (FLO certification) and market transformation (IFAT and FTOs) (for more detail see Chapter 7). As a result of these different ideological positions, FLO and IFAT pursue fair trade in different ways. These positions are depicted in Figure 5.3.

As Figure 5.3 shows, FLO and the LIs aim to consolidate Fairtrade-certified products throughout mainstream distribution and retail outlets (involving conventional retail supermarkets and brand companies). By contrast, IFAT and FTOs are building the movement of 100 per cent fair trade organisations (not Fairtrade-certified products *per se*), whose explicit mission is to transform international trade relations and terms for marginalised and disadvantaged small-scale producers in developing countries. As such, their focus is on supporting small-scale farmers and craftspeople, whereas FLO's focus is increasingly on factory and plantation workers (Dalvai, 13 April 2005, fieldwork notes). FTOs aim to mainstream a more radical interpretation of fair trade: expanding the number and market

Fair trade market
mission: to
transform existing
marketplace

Conventional market
mission: to increase the
presence of fairtrade
products in mainstream
consumer outlets

IFAT: FTOs &
producer cooperatives

FLO: LI

*Figure 5.3   IFAT and FLO at opposite ends of a fair trade ideological
            spectrum*

value of FTOs and producer cooperatives with consumers to bring about
social change (see Chapters 6 and 7).

Whilst related, these missions are not the same (see Chapter 7). As
one respondent noted, there is 'overlap' between the missions of LIs
and FTOs, but their missions are 'not synonymous' (Tiffen, 25 October
2005, fieldwork notes). None the less, these more radical nodes coexist
alongside the conservative nodes of FLO and the LIs in the decentralised
network structure of the broad fair trade movement (see Chapters 6 and
7). For their part, FLO and the LIs are key protagonists in the recent
spread of Fairtrade products into international 'mainstream' outlets and
by large conventional brand companies/traders.[3] Those in the fair trade
industry/movement refer to FLO and the LIs as the 'FLO family'.[4] The
FLO family is seeking to consolidate the Fairtrade system by gaining
acceptance among conventional market traders whose market power is
entrenched. Seen as the movement's 'resisters', the LIs are structurally
located in capitalist market institutions and seek to institutionalise alternative models into capitalist institutions – undertaking the 'hard sell and
execute model implementation' (Braithwaite, 1994) – but not to transform
these institutions.

The account of fair trade's 'resisters' tells a more complex story still. The
first half of this chapter untangles this complexity and in so doing it magnifies how knowledge and organisational structure respectively operate in the
distinct evolutionary phase of consolidation. In this context is the second
level at which the political and practical dynamic in the fair trade movement exists. Among FLO's LI membership reside two distinct subcultures
that nurture the broader ideological tension between IFAT and FLO.
These subcultures play, and have played, pivotal roles in the development
and evolution of FLO's system, and have determined the way in which
FLO responds to the outside world (see below). Respondents' comments
illuminated the existence of these two subcultures:

> within FLO you have NIs that are saying 'we are the Anglo-Saxons' with a
> 'business model' approach. It seems to be another culture. And then you have

the French, Belgian, Europeans saying, 'okay use the business model to *dem-onstrate* something, but once we have done this, we need to take [Fairtrade] onto another level which is advocacy and . . . a society approach'. (Former LI director, fieldwork notes)

our attempt [at Transfair USA is] not to overthrow global capitalism, but to work within the mechanisms of global capitalism, to shift its *benefits* to people in the countries where many of the products we consume originate. We're not anti-WTO protestors, we're not throwing rocks at Starbucks or other compa-nies . . . we're very much working *with* these companies and see them as actual or potential allies and friends to work with us to develop the growth of Fair Trade, and simply to shift more of the benefits back to poor farmers. . . . we're very business oriented and free-market oriented, and we believe strongly that for Fair Trade to work in the United States, we have to understand the market and we have to embrace it and we have to work within the free market. (Sellers, former Chief Operating Officer, Transfair USA, 10 May 2005, fieldwork notes)

The first respondent describes FLO's two distinct LI subcultures and the tension between the two approaches: the 'advocacy' LIs view Fairtrade as a means to an end (that Fairtrade certification merely '*demonstrates*' something) whereas the 'business model' LIs view Fairtrade certification as an end in itself. The LIs from continental European countries consti-tute one subculture (the 'advocacy' approach). The so-called 'Latinos' (Italy and Spain) are also part of this subculture (VanderHoff Boersma, 7 January 2006, fieldwork notes). The USA, the UK, Switzerland and to some extent the Netherlands, the 'Anglo-Saxon' members, form a 'busi-ness model' subculture. Sellers's comment illustrates the Anglo-Saxon LIs' market-oriented perception and promotion of fair trade: Transfair USA 'embraces' and 'works within' the confines of existing market norms, the idea being that if it were to act more radically, Transfair USA would be viewed negatively as 'rock-throwers' by the corporate sector.

This highlights market-oriented LIs' aim to be 'allies' of the corporate sector. Transfair USA does not appear to view the existing trading regime in a critical light or see a need for it to change. As one producer described it, the 'business model' LIs (of which Transfair USA is a key one) are 'pragmatic', 'market-driven' and 'do not like discussions on a political level'. To the extent that producers' disadvantaged position is caused by the institutional structures that govern the international trade regime, Sellers's comment suggests that 'business model' LIs are not seeking to bring about significant change, at least if Fairtrade is going to 'work' in the mainstream conventional market. Indeed, the same producer observed that the 'Anglo-Saxons' are quite 'happy with the way of the neoliberal economic approach' and operate the Fairtrade system as a paternalistic 'charity organisation' instead of as an empowering trading system for

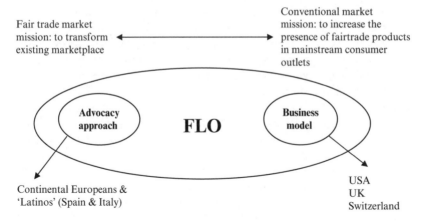

Fair trade market
mission: to transform
existing marketplace

Conventional market
mission: to increase the
presence of fairtrade products
in mainstream consumer
outlets

Advocacy
approach

FLO

Business
model

Continental Europeans &
'Latinos' (Spain & Italy)

USA
UK
Switzerland

*Figure 5.4   Microcosm of fair trade movement's broader ideological
spectrum within FLO*

producers (VanderHoff Boersma, 7 January 2006, fieldwork notes). By contrast, the 'advocacy approach' subculture, while also operating within convention with FLO's system, is more suspicious of the market, and strongly advocates change to the terms and rules of international trade for producers (VanderHoff Boersma, 7 January 2006, fieldwork notes). Figure 5.4 illustrates the micro-ideological spectrum among LIs that reflects broader IFAT–FLO differences.

While in the context of the wider movement the LIs can be collectively conceived as the movement's 'resisters', the portrait of resisters here shows that they form a heterogeneous rather than homogeneous group. Spread along an ideological spectrum, the 'advocacy' LIs are situated (philosophically) closer to the wider movement than to the 'business model' LIs, and the 'business model' LIs gravitate towards conventional market actors rather than 'advocacy' LIs. This illuminates the complexity within social movement narratives that a defiance lens aims to better capture.

The ideological differences between these two subcultures of resisters, and the more macro-movement perspectives they reflect, hinge on competing views of the efficacy or authority of the existing neoliberal economy and the role of the Fairtrade certification model in empowering small-scale producers within the market. Fundamentally, this is a competition between different types of knowledge – one that dominates the conventional marketplace; the other alternative and marginal to this prevailing discourse. Evolutionary economists observe that, as new ventures grow over time, they come to reflect dominant bodies of knowledge (see Ramazzotti, 2001: 76). This organisational and ideological evolution

comes at the cost of the organisation's adaptability and responsiveness to
new ideas and information (see McGrath and MacMillan, 2000; Schaper
and Volery, 2002: 269). These observations about organisational evolution
and its effect on knowledge are illustrated here. Interestingly, decentralised, networked organisational and governance structures are generally
complimented for their superior information-processing, flexibility and
adaptability in contrast to integrated, hierarchical structures of governance (see Achrol and Kotler, 1999; Doherty and Meehan, 2004). These
two types or styles of organisation are attributed to different market
environments: disintegrated, 'organic' forms of organisation in volatile,
unpredictable contexts; and integrated bureaucratic, 'mechanistic' forms
of organisation in predictable, stable environments (Nooteboom, 2001:
51). The superiority of the former in contemporary times, however, arises
from the information-rich nature of the knowledge economy (see Achrol
and Kotler, 1999). For Achrol and Kotler (ibid.: 146), networks are better
adapted to knowledge-rich environments because of their superior information-processing capabilities. As they claim:

> The network organisation is . . . a superior learning organisation . . . [compared
> with] hierarchy [which] creates strong ties within and among functional units.
> Strong ties cause members to think and act alike, and thus, information that
> flows in the system becomes largely redundant over time. In contrast, networks
> create dense but weak ties with members with different functions, interests and
> knowledge bases. Each link transmits new and different information, and for the
> network as a whole, this means superior knowledge assimilation. (Ibid.: 147)

Be this as it may, we have just seen that networked organisational structures are not immune to hierarchical formation in the process of market
evolution. Nodes within networked governance structures appear to
exhibit the evolutionary capacity to consolidate and build centralised,
hierarchical structures for governing knowledge; nodal hierarchies can
form and produce discrepancies and inefficiencies in knowledge flows (see
Chapter 7). The effect of nodal hierarchies is considered below; suffice to
say here that this empirical insight adds refinement to the idea of network
organisations as sophisticated and desirable structures of governance
for knowledge. Indeed, Chapter 6 shows that, in the face of conservative
nodes, nodes within the wider network have continued scope for innovation, and Chapter 7 reveals alternative institutional network structures that
nurture trajectories of continued innovation and thrive in information-rich
environments. These processes are important for understanding how the
political obstacles to triggering market transformation are overcome; the
response of innovative nodes is crucial to understanding the evolutionary
success of alternative narratives (see Chapters 6 and 7). The following

section examines in more detail how FLO's organisational model gives exclusive control to market-oriented interests, and considers its impact on FLO's evolutionary capacity.

INSTITUTING ORTHODOXY: GOVERNANCE AND FUNDING

Dependency theorists posit that an organisation's need to survive and acquire resources for growth encourages conformity to the external political climate. As McGrath and MacMillan (2000: 141) write:

> Most firms . . . are predisposed to seek efficiency rather than undergo the high costs of generating variety in their portfolios through the pursuit of new business models . . . firms are driven to respond to the external environment in ways that allow them to gain essential resources. Thus they are highly constrained in the actions they may take and are continually engaged in political negotiations to acquire more resources.

This view is insightful in this case. While a pragmatic market-driven view constitutes only one perspective of expanding fair trade markets, it none the less commands a greater degree of influence over the radical fair trade discourse. This power imbalance between FLO and IFAT is predicated on their different ideological positions: FLO's relative authority and influence over IFAT is justified by FLO's explicitly conventional market-oriented approach, one that does not question or criticise the authority of the existing market. As one respondent explained, FLO and a few particular LIs (see below) exert decision-making power without first seeking FTOs' views or support because they view the FTO movement's vision as too 'old fashioned' and 'traditional' to succeed in the marketplace. Describing this power imbalance, one respondent observed:

> there needs to be more dialogue between IFAT and FLO. Because at the moment it is not good – we [IFAT] have to bargain with FLO. For me it is a bargaining game, we have to ask certain rights . . . to be recognised or if we want to influence the standards, such as after we discussed with [banana, coffee and cocoa] producers the introduction of plantations – [they] were completely against FLO [on this issue]. (IFAT member, fieldwork notes)

This description of the 'bargaining game' that IFAT is forced to play with FLO illustrates the unequal power relationship between their competing discourses in governing the development of fair trade. FLO's is a liberal style of power ('power over') – reduced to bargaining and power plays – rather than a 'post-liberal' exercise of power ('power with') embodied in collaboration, deliberation and cooperation (see Mouffe, 1992). In fact, FLO can be seen to gain much 'power with' from mainstream actors by conforming to prevailing market norms; its interpretation of Fairtrade is more accessible to conventional market actors than IFAT's transformational model. Moreover, FLO appears to be using this 'power with' to exert 'power over' the wider fair trade movement, a notable political trend in new institutions that adopt top-down decision-making structures and bureaucratic relations (VeneKlasen and Miller, 2002: 45).

GOVERNANCE

As we have already seen, the pragmatic market-driven LIs constitute only one subculture among FLO's LI members. Despite this, they have been an all-powerful minority in FLO's decision-making, heavily influencing how FLO responds to the outside world (particularly towards IFAT). The authority their perspective has assumed in FLO's governance has developed in two ways. The first is through the LIs' legal ownership over the organisation.[5] In spite of being only one of a number of stakeholders in the Fairtrade system, the LIs have had constitutional power over producers in the governance of FLO since its creation which, as respondents claimed, has given the LIs undemocratic and largely unaccountable influence over FLO's development:

> the dynamic in FLO is not always easy to understand because . . . the power in FLO lies with the National Initiatives. FLO cannot impose the politics on the National Initiatives. This has to do with the history of how FLO started. All of this began with the National Initiatives, and only then they came together to make FLO, but they did not give their power to FLO. FLO [does] standards, yes, FLO [does] the [product] registers, yes, the monitoring, sure . . . but the *power*? It is not [given to FLO]. Or the criteria which makes Chiquita a yes or no [in FLO's system], it is not [FLO's decision]. . . . there's a huge criticism about FLO now from producers . . . [that] there is no participation, well there is participation, but when it comes to *decision*-making, they [producers] are in a minority, because the National Initiatives have this majority. (IFAT member, fieldwork notes)

> legally, the National Initiatives (NIs) are the owners of FLO International . . . This . . . point has important consequences for the situation we find ourselves in today; the people who actually make the decisions within the Fairtrade system are the NI Directors. At the NI Director meetings (called the Meeting of Members – MoM), neither the producers nor any other Party can participate . . . these meetings [of members] do not take place within the structure of FLO, despite the fact that they make all the decisions pertaining to FLO. . . . FLO's Board of Directors is composed of 6 members representing the NIs (appointed

by them and they also vote for the President) and they possess 50 per cent of the votes. In other words, although FLO's Board of Directors includes 4 producers and 2 industry representatives, the NIs have enough votes themselves to approve or deny any point of action. All final decisions are made at the MoMs and sometimes they even revoke decisions made by the Board. (Denaux, 25 November 2004)

These accounts highlight the pervasive control the LIs have exerted over FLO by virtue of their constitutional ownership. LIs have represented a majority on the Board – and been FLO's legal owners – which means that despite producers' board participation they have been unable to influence FLO board decisions. In fact, in spite of a seemingly representative governance structure and FLO's (original) spirit of consensus-based decision-making (Renard and Pérez-Grovas, 2007: 149), the Meeting of Members (MoM) (the exclusive meeting between LIs) has been the actual and final decision-making forum in FLO (Pare, 4 July 2005, fieldwork notes; Bretman, 3 May 2005, fieldwork notes).

This evolution in FLO's governance can be seen to reflect deliberative democracy theorists' observation that governance mechanisms are not value-free and that the relative validity of competing perspectives in decision-making processes is a political contest. According to Dewey, for instance, institutions are no longer helpful – indeed they are a 'problem' – when within them a 'cadre of experts' forms and becomes 'shut off from knowledge of the needs they are supposed to serve' (cited in Pimbert and Wakeford, 2001: 26). One respondent described FLO as heavily influenced by a 'small cadre of people' whose interests are market-driven, a clique that, in the last several years, has attracted growing criticism from producers for undermining their developmental needs and interests.

To the extent that FLO is governed by traditional 'top-down' or one-way information flows, its governance model can be seen as an institutional impediment to change in markets (see Chapter 7 for further analysis). Loasby (1999: 27) points out for instance that 'economic systems, like political systems, are likely to generate more knowledge and to use it more effectively if they are open societies'. The above empirical accounts speak indeed to the need for the more 'open' mode of organisation in FLO to facilitate an evolution in knowledge (beyond the prevailing discourse of 'markets') and to enable the institution to operate more effectively. Focusing on the political dimensions of the organisational evolution of 'knowledge', deliberative democratic theorists highlight that 'open' governance structures and processes help to mediate the power struggle that underscores the generation, distribution and use of knowledge, particularly where social power relations are shaped by its ownership and control (see Gaventa, 1993). Thus the political implication of 'large, vertically

integrated hierarchies' (Achrol and Kotler, 1999: 147) such as FLO's is
the re-creation of traditional relations of power and ownership that stall
processes of change in the broader economic system.

FUNDING

While FLO's governance structure has excluded non-LI voices from
shaping the development of fair trade markets, FLO's funding model
has further marginalised non-market-oriented LI voices from this group
of decision-makers. By way of explanation, Figure 5.5 (a hypothetical
example of FLO revenues from the certification of a coffee chain) depicts
the three revenue streams that have given authority to the 'business model'
development of Fairtrade:

Revenue x

LIs receive income from licensees of the Fairtrade Mark (who include any
market actors who wish to affix the Fairtrade Mark to a product). Licence
payments are calculated as a percentage of a trader's market share, sales
or volumes (depending on each LI's particular fee structure). By virtue of
their size, the largest traders in the LI market represent their largest potential source of income. This has disadvantaged FTO traders (financially and
philosophically) who, though the most committed and longest-standing
actors in fair trade markets, are far smaller than conventional traders
(Raynolds, 2007: 76). LIs have also worked directly with retailers (and
mobilised consumer pressure on supermarkets) to convert all own-brand
coffees to Fairtrade and thereby put pressure on conventional brand manufacturers to source Fairtrade if they want access to consumers.[6] This is the

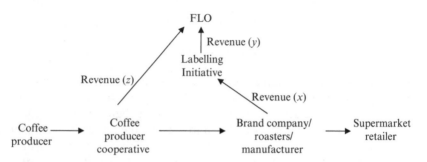

Figure 5.5   Three key funding streams within FLO

first plank in the LIs' and FLO's growth strategy: the focus on large-scale conventional companies as revenue-raisers.

Revenue y

LI members contribute licence-fee revenues to FLO for its operating budget.[7] The LIs with the most money – those that concentrate on working with the largest market traders – have exercised the most influence over FLO's decision-making and policy development, not least because they largely determine FLO's organisational activities through the funding they grant or refuse to provide (see below). By contrast, the 'advocacy' LIs, which are reluctant to draw MNCs into FLO's system given their more radical ideological disposition, have fewer funds to give to FLO and thus less 'buying power' in FLO's system. As one LI director stated:

> And which are the strong NIs within FLO? The US, the UK, Switzerland, and to a lesser extent, the Netherlands . . . And the big ones [LIs] are the Anglo-Saxons, because in business, it's like that . . . [that's] the difference between me [as an LI with a small Fairtrade market] and them [the 'Anglo-Saxons'], they're big and rich and I'm not. . . . (Former LI director, fieldwork notes)

This candid account demonstrates how FLO's funding model effectively subordinates non-market-oriented LIs' voices within Fairtrade's govern-ance. This financial model has at least two pernicious consequences. The first is that the LIs and FLO are financially dependent on MNCs for market growth and survival (which in turn has given MNCs significant 'power over' the LIs and FLO). The second, highlighted by respondents, is the political influence it has had on the Fairtrade certification system itself:

> one of the major problems with the 'greenwashing question' is that FLO and Transfair USA refuse to address it publicly. Their probable reasoning is obvious: these companies [that are] doing the damage provide most of the cash for their operating budgets. . . . (Earley, 11 February 2005)

> FLO hasn't managed to cultivate an environment where a principled applica-tion of the label doesn't prevent growth but at the same time doesn't allow the corporatisation of fair trade. [It's] not 'corporatised' because they [MNCs] can carry the label, but because they're allowed to define the rules of the game. (Gorman, 12 July 2005, fieldwork notes)

> the Anglo-Saxons [within FLO are] saying, 'we need a business model, so we need a service-provider . . . [FLO] do your job' . . . [But] if you want to be ideo-logical [as an LI]? That's an issue . . . [because] if you want to do something on a political level . . . you . . . need to be centralised, you need to coordinate your campaigns and efforts and so on. Well the Anglo-Saxons say 'no priority, we

are not going to fund this'. How can I justify to my license holder that he is also going to pay for my lobbying? I can't say that, no way.' (Former LI director, fieldwork notes)

As these comments illustrate, through fear of jeopardising major licensees' uptake of Fairtrade, the Fairtrade certification system's demands of traders and of the broader political environment have diminished. FLO and the market-oriented LIs have pursued a model of growth in a way that has led to decision-making and rule-making that serves the interests of conventional market actors at the expense of fair trade principles. As Gorman phrased it, Fairtrade is 'corporatised' because MNCs are 'allowed to define the rules of the game'. This is the second plank in financing a 'resistance' model of fair trade: the interests of FLO's most powerful decentralised organisational nodes are favoured and the power of those nodes is the product of their support for the *status quo*.

Revenue z

Fairtrade producer cooperatives pay for certification in order to gain access to Fairtrade markets. Previously, licensee payments covered producers' certification costs, providing a subsidy for producers to access Fairtrade markets. Licensee payments no longer subsidise producer certification.[8] Producers' new need for capital to become part of Fairtrade markets has excluded, and created an obstacle for, many small-scale producers who cannot afford the high costs of achieving certification. This policy change has been seen as undermining fair trade principles by reducing the costs of Fairtrade product certification for market traders at the expense of producers' market and developmental interests and needs (see Doppler and González Cabañas, 2006). As one producer explained:

> FLO is allowing itself to be run by the market. In the beginning, FLO's (Max Havelaar) only objective was to develop organisations of small producers. Also their other activities served this purpose – the [Fairtrade] certificat[ion], the criteria, the market, the inspections, the support the National Initiatives and the certification committees. But now, it appears that FLO's only goal is the 'market' and [to show that] all [in the existing market] is well . . . [For] the NIs – if the market requires ISO 65, we [FLO] give it to them, if the market requires plantations, we give it to them, if the market requires us to work with the MNCs, we do it. And now that FLO Cert. has become independent from FLO e.V., producers must pay for their certification . . . certification is no longer part of the support provided to help develop producer organisations. Rather, certification shows the market [that] 'all is good'. (Denaux, 25 November 2004)

This observation clearly highlights that, while the system was designed to subsidise producers' market access, and certification was intended to be part of a process of meaningful trade capacity-building, FLO certification (particularly since the creation of FLO Cert.) has become more bureaucratic, complex and anonymous, displacing FLO's founding producer-oriented prerogative and organisation (Renard and Pérez-Grovas, 2007; Renard, 2005). As was articulated by Franz VanderHoff Boersma, one of the founders of Max Havelaar and a farmer with UCIRI,[9] 'the 'market driven' approach [of FLO] at almost all costs [has] created many questions in the field [for] producers who feel left out [of FLO's system] and funneled into a market approach they are struggling against' (23 December 2005, fieldwork notes).

This is the third plank to FLO's growth – making producers pay for access to Fairtrade markets. Since small producers' material disadvantage bars them from access to the (now) costly Fairtrade market system, a policy of producer certification payment filters out and rewards cooperatives with sufficient capacity and capital from those that are smaller and in need of financial and capacity-building assistance. Reinforcing this barrier to entry is the growing tendency to certify large traders' own plantations over smaller Fairtrade co-ops. While FLO originally agreed that certification of plantations would only be allowed in commodity sectors based on plantation-farming (such as tea) and not allowed in those where small-scale production occurs, FLO has increasingly relaxed this rule in industries where small production exists, such as bananas and tropical fruits (see Raynolds, 2007; Wilkinson and Mascarenhas, 2007a; Renard and Pérez-Grovas, 2007). As fair trade pioneer Pauline Tiffen observed, large conventional traders in FLO's system prefer to work only with larger Fairtrade producer cooperatives (or plantations), which guarantees them the economies of scale and volumes they need but is 'not very developmental' for smaller, more vulnerable producer groups who have 'worked really hard and [have] needed the break' to access markets. As Tiffen described the situation, 'you can lead a horse to water, but you can't make it drink' (25 October 2005, fieldwork notes).

Rather than create an alternative incentive structure for MNCs to work with small producers, the FLO certification system has advanced 'business-as-usual'. FLO's policy of producer-certification fees poses an immediate barrier to entry into Fairtrade for poor producers, as does its policy to certify plantations, particularly for small producers in securing contracts with traders.

Organisational theorists and (social) psychologists have observed the strong motivation among individuals and groups to conform to sources of authority when doing so guarantees financial survival or social acceptance (see McGrath and MacMillan, 2000; Robert and Weiss, 1988; Milgram, 1974). Viewed in these terms, the LIs can be seen as conforming to the norms and processes of the dominant market system to secure their market growth and survival. This evolution has resulted in a more conservative vision for, and version of, Fairtrade. For instance, one Fairtrade farmer noted how the 'story' that some LIs tell – that MNCs must be accommodated however small their commitment to stocking Fairtrade products – simply 'disguises' the 'economic interest of FLO and NIs': 'selling more [means] higher incomes for the NIs and FLO' through the payments from licensees. Indeed, 'business model' LIs have argued that FLO cannot exclude MNCs on (radical) ideological grounds and must accommodate their requests to either become licensees or to certify their current production sites/plantations. Their rationale has been that if excluded or thwarted in their attempts to sell Fairtrade products, MNCs will be made to feel like the 'bad guys' and would have a reason to exit the Fairtrade system or ignore it and create a competing 'fair trade' mark (Paulsen, 7 July 2005). This clearly demonstrates how FLO's funding model compromises their capacity and motivation to defy the economic *status quo*.

This development highlights a key paradoxical theme in this chapter: in the process of social change, the fair trade movement's 'resisters' have built structures that pacify the movement's influence but fuel their own organisational growth. One fair trade producer described this paradox vividly when he said that 'they [the LIs] profess lip service to the struggle [that we producers face] against the dominant neoliberal imperial economy', but that, despite their words, the LIs have actually 'lost [the] mission of Fair trade . . . [and] dare to say that the neoliberal economy and market is a reality and you have to stick to it and [it] cannot be changed; only marginal work can be done' (7 January 2006, fieldwork notes). This response brings into sharp relief that the business model LIs are exerting 'power over' the Fairtrade system to maintain and benefit from 'business-as-usual'.

Evolutionary economics tells us that organisational and institutional structures that promote 'disagreement' are essential for progressing human knowledge, based on a Popperian view of knowledge that 'economic and human activity changes knowledge . . . and every change in knowledge opens up the conditions for changes in activity and, thus, further changes in knowledge *ad infinitum*' (cited in Foster and Metcalfe, 2001: 4). In Popperian terms, the development of FLO's governance and funding structure can be seen to frustrate the evolutionary process by giving preferential treatment to market 'orthodoxy'; these structures have stifled disagreement and debate and made FLO/the LIs immune to the diffuse and contextual knowledge circulating in the broader fair trade system. In the following section we turn to consider precisely how this structure has undermined the movement's capacity to transform economic structures with Fairtrade certification.

MAINSTREAMING THE *STATUS QUO*? THE VALUE CHAIN AND THE FAIRTRADE 'BUSINESS MODEL'

Working out 'what works' in order to become dominant in the market tends to be an uncertain process of trial and error, and repeated model adaptation is commonly required. As Loasby (1999: 28) claims:

> contrary to the Schumpeterian image of the innovator who drives the original conception to success, most imaginative conceptions which succeed are substantially changed along the way. As in biological systems, selection is mainly rejection, but in economic systems it sometimes takes the form of adaptation and redesign, leading to another set of trials, which may result in further adaptation, or eventual rejection.

However, the adaptation process is as much political as it is pragmatic (see Chapter 7). Organisational theorists explore the organisational evolution of power through the idea of organisational inertia and tendency towards hierarchical and bureaucratic formation, in which '[a]daptation [to change] is slow and costly because of entrenched interests eager to preserve their power and prerogatives' (Achrol and Kotler, 1999, 146; see also Robert and Weiss, 1988; McGrath and MacMillan, 2000). The idea of organisational inertia can be demonstrated in the evolution of FLO's organisational development and strategy of 'resistance'. FLO's tendency is towards market preservation rather than market innovation. Figure 5.6 depicts a Fairtrade 'value' chain that charts the distribution of value among principal Fairtrade coffee supply chain actors: coffee producers, producer cooperatives, traders and retailers. FLO and the LIs rely on this model for market scale.

Similar to the income stream of FLO, the distribution of value in the Fairtrade 'business model' approach advocated by market-oriented LIs can be seen to reinforce existing power/value inequities in the trading chain. Figure 5.6 illuminates that roasters still capture the lion's share of the dollar value; in this illustrative example, roasters receive 13 times more than individual producers and 22 times as much as the cooperative. Whilst FLO's system may pay producers a relatively higher price for their coffee, producers' remuneration remains marginal to that systematically accrued by market players who control branding and distribution. It also remains tied to commodity production – a depreciating unit of value-adding activity in international trade (see Chapter 2).

On the one hand, this model re-creates the same problem for producers

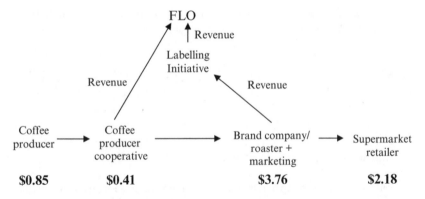

Source: Adapted from Nicholls and Opal (2005: 83). The stages of roasting and marketing have been lumped together here to show the entire value accrued by brand manufacturers.

Figure 5.6   The coffee value chain upon which the Fairtrade system depends for scale

that exists in conventional international commodity markets, whereby their limited value-chain mobility is forcing producing countries to export increasingly large volumes of raw commodities in order to sustain their income (UNDP, 2005: 118). On the other hand, the LIs prolong producers' political-economic status by refraining from challenging MNC power and merely encouraging MNCs to increase the volume of Fairtrade they stock.[10] Two informants described how this limits FLO's capacity to promote market evolution:

> [increasing] volume is great, volume is excellent, but volume is not a strategy . . . volume *can't* be a strategy [for social change] *in itself*. (Earley, Co-founder, Just Coffee, 23 June 2005, fieldwork notes)

> it's not all about volume and signing up more MNCs, there's something else. Signing up more companies doesn't address ideological issues . . . FLO needs to push companies not just to address the price issue, but fundamental issues of inequality in the supply chain . . . that's tough because it's easy to ask a company to write a cheque, but to hand over power, I think that's where the challenge lies. (Petchers, Coffee Program Manager, Oxfam America, 19 July 2005, fieldwork notes)

As these comments help to illustrate, FLO's volume-based model is inadequate for the fair trade movement's mission of producer empowerment. As Petchers puts it, 'there's something else' beyond 'volume' and scale that FLO's system neglects: market power. Others concurred and raised concerns that this model and FLO's strategy has diluted or reduced fair trade principles:

for reasons of corporate adoption and for ease of consumer access, [fair trade] is something that has been boiled down to 'Fairtrade means producers get a fair price'. But in actuality, it's about almost everything *but* that . . . [fair trade] is actually not about what you're paying so much as the fact that you are engaged in direct, long-term relations with producers, where the objective is to maximise benefits going back to the most vulnerable people in the supply chain in ways that challenge the existing terms of trade. So it's really process-oriented, it's really a long-term project . . . that's not something that you can easily do by saying 'yep here's your seal and put it on your bag and pay 1.26 and be done with it'. . . . even though you can get people to pay a better price when you get these large corporations on board . . . what you *lose* is . . . the *power* of what *could* come if they really understood what they were buying into . . . if you could really get Procter & Gamble to understand that it's not just about paying a Fairtrade price, it's about developing long-term relationships, it's about really investing in these communities, it's about seeing the sustainability of *your* business being tied to the sustainability of *their* business . . . [then] we'd have a much different story to tell. . . . (Gorman, 12 July 2005, fieldwork notes)

if we're allowing companies to participate [in Fairtrade] and not asking anything in return other than to pay a higher price for their coffee, we're not asking them to change their business practices in general, we're not asking them to do pre-financing in general, we're not asking them to commit to forming long-lasting relationships with these [producer] communities. What we're doing is we're giving people this false sense of doing something to change an unjust economy . . . when we allow these companies to participate without asking them to change their practices or even for the same level of transparency that the farmers have to go through [in FLO's system], then in effect what we're doing is we're watering [fair trade] down. (Earley, 23 June 2005, fieldwork notes)

As Gorman suggests, the movement's power lies not in getting MNCs into the system *per se*, but in the system's effective promotion of its 'longer-term project' among MNC participants: to transform corporate thinking and practices and thus trigger economic change. In this sense, the market power that FLO and the LIs have gained from adapting to the worldview of MNCs gives MNCs 'power over' them and the Fairtrade market. This change in the Fairtrade system demonstrates that the organisational structures that resisters are motivated to build are ill suited to the aim of market evolution and, as we are about to see, in fact endanger their own institutional survival.

DUPING FLO TO DESTROY FAIRTRADE

According to Harper (1996: 5, 38), the market is more than a system for resource allocation; it is a learning process, and entrepreneurship a 'problem-solving activity'. Learning occurs 'in the light of experience and feedback from the market', whereby entrepreneurs 'may retain some part of their systems of knowledge while modifying the rest' or may 'devise entirely new systems to replace their original ideas and strategies' (ibid.: 6). In this way innovation is the product of insight born from continuous trial and error and the concomitant expansion of human knowledge.

Yet since new knowledge is potentially capable of destabilising market structures, the desire to acknowledge and exploit new information is not universal. As organisations move into a phase of consolidation, the experience of initial market success can be so seductive that the perceived need to continue learning and exploiting new information diminishes and becomes more difficult (see Robert and Weiss, 1988; McGrath and MacMillan, 2000). Different actors also have different interests in, and intentions for, the use of knowledge (see Gaventa, 1993). For instance, powerful market actors value knowledge for profitability (and in some cases preventing others' ability to profit from knowledge), not for the purpose of discovering new and more sophisticated models of equitable market governance of international markets.

While market-oriented LIs see MNCs as their 'allies' in their project of consolidating Fairtrade (Sellers, 10 May 2005, fieldwork notes), corporations see the LIs and FLO as allies for a completely different objective. MNCs have sought to be associated in consumers' minds with the Fairtrade image – the Fairtrade Mark – to give the appearance of sharing the Fairtrade identity. As several corporate respondents observed, Fairtrade is very well known by 'everybody' (Meyer, Corporate Affairs, Kraft Europe, 27 June 2005, fieldwork notes); the Fairtrade Mark carries with it widespread popularity and a certain *cachet*. Hence associating their brand with the popular image of the Fairtrade Mark offers companies a means of enhancing their brand image – goodwill – with consumers (see Chapter 2). This is nevertheless a fine line to tread since companies want consumers to give preference to their products because of the desirability of their brand, not because a product carries the Fairtrade Mark (Leheup, Commodity Sourcing Manager for Coffee and Beverages, Strategic Business Unit, Nestlé, 18 April 2005, fieldwork notes).

So in recent years, prominent brand companies such as Procter & Gamble and Starbucks in the USA, and Nestlé in the UK, have begun to purchase small percentages of Fairtrade-certified coffee as the Fairtrade market and its popularity have increased across continental Europe, the UK, the USA and Canada. The brand companies' Fairtrade coffee lines have been presented as new specialty coffee brands for the company rather than offered in their existing or mainstream coffee lines. McDonalds, the largest global food-service/quick-service restaurant chain, and Dunkin' Donuts, a global coffee and baked-goods chain, as well as global supermarket retailers such as Tesco, are other global brand companies that have begun to stock Fairtrade coffee. In other product industries such as bananas, Chiquita and Dole have begun to offer Fairtrade bananas, and Cadbury–Schweppes recently bought out the growing chocolate brand Green and Black's (the first company to be awarded the Fairtrade Mark for their 'Maya Gold' chocolate brand line).

Corporates' minimalist strategy in the Fairtrade system is indicative of their underlying concern that the Fairtrade Mark threatens brand control by making the brand logo secondary to the Fairtrade Mark in influencing consumers' purchasing decisions. As such, the Fairtrade Mark is another 'brand' competing for market share. As Jeroen Douglas of Solidaridad noted:

> if you have three coffee roasters – all of whom deliver Max Havelaar coffee – but you cannot as a consumer distinguish the three [roasters] from each other, then those roasters are not interested at all in the Max Havelaar brand because they're investing in their competitor. (12 April 2005, fieldwork notes)

Douglas captures the threat that Fairtrade – or any certification label popular with consumers – poses for brand companies: the dilution of the brand value in favour of the certification mark. Brand companies would rather increase the value of the brand (which they exclusively control) than leverage the value of a certification mark (which they do not control) in the mind of the consumer. Confirming this was a respondent from a multi-stakeholder initiative who proposed that certification will never be the 'main game' for industry since they perceive their brand value to be diminished in the consumer's eyes by the certification label:

> I really think it is important what companies say, that they see the value of their product in their *brand*, and not in the label. But the certification schemes of the niche markets, Rainforest and Utz Kapeh and Fairtrade . . . they are building their marketing aspects on labelling a *product* . . . I mean, imagine you go to a supermarket shelf and you see the product of Sara Lee and Nestlé and Kraft . . . all standing close to each other, and they all have the [certification] label [from a particular certification body such as Fairtrade] on the product . . . [from the consumer's viewpoint] there's no credibility in the brand then, because consumers will assume that a product that has been labelled has a very high value . . . [and that the label] is *the value* of the product [not the brand] . . . So this is important to understand why the companies did not go for certification and labelling, and why they do not have an interest to transfer one of the existing certification systems to the mainstream. (Anon., fieldwork notes)

The threat Fairtrade poses is its capacity to undermine brand differentiation – the very core of brand companies' market power. It would make corporate investment, legal protection and advertising strategy completely meaningless. Brand companies would never willingly subordinate their means of market control and value to Fairtrade.

Unlike conventional means of annihilating market competition such as acquisitions or mergers (see Chapter 2), however, FLO is not a single company but a decentralised network of governing nodes. Thus no one brand company can 'take over' the Fairtrade Mark. The best companies can do in this situation is to cooperate with other brand companies to bring about FLO's destruction. One Fairtrade producer described this corporate strategy: 'TNCs have never liked Fairtrade. The war never ended, the strategy just changed – if you can't beat 'em, join 'em. Then get rid of 'em . . . ' (VanderHoff Boersma, in Paulsen, 7 July 2005).

Upon reflection on the way in which MNCs are using the Fairtrade system, respondents described how many of the huge brand companies beginning to tap the Fairtrade market are simply 'window-dressing': making a minimal commitment to Fairtrade to profit from association with the Fairtrade image but leaving untouched the company's wider business operations and philosophy. As respondents observed,

> brands like McDonalds . . . [now] own these other brands which have no association with the main brand and introduce [Fairtrade] there. You see that with Procter & Gamble's 'Millstone' in the US . . . that Millstone thing is completely hypocritical [by contrast with the rest of the company's philosophy]. (Rosenberg, Director, Utz Kapeh, 7 April 2005, fieldwork notes)

> when you're talking about markets [like fair trade] that are *that* small and emergent, there's interest in the business sector in getting *into* those niche markets for the traditional business reasons like 'what does that represent in terms of growth potential', 'if I can secure a place here, what does it mean in terms of long-term profitability?'. But there's *usually no* interest in putting marketing or advertising dollars or consumer education dollars *behind that* [speculative business venture]. . . . So I think [big corporations] see [Fairtrade] as a way of buying themselves a CSR profile. They see this as a way of saying 'we're a responsible company *because* we carry these products'. And in some ways, [the Fairtrade Mark] then becomes [the company's] own marketing. So the [companies] are not buying [Fairtrade] because they're trying to develop a new product, they're buying it – and they're selling it – because it's *PR*. And you don't spend PR dollars to promote your PR. . . . (Gorman, 12 July 2005, fieldwork notes)

A vivid example of this trend is Nestlé UK's recent launch of its 'Partner's Blend' Fairtrade-certified coffee brand. While gaining association in the mind of the consumer with Fairtrade and entry into the UK's lucrative Fairtrade market, 'Partner's Blend' accounts for only one tenth of 1 per cent of Nestlé's total volume, and involves just over 200 of the 3 million producer groups around the world dependent on Nestlé for a living. As

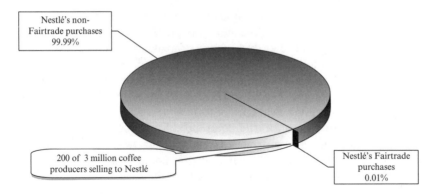

Nestlé's non-
Fairtrade purchases
99.99%

200 of 3 million coffee
producers selling to Nestlé

Nestlé's Fairtrade
purchases
0.01%

Figure 5.7 *Percentage of Nestlé's total volume of coffee certified as*
Fairtrade

shown in Figure 5.7, this 'commitment' to producer empowerment is
questionable.

Figure 5.7 powerfully illustrates how large-scale traders are subverting
the Fairtrade Mark to a subsidiary brand to maintain market control. In
this strategy, the Fairtrade Mark becomes MNCs' 'own marketing' in the
sense that carrying a few Fairtrade products equates to a responsible corporate image. Rather than using the Fairtrade Mark as a tool for connection and communication between producers and consumers in a globalised
marketplace, brand manufacturers are using it as an advertising tool to
reassert their market influence.

This strategy can be described as symbolic imitation, an institutional
response (see Chapter 7 for further examination) that is possible – and
effective – because FLO and the LIs have not demanded a quantifiable shift
in corporations' existing business practices in order to use the Fairtrade
Mark (Earley, 23 June 2005, fieldwork notes).[11] As the last section illustrated, instead of addressing the inadequacies of the Fairtrade model to
empower commodity producers in heavily branded markets, the LIs have
ignored it and pursued the model's consolidation. While FLO/the LIs
are gaining increasing scale in mainstream markets, they are gaining less
ground on the movement's aim to shift mainstream corporate philosophy
and practice. Corporations see the model merely as an opportunity for
MNCs and retailers to make profit, not to democratise the distribution of
power and value in international commerce. Corporate informants' comments reflected their traditional business interest. Some suggested that their
company would only source Fairtrade coffee if their consumers demanded
it, or in other words, if the Fairtrade market were to recede, the company
would cease to offer Fairtrade coffee (Atorf, Coffee Manager, Procter &

Gamble, 27 July 2005, fieldwork notes). Other respondents from the coffee industry suggested that since the market price of coffee had begun to rise, the value proposition of Fairtrade would decrease and become 'less necessary' in the eyes of conventional buyers and sellers (Mecklenburg, Vice-President, Sustainable Procurement Practices, Starbucks, 12 July 2005, fieldwork notes; Lingle, Executive Director, Specialty Coffee Association of America, 6 July 2005, fieldwork notes).

As a result of FLO's/the LIs' approach, MNCs are able to reassert market control in the Fairtrade market through their participation in FLO's system. The Managing Director of a commercial FTO identified just some of FLO's vulnerabilities to MNC's influence:

> You've got to actually work out how you're going to engage with a multinational corporation in a meaningful way. How are you going to make sure that they deliver on the commitments that they're apparently making? . . . Part of when you get the Fairtrade Mark on a product is that you're [as a company] saying that you're not going to cannibalise somebody else's market, you're going to *grow* the market and you're committed to see growth year on year – i.e. you're not just putting this [Fairtrade product] there as a blocking position . . . Are the sorts of people who are running the Fairtrade marking system throughout Europe in *any* position to do *that* sort of negotiation with organisations with bigger resources than these [LI] organisations? . . . [in this situation] you [as an LI or FLO] are running before you can walk in terms of who you're engaging with. Because how do you make sure that they [MNCs] do that, and how do you do it in a timely fashion, how do you do it so that you don't realise too late that they [the MNC] actually were taking the piss in terms of what they said they intended to do, and are just blocking [other market entrants] so that they can take the Fairtrade slot on the shelf, remove *somebody else* out of it, and then eventually *drop out* of it [the Fairtrade market]. (Anon., fieldwork notes)

This comment highlights how the Fairtrade system can be weakened by corporations' many strategies to maximise profit and dominate the market because the model depends on them; MNCs have a stronger bargaining position in negotiating with LIs what the company's commitments will be (and what they turn out to be in practice). While market-oriented LIs view corporations' uptake of Fairtrade products as being in the fair trade movement's interests, these empirical observations suggest that corporations will never 'mainstream' Fairtrade products on a wide scale. The MNCs can assure the LIs with which they deal that the company intends to make significant commitments to the system in the future while in the meantime they block other companies' entry into the Fairtrade market and limit the growth potential of the Fairtrade market. They will do so to maintain their market control. Figure 5.8 illustrates the above-mentioned corporate strategies to bring about FLO's destruction and use it for their own ends.

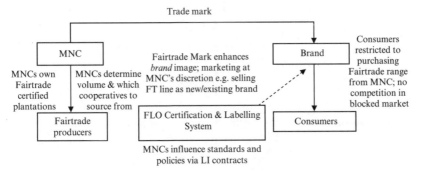

Figure 5.8   Emerging sites of exploitation of FLO's system by MNCs

While static adaptation may fast-track market consolidation, the empirical accounts in this chapter suggest that the particular evolutionary trajectory of resistance has made FLO susceptible to industry 'capture' (Ayres and Braithwaite, 1992), enabling brand companies to reassert their market control. FLO's weakness results from the fact that it no longer appears to set the terms in the Fairtrade market. Rather, it has allowed its rules for trader participation to be shaped heavily by conventional traders' interests and practices.

THE SYMBIOTIC DANCE OF RESISTERS AND GAME-PLAYERS

If we accept that the market process is 'a continuous sequence of conjecture and exposure to refutation, a learning procedure for generating and testing entrepreneurial ideas' (Harper, 1996: 38), it follows that governance structures that nurture learning and enable the flow of new and alternative information in a knowledge economy are essential for evolution (see Achrol and Kotler, 1999; see Chapter 7). Those that constrain this flow – the hierarchical, vertically structured forms suited to market predictability such as those analysed in this chapter – are problematic for evolution. In fact, business theorists see this state of inertia as a prelude to the organisation's 'decline' in the market. Innovation – the exploitation of new knowledge – is the means of market renewal (Robert and Weiss, 1988). This organisational tendency emerges in the context of resistance in the sense that the resister's relevance and survival is under threat if they do not capitalise on new information and ideas about the system's weaknesses. As Gorman claims,

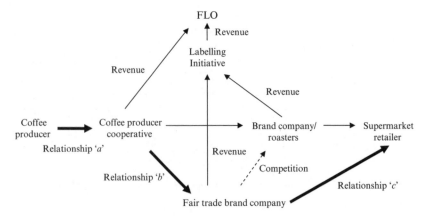

*Figure 5.9   Fair trade pioneers' means of bypassing MNCs' market
power in FLO's system: the introduction of fair trade brand
companies*

where I *hope* ultimately Fairtrade will end up proving itself . . . [is that] it can
demonstrate that it can be responsive to new and emerging needs, and that it
has a way of being critical and not stagnant. For example, the next horizon
of fair trade is really dealing with the issue of ownership. Because for cocoa
farmers . . . the dollar value of cocoa in a bar of chocolate that costs 1 dollar is
about *eight cents*. So you can be paying a cocoa grower a fair wage with respect
to the local market, but [the producer] is not actually able to capture the value
that their labour has directly and indirectly generated because all the value
happens further in the supply chain – it's in the brand. So companies like the
Day Chocolate Company in the UK which sells Divine Chocolate is one third
owned by the farmers that grow it. So they get the value from the Fairtrade
premium, they get the value of the *brand* . . . I think that Fairtrade will only be
successful and sustainable if it can adapt and respond to *emerging* difficulties
that producers face. (Gorman, 12 July 2005, fieldwork notes)

Gorman links FLO's neglect of the politics of producer (brand) ownership with the idea of becoming 'stagnant' in the market, suggesting that
Fairtrade's weaknesses, if left unresolved, will threaten its institutional
survival. At the same time, Gorman alludes to the movement's actors who
are critical of sustaining and reviving the prospect of economic transformation in the context of capture: fair trade's innovative pioneers who are
building fair trade brand companies. These actors – who can be seen as
the fair trade movement's 'game-players' – have exploited insights about
FLO's weaknesses and are bypassing the Fairtrade certification model as
a mechanism for market transformation. Figure 5.9 illustrates fair trade
pioneers' revised strategy for changing conventional business in the form
of new, stronger commercial fair trade relationships.

As Figure 5.9 shows, the strategy of 'game-playing' in fair trade involves working directly with producer cooperatives (depicted as line 'a') and giving them both ownership in the brand and a direct long-term trading relationship with their 'own' FTO trader (shown as line 'b'). The FTO brand company then deals directly with the retail supermarket or other outlets (thus competing directly with conventional brand companies) (illustrated as line 'c'), and as it grows in the marketplace, creates competition for conventional players (indicated by the dotted arrow). This innovation exploits an alternative discourse that articulates and validates producers' worldview. The power of this innovation – in fact any innovation – is a capacity to disrupt market norms (see McGrath and MacMillan, 2000) and in so doing define new terms and standards of competition to which conventional market actors must respond if they are to survive. The movement's pioneers are innovating in new models of fair trade to create the market conditions in which conventional companies are 'forced to change or exit' the market (Tucker, Managing Director, Third World Information Network, 16 June 2005, fieldwork notes).

The significance of this new business model relates indeed to the growth of knowledge gained from the Fairtrade certification system's experience in the market. The pioneers' brand model of fair trade seeks to overcome the Fairtrade system's political weaknesses in the market. As Gorman argues, this innovative business model addresses issues of producer ownership in the company and brand equity, long-term and direct trading relations and value (in short, empowerment in supply chain relations). Moreover, these models create actual competition for conventional brand companies to raise their commitment to fair trade principles.

The (political) elements that are exploited in this innovation in business organisation are those that the movement's resisters have failed to incorporate into the certification system. Analysed in closer detail in Chapter 6, this innovation – or innovative adaptation to the development of the certification model of fair trade – has derived from careful observation and learning (see Nooteboom, 2001; Harper, 1996). In this way resisters and game-players appear to be engaged in a symbiotic dance choreographed to the rhythm of the evolutionary cycle. This chapter has examined resisters' moves in this dance sequence, which are as follows: game-players create new innovations; resisters consolidate them in the existing market structure through static adaptation, which recreates conditions of (political) stasis in markets. These conditions – in which resisters ignore emergent knowledge – encourage and become the basis of game-players' next innovation. Chapter 6 analyses the movement's game-players who take part in this symbiotic dance, and the innovative models they have spawned since the introduction of the certification system.

CONCLUDING COMMENTS

This chapter has examined the evolution of resistance in fair trade through the institutional development of FLO and the LIs. The empirical analysis highlighted the pernicious effects of FLO's increasingly market-oriented approach to fair trade growth, which has been supported by governance and funding structures that together have effectively invalidated producer and FTO voices/knowledge. The gradual evolution of their unique networked structures of governance offered insight into the (political) evolutionary pressures to which network organisations are subject. This refines our understanding of networks, which conventionally are reputed for their superior ability to acquire, govern and utilise information in information-rich environments. The story of fair trade's expansion in this chapter told of the nodal hierarchies and information inefficiencies that evolutionary dynamics can produce. None the less, networked governance permits the coexistence of both radical and more conservative nodes (see Chapters 6 and 7).

As the chapter has shown, FLO's institutional preservation of 'orthodoxy' emerges from ongoing political judgements inscribed in its knowledge output (in the form of new standards, decisions, policies) made by a select group of actors who are seeking to gain wider market acceptance for Fairtrade. This supports democratic theorists' insight that organisational structures that govern knowledge – and the particular bodies of knowledge they reflect – are not value-free (see Gaventa, 1993; Hayward, 1998; Lefebvre, 1991). An empirical account of how power operates in this context illuminated the power struggle that underpins contests over knowledge production and governance. In the context of resistance, social movement actors gain power by collaborating 'with' MNCs. Yet this route to accessing power is highly precarious and based on MNCs' 'power over' them.

This analysis has demonstrated how market evolution is dependent on the evolution of knowledge (Loasby, 1999: 25–8). Given the political nature of knowledge, organisational forms that effectively govern the production, spread and exploitation of new information and ideas are crucial to the process of change (Achrol and Kotler, 1999). The centrality of knowledge in economic evolution makes this cyclical shift – from the organisational form that supports innovation to that which drives consolidation – a highly political process; 'contests for knowledge are contests for power' (Pimbert, 2001: 81). Braithwaite's defiance framework, from which the category of resistance derives, enables a deeper analysis of agency and power that captures the heterogeneous ideologies and strategies of different social movement actors and their roles in the process of change (see for example Bevir and Rhodes, 2005; Nygren, 1999). To this end, this chapter reveals even greater nuance among resisters and complex dynamics between them and other defiance categories in change processes (specifically game-playing).

While resisters are a threat to their own organisational survival, they play the role of creating new conditions of market stasis. In this sense, their capacity to bring about change through markets is limited. In fact, resisters can be seen as dangerous to the extent that they seek to maintain market stability, however great the cost to those disadvantaged by the *status quo*. For this reason, resisters must be kept off-balance (thrown into a state of market volatility). The chapter showed how power lies in exploiting new knowledge because innovation sets the terms of competition: new knowledge has the opportunity to become dominant (valued) in the marketplace. Game-players play this role. Game-players act in conditions of market stasis to liberate alternative discourses that are suppressed in this static environment; they capitalise on the knowledge and information that is undervalued in resisters' institutions. In this way, game-players ensure that market evolution continues. Empirically, the fair trade pioneers (game-players) are spawning new fair trade brand companies. We now turn to explore their role (and power) in the process of social change.

NOTES

1. Evolutionary economists look to biology to explain this pattern (termed 'natural selection') and economic evolution more generally (see especially Nelson and Winter, 1982). The basic idea is that in nature, 'selection mechanisms favour one variety (e.g. a species) over another, from which one species is eliminated and the other prevails, based on its adaptability . . . selection mechanisms bring to the fore techniques, organisational routines and products that are best adapted to their respective environmental contexts' (Foster and Metcalfe, 2001: 1).
2. This section deals with empirical material on FLO's governance before the FLO Board Meeting of November 2006 at which the Board made structural changes to its governance structure. The analysis of this section reflects this former state.
3. IFAT is analysed in greater depth in Chapter 7.
4. Not all of the 20 LIs were interviewed for this research, though those of historical and contemporary significance in the regions chosen for this fieldwork were included, whether by face-to-face interview or telephone/email correspondence. These included LIs across Europe (such as Max Havelaar Netherlands, Belgium, Switzerland, France), the Fairtrade Foundation in the UK, Transfair USA, and FLO in Germany.
5. In November 2006 the LIs adopted a new constitution that aims to broaden FLO's ownership structure. This chapter documents and analyses the historical context of this evolution, which itself is examined in Chapter 7.
6. While integrating Fairtrade into supermarket own-brand ranges for chocolate or coffee or fresh fruits has stimulated consumer demand, the gains of this strategy for producer development are not universal and in some cases are highly questionable (see Barrientos and Smith, 2007).

7. Member contributions are a key revenue source for FLO. In 2005 they accounted for more than two-thirds of FLO's income, and just under two-thirds in 2006 (see FLO, 2007a).

8. Producers originally accepted the proposition that they should pay for certification as a way of increasing the Fairtrade system's efficacy as an independent third-party certification body. Their opposition since has been triggered by the decision-making process surrounding the agreement. In September 2003 the FLO Forum achieved consensus for a system of producer payments that was overturned by a subsequent decision passed in an FLO Operational Board meeting in November 2003 (from which producers were absent). After a series of threats made between producers and the LIs, temporary reconciliation has been achieved (see Renard and Pérez-Grovas, 2007: 149). Irrespective of this, producer payments remain a financial hurdle for many small-scale producers.

9. UCIRI is a pioneer Indian producer union in the Fairtrade system, located in South Oaxaca, Mexico.

10. Interestingly, this conflict of interest emerging from revenue flow x comes in the wake of market-oriented LIs' criticism of more political or 'activist'-natured LIs and the 'traditional' or non-profit approach characteristic of the wider movement and earlier periods in the fair trade movement's history. The criticism of advocacy-oriented LIs has been that by siding with the wider movement of fair trade campaigners and activists, LIs marginalise industry and are insufficiently impartial for the role of a certification body. By the same token, the data above suggest that a market-driven disposition among the LIs makes them insufficiently committed to the fair trade mission of producer empowerment in the trading relationship.

11. This is particularly the case with supermarket retailers. While these enormous market actors occupy an increasingly prominent role in FLO's system, they do not fall under FLO's definition of 'trader' and so are not bound by contractual agreements to abide by and support fair trade principles. Unless a supermarket retailer has a unique commitment to fair trade principles, this definitional oversight in FLO's regulatory system encourages, and subjects small producers to, purely commercial prerogatives and practices in the Fairtrade market (Barrientos and Smith, 2007).

6.   Fair trade as game-playing

Game-players are radical and 'bold' actors. They seek to transform the regulatory environment rather than acknowledge convention and accepted norms. The game-player 'imagines' another regulatory world by 'think[ing] outside the square', and transcends existing regulatory constraints by accurately perceiving, 'moving around and redefining the rules' (see Braithwaite, 2009; Braithwaite et al., 2007: 291). The ability of the game-player to manoeuvre around institutional and structural constraints as well as lead the creation of new ones mirrors that of the entrepreneur. Like game-players, entrepreneurs desire structural change: entrepreneurs disrupt the 'rules of the game' with innovative business models to 'break down barriers that cause the current market to be structured as it is' (see McGrath and MacMillan, 2000: 94). Entrepreneurs are described as 'visionary', 'creative' and 'convention-defying' actors (see Cauthorn, 1989: 15; Goyder, 1998; McGrath and MacMillan, 2000). They are thought to display 'alertness' within their environment, which enables them to 'transcend an existing framework of perceived opportunities' (Kirzner, 1985: 7). Schumpeter (1934) described entrepreneurship as the 'gale of creative destruction' that overturns accepted industrial patterns.

While theories of entrepreneurship go some way to explaining the game-player's psychology and behaviour, their utility ends when it comes to extrapolating how game-players actually annihilate and restructure market structures. Schumpeter (1934), for instance, took greater interest in the effectual role of entrepreneurship in the evolutionary process than in explaining the causes or preconditions of innovative acts (Binks and Vale, 1990: 28). An analysis of the fair trade movement's pioneers can be seen to offer insight into game-playing and, through it, the political microprocesses that underpin market transformation.

A CAST OF UNIQUE CHARACTERS: GAME-PLAYERS AND THE 'POWER WITHIN'

Since the original Max Havelaar model was established, those who created it have moved on to other fair trade projects. Based primarily in the Netherlands and Mexico, these individuals and ATOs are among a handful of radical innovators in the fair trade movement. As discussed below, these innovators are uniquely positioned both within the wider ATO movement and also in relation to conventional corporate firms. The term ATO has multiple meanings and manifestations (see for example Barratt Brown, 1993; Tiffen and Zadek, 1998; Tallontire, 2000; Nicholls and Opal, 2005). ATOs originally experimented with direct trade relationships and better trading conditions for small-scale producers who were not benefiting from existing business and trading links. While novel for their time, ATOs' 'alternative' status has been brought into question as the accessibility of Fairtrade products becomes more widespread.

Nevertheless, the term 'ATO' (now FTO) remains useful in that it distinguishes still-relevant and distinctive characteristics of FTOs. For instance, the term 'FTO' distinguishes those organisations set up explicitly to serve and empower producers in trading relationships from 'second-mover' companies that engage with Fairtrade in response to consumer pressure for Fairtrade by carrying a few Fairtrade products (Traidcraft, 2003, 2004). Also, FTOs' primary goal is not to maximise profits, but to maximise producers' income and value.[1] In addition, all (or nearly all) of FTOs' products are produced according to fair trade principles (including fair prices, direct trading, long-term relationships and pre-payment). Finally, nearly all FTOs are registered with FLO to carry products for which FLO has standards.

While the term FTO helps to distinguish these so-characterised organisations from conventional companies, it none the less describes a diversity of organisational structures including not-for-profit associations, not-for-profits with guardian shares in a for-profit company, worker-owned cooperatives, part-producer-owned companies, a company limited by shares, and privately held companies (Nicholls and Opal, 2005).

FTOs' experimentation with structures of corporate governance and fair trading principles aims to show to mainstream corporations the commercial viability of fair trade and progressive stakeholder governance arrangements whereby producers and/or employees are part-owners of the company. Some FTOs – such as Divine Chocolate Ltd, Equal Exchange or AgroFair – aim not only to demonstrate the viability of fair trade principles as the basis of a company, but also to act as a catalyst for change in their industry (see below). With this purpose an FTO could make itself redundant if it achieved its organisational mission to transform the industry. This end-goal sits oddly with economic theories of corporate monopoly (Nicholls and Opal, 2005).

Historically, FTOs' manner of pursuing their mission has not always been so diverse. During the 1950s and 1960s, FTOs were primarily religious- or charity-affiliated, working closely with small-scale producer groups for development and emergency relief (Kocken, 2003). Given these historical roots, many FTOs continue to be non-profit organisations. For instance, in 2000, 38 per cent of FTOs were not-for-profit organisations (Nicholls and Opal, 2005: 96). During the 1970s and 1980s, FTOs took on a more politically active nature, fuelled by Northern consumers' and grassroots' political motivations. These groups had made connections with developing-country producer groups that were part of solidarity and national liberation movements (Kocken, 2003).

By the mid-1990s, FTOs' aspirations for development-through-trade were, in the main, having little impact on mainstream firms' behaviour. Not only were traditional FTOs proving economically unsustainable (see Redfern and Snedker, 2002), but also (by now) brand power was well entrenched and brand value was on the rise (see Chapter 2). Perceiving these structural changes, a few new radical FTOs began to express themselves through a more commercially oriented form in the 1990s by focusing more seriously on consumers. This move echoes Drucker's (1985) observation that entrepreneurial actors perceive and exploit change in their external environment. In fact, whereas some not-for-profit FTOs went out of business in this changing era, a small circle of pioneering alternative traders seized the opportunity to reinvent the profile of the FTO with a brand model designed to prosper in a commercial setting. The new innovations are distinct among traditional non-profit FTOs. As respondents observed:

> Some of the [fair trade] companies – like Divine Chocolate Ltd and Equal Exchange – those are great models, but that's not the norm in the fair trade world. (De Carlo, 30 June 2005, fieldwork notes)

> our success [at Divine Chocolate Ltd] comes quite heavily down to the fact that we've taken a *branded* route, so that the Fairtrade products from Cafédirect and Divine Chocolate are coming from companies that specialise in the commodity that they're dealing in and are coming to the market with a *brand* which is what people can associate with. And I think that's quite distinct from . . . GEPA in Germany – they appear to me to be the equivalent of . . . Oxfam – coming to the market with a chocolate [not a brand], and that [approach] is . . . much harder to crack [in the market]. You get your initial core supporters – obviously people interested in development are Oxfam supporters [and will buy the chocolate], but if you actually want to break it wider than that [in the market], then you actually need to have something that communicates something with the broadest range of the population . . . . (Tranchell, Managing Director, Divine Chocolate Ltd, UK, 5 May 2005, fieldwork notes)

The individuals and FTO actors who have launched unique FTO brands can be seen as the movement's game-players. They have innovated in the traditional FTO with commercial and legal tools such as branding and marketing. Below, some of these 'game-players' and the models they have built are introduced.[2]

Solidaridad

Solidaridad is one such fair trade pioneer. The Netherlands-based organisation was instrumental in setting up the original Max Havelaar certification system with UCIRI, the indigenous Indian farmer union in Mexico. As Chapter 5 showed, the FLO architecture is the Max Havelaar organisation's (now expanded) progeny. Following the establishment of the Max Havelaar system in the Netherlands, Solidaridad moved on to other fair trade projects. In collaboration with producer cooperatives in Latin America, Africa and Asia, Solidaridad has helped producer organisations to set up commercial fair trade companies including AgroFair (1996) in the banana – then wider fresh fruits – sector, and Kuyichi (2000) in the cotton/textile industry.

AgroFair

The first of these companies, led by Wim Nienhuis (CEO), is a fair trade fruit company co-owned by its farmers. As the company website describes, this co-ownership structure ensures that farmers have a 'fair say, fair share, fair price'. AgroFair was founded by Solidaridad in 1996 in partnership with groups of fruit farmers and farmer cooperatives located in Ghana, Ecuador and Costa Rica. Initially, a Dutch company owned one-third of AgroFair, but Solidaridad later bought back these shares to restructure the company (Nicholls and Opal, 2005: 91), so that now AgroFair shareholders decide on the distribution of profits and producers receive 50 per cent of the dividend (AgroFair, 2006). Twin Trading, CTM Altromercato (see below), Solidaridad, and ethical investors Triodos Innovation Fund and Viva Trust, hold AgroFair's remaining share capital and ensure fair trade principles are upheld (AgroFair, 2006). Some are also involved in marketing and sales through ownership in AgroFair subsidiaries in Italy, the UK/Irish and US markets to support the expansion of AgroFair fruit into other markets.[3] The AgroFair Foundation exists to 'improv[e] the social and environmental conditions for producers of tropical fruit' (AgroFair, 2006).[4]

This corporate governance model benefits AgroFair's farmer–owners not only through the sale of their raw products but also through their involvement in value-adding activities including the sales and marketing strategy of AgroFair fruit throughout Europe. This model of co-responsibility in marketing strategy radically defies the trend in Western corporations' organisation and structure of logistics and production by increasing producers' integration in, and control over, the value chain (see Figure 6.1).

> With the traditional players you can see a trend: western companies are integrating the supply chain, getting closer and closer to the global South. They do not focus only on selling bananas – they also dominate production and logistics. What AgroFair is doing can be called 'reverse supply chain integration': the Third World producer is integrating the supply chain in his own interest. The producer is dedicated not only to growing product, but to organising logistics, and having at the same time a voice and vote in the sales strategy. In contrast to normal opinion, AgroFair has shown that involving Third World producers in business structures, making them co-responsible for the marketing strategy, is a viable aspiration. (Roozen, cited in Nicholls and Opal, 2005: 91)

Viable it is indeed. AgroFair fruit, particularly bananas (the first and most established product in AgroFair's range), is the darling of one of the two national retailers in Switzerland, Coop, which switched its banana supply to 100 per cent Fairtrade (AgroFair, 2004: 4). AgroFair has become the second-largest banana supplier in Switzerland as a result and, until mid-2007, sold more Fairtrade bananas than any other supermarket retailer in the world (ibid.: 24).[5] In 2004, AgroFair's turnover increased by 47 per cent to €37.6 million, up from €25.6 million in 2003. In 2006, the company grew a further 40 per cent, with a turnover of €62 million and a share dividend of €236 000 (half of which has gone to producers).

Kuyichi

The second of Solidaridad's farmer-owned brand company ventures, Kuyichi, is a fair trade jeans fashion brand for the 'young urban consumer' (Kuyichi, 2007a). According to Solidaridad Director, Nico Roozen:

> After Max Havelaar coffee and Oké bananas, fashion produced in a sustainable manner is our third major fair trade initiative. Why clothing? Because – as everyone knows by now – the textile industry is a tough sector where cost price takes priority over people and the environment. (MADE-BY, 2005a)

Set up by Solidaridad and cotton producers in 2000, Kuyichi's mission is to make organic cotton production and fair trade manufacturing processes the norm in the fashion industry. Kuyichi promotes itself as being '1st for Organic Cotton' and is a strong advocate of producer share-ownership. According to the company website, 'Fair Trade is about commercial relationships between people. We don't buy "things", we buy from "someone" . . . Kuyichi is a fair price, fair say and fair share' (Kuyichi, 2007b). The

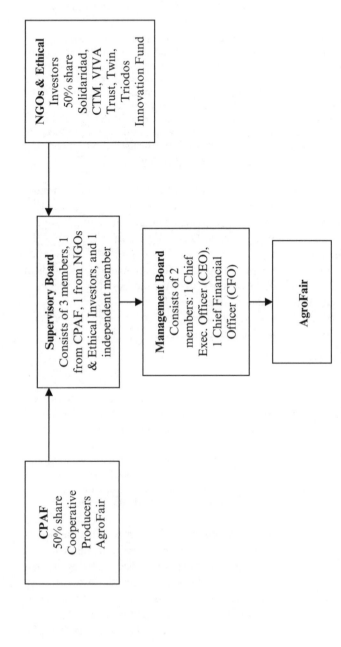

Note: In this two-tiered corporate structure, the Management Board is responsible for the company's management, and overseen by the Supervisory Board (instituted in 2006). Both boards are accountable to the General Meeting of Shareholders.

Source: AgroFair (2006: 7).

Figure 6.1 AgroFair corporate governance structure

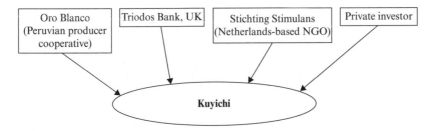

Figure 6.2   Kuyichi corporate governance structure

company is co-owned by the Peruvian cotton farmer cooperative, Oro Blanco, which produces the high-quality biological cotton for Kuyichi clothes and jeans.[6]

A unique way in which the company pursues its mission through this business model is by offering consumers a system for tracing or tracking their purchase to the (multiple) producers of that good. Termed 'Track&Trace', Kuyichi garments carry a code that consumers can enter into the MADE-BY system.[7] The online system retrieves information correlating to that garment, such as the cooperative that picked the cotton, the workers who sewed the garment, and who designed the item (Kuyichi, 2007c). Aside from Oro Blanco, Kuyichi's co-owners include the UK's Triodos Bank (a social investment bank), Netherlands-based NGO Stichting Stimulans, and a private investor (see Figure 6.2). The Kuyichi brand currently sells in several countries across Europe.

Kuyichi also actively encourages its young consumer market to become 'agents of change' in 'Dance4Life', an 'interactive and positive international project aimed at providing an opportunity and platform for young people to become more actively involved in the fight against HIV/AIDS'. Kuyichi provides organic T-shirts for this new global youth initiative.

Twin Trading

Twin Trading, a London-based FTO that provides financing for fair trade businesses and farmer cooperatives, is another fair trade innovator. Founded by the Greater London Council in 1985, Twin Trading (formerly managed by pioneers including Albert Tucker and Pauline Tiffen) has been one source of innovation in commercial fair trade brands and businesses that today are leading (fair trade) brands in the UK market. These companies include Cafédirect (1991), the UK's largest Fairtrade hot drinks brand company, and Divine Chocolate Ltd (1997), the UK's largest chocolate brand company.

Cafédirect

Cafédirect, managed by Penny Newman, was founded by Equal Exchange UK, Traidcraft, Oxfam and Twin Trading. The company operates with the belief that the company is 'doing today what many will do tomorrow': fair trade businesses are the companies of the future. The company's mission is to be the 'leading brand which strengthens the influence, income and security of producer partners in the south and links them directly to the consumer' (Cafédirect, 2006). To date the company has done this remarkably successfully. From offering one coffee product in 1991 to now 41 products, ranging from drinking chocolate to gourmet and specialty coffees and teas, in 2004 the company's turnover was £13.6 million (Twin Trading, 2006). It is the UK's fourth-largest coffee company with an annual growth rate of 20 per cent. The company's fair trade mission manifests in its direct and long-term partnership with its tea and coffee producers and paying Fairtrade prices and premiums as well as the reinvestment of a substantial proportion of its profits into producer capacity-building (see note 1). The company works with 33 producer organisations in 11 countries, involving over a quarter of a million producers in its effort to gain producers a better deal from trade in tea, coffee and cocoa. This business partnership has enabled the wider communities' independent social development projects in local infrastructure, schools and health care facilities.

Since 2003, in a reorganisation of Cafédirect's ownership structure and capital venture, Cafédirect's producers have also had more active influence over the company and its future through ownership of shares and representation on the company's board (Cafédirect, 2004) (see Figure 6.3). In 2004, Cafédirect offered a share issue to raise capital and make its ownership structure more inclusive. To ensure that, in going public, the company's fair trade purpose remains sacrosanct, public shareholders have limited voting rights and its founders retain guardian shares of the company (see Figure 6.3).[8]

Divine Chocolate Ltd

Divine Chocolate Ltd, managed by Sophi Tranchell (in the UK), was set up between Twin Trading and the Ghanaian cocoa cooperative, Kuapa Kokoo. At its 1997 AGM, Kuapa Kokoo farmers decided to create their own chocolate bar (Divine Chocolate Ltd, 2005). The innovative nature of Divine Chocolate Ltd – other than being a commercial fair trade brand company – was its radical governance structure: Kuapa Kokoo producers are board directors of the company and shareowners in brand equity. The mission of Divine Chocolate Ltd is multiform: to 'take a quality affordable range of Fair Trade chocolate bars into the

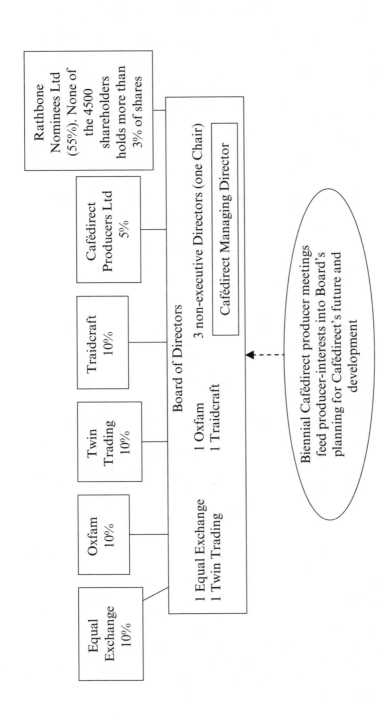

Equal Exchange 10%
Oxfam 10%
Twin Trading 10%
Traidcraft 10%
Cafédirect Producers Ltd 5%
Rathbone Nominees Ltd (55%). None of the 4500 shareholders holds more than 3% of shares

Board of Directors

1 Equal Exchange
1 Twin Trading
1 Oxfam
1 Traidcraft

3 non-executive Directors (one Chair)

Cafédirect Managing Director

Biennial Cafédirect producer meetings feed producer-interests into Board's planning for Cafédirect's future and development

141

Source: Adapted from Just Business (2007a).

Figure 6.3   Cafédirect corporate governance structure

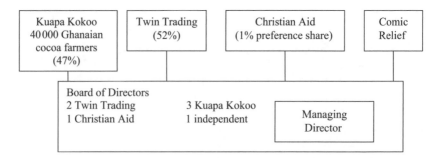

Note: Until July 2006, The Body Shop, a board member, held ownership of 14 per cent of shares, and Kuapa Kokoo only 33 per cent. Since then, The Body Shop has donated its 14 per cent of shares to Kuapa Kokoo, which now owns 47 per cent of the company.

Source: Adapted and updated from Just Business (2007b).

Figure 6.4   Divine Chocolate Ltd corporate governance structure

mainstream chocolate market'; to 'raise awareness of Fair Trade issues amongst UK retailers and consumers of all ages'; to 'be highly visible and vocal in the chocolate industry and thereby act as a catalyst for change'; and to 'pay a Fair Trade price for all the cocoa used in the products' (see Figure 6.4).

Positioned consciously among other normal 'mainstream' chocolate bars in terms of price and availability, the company's chocolate brand range competes directly with the likes of Cadbury and M&M/Mars. Its brand comes in a range of flavours and seasonal chocolate products, such as Christmas coins and Easter eggs. In 2000, the company launched the Dubble chocolate bar (inclusive of an array of educational materials and website resources), a Fairtrade chocolate bar specifically for the children's market – the first of its kind for Fairtrade product markets. Divine Chocolate is available in 5000 stores in the UK, including Sainsbury's, the Co-op and Tesco supermarkets. Its private-label ventures have helped to increase its availability. In 2000, for instance, the UK's Co-op supermarket retailer launched with Divine Chocolate Ltd a co-branded private-label chocolate, later changing its entire own-label chocolate to Fairtrade. Similarly, in the same year, Starbucks changed all its own-brand chocolate to Fairtrade certified, co-branding it with Divine. In 2003, the company reached profitability, and has continued to do so year on year. In 2006, with 18 per cent annual growth, the company achieved a post-tax profit of over £450 000, and after ten years of business, in 2007 the company paid its first dividend of £500/share (Martyn, 2007).

Twin Trading, the incubator for these two now highly successful UK fair trade brand companies (which continue to move into other consumer markets, such as the US), provides market distribution for other fair trade brand companies and traders, such as AgroFair, based outside of the UK market. Twin Trading also operates as a trading arm for Cafédirect.

CTM Altromercato

Mentioned above in this network of pioneers is CTM, an Italian-based cooperative union founded in 1988 in Bolzano, Italy. CTM operates the Altromercato chain of fair trade retail shops throughout Italy. CTM is the largest FTO in Italy and the second-largest FTO worldwide. It aims to participate in, and promote, a fair trade business structure in international trade. CTM covers more than 60 per cent of the fair trade market in Italy, with 140 member organisations in its cooperative which together operate more than two-fifths (260) of the world shops in Italy (Dalvai, 9 November 2005, fieldwork notes). The world shops are FTOs that, in addition to trading, undertake active consumer education about fair trade and trade-related issues. CTM, like the other pioneering organisations creating commercial viability for radical fair trade business models mentioned above, continues to be a 'key ally' for producers in the fair trade movement and an important innovation in new fair trade markets (VanderHoff Boersma, 23 December 2005, fieldwork notes). CTM has developed over 200 food products and 3000 handcraft products that are sourced from 150 producer organisation partners in developing countries (Nicholls and Opal, 2005: 139). As of 2002/3, the CTM family raised US$39.7 million, a near-50 per cent increase from the previous year. Because of the long-standing consumer trust in the CTM name, the company has not taken up FLO certification for its products (see Figure 6.5).

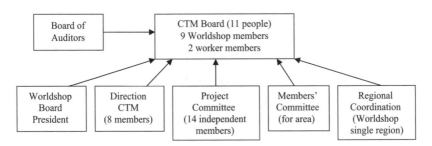

Source: CTM Altromercato, 30 January 2006.

Figure 6.5   CTM Altromercato corporate governance structure

Equal Exchange

Another actor in this circle of innovators in the fair trade movement is
Equal Exchange, co-founded in 1986 in the USA by Jonathan Rosenthal,
Rink Dickinson and Michael Rozyne. Inspired by liberation struggles in
Latin America and Africa in particular, the founders set up the USA's first
commercial ('for-profit') fair trade organisation that would 'be a support
mechanism for . . . countries once they achieved national liberation and had
set up an economy' (Rosenthal, 6 July 2005, fieldwork notes). The founders
were front-runners with fair trade in the commercial US market, a novelty
for both the conventional commercial market and the US fair trade movement. Until their arrival, all other alternative traders in the US fair trade
movement were explicitly non-profit, often religious organisations, and
dealt primarily with handcrafts and textiles.

Launching a commercial fair trade coffee company, Equal Exchange
was anathema not only to the conventional market, but also to the wider
fair trade movement in the USA. The company has a strong commitment
to its fair trade partnership with producer cooperatives, not only paying
Fairtrade prices, but also providing pre-financing and trading directly
with farmer cooperatives to link them directly with consumers. What is
particularly novel about this FTO's company is its worker-owned cooperative structure (see Figure 6.6). Structuring the company in this way

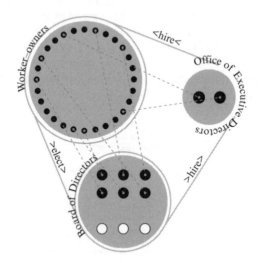

Source: Equal Exchange (2006).

Figure 6.6   Equal Exchange governance structure

from its inception, the founders reduced their control of the company by providing each employee with one share and one vote. All employees are offered membership, and all employees own the same share and receive the same share of the company's profits. Employees nominate and elect the company's board candidates, themselves holding six of the nine director positions. The Board hires and supervises management. Furthermore, the top executive can earn no more than three times as much as the lowest-paid employee (North, 2003a). In addition to selling Fairtrade coffees, the company diversified in 1998 into Fairtrade teas, in 2002 into cocoa, and 2004 into chocolate bars and, in 2005, sugar. Although it has unconventional governance and profit structures, the company is thriving commercially, sending a clear message to the wider industry that such a model is possible – and successful. In business for 20 years, the company has made a profit in the last 16 of 17 years (Equal Exchange, 2005a). The company generated US$10 million in sales at the end of 2002 and US$20 million in 2005 (ibid.), winning numerous awards for making a commercial success of an unorthodox and 'ethical' business – a point that the fair trade pioneers want to prove (Nicholls and Opal, 2005).

These mini-portraits of several fair trade pioneers and their unique fair trade businesses offer a glimpse of the radical company structures and *modus operandi* of fair trade's 'game-players', who, as we are about to see, generate and use power in distinctive ways.

ON POWER

As seen above, fair trade's pioneers harness fair trade business models to transform perceptions of what is possible and viable in global trade. Of course, the mere existence of these alternative models – let alone their commercial success – conflicts with the hegemony of the modern corporate entity and purpose (see Chapter 2). Whereas in fair trade companies fair trade principles and prerogatives inform their operating policies, goals, benchmarks and decision-making criteria, in conventional MNCs, even where MNCs engage in 'corporate social responsibility', 'charity' or selling Fairtrade-labelled goods (Traidcraft, 2004), the business model remains intact. As pioneers within the movement claimed:

> Fair Trade is *absolutely integral* to the [Divine Chocolate] company . . . there would not be a [fair trade] company without our Fairtrade proposition and without our fantastic farmers we work with. Whereas CSR is *not that*. They [conventional companies] aren't companies that have been set up to do *that* [fair trade], they've been set up to do whatever it is they've been set up to do, and then they're doing something nice on the edge. And that is something with

an *incredibly* different proposition . . . it's *so* different on every level, how you measure success is different, what the emphasis of your executive and the skill base of your executive is is different . . . and the idea that you *cannot* separate [fair trade] from what you [as a fair trade company] are doing . . . means that you have to make a success of it. (Tranchell, 5 May 2005, fieldwork notes)

we know that strong farmer businesses can do things, they can build roads, they can build schools, nobody has to go and do that for them . . . When farmers can get better return or value out of trade, they will invest in roads, they build warehouses . . . but we don't have to provide that under charity if we put that value back by the way that we trade. . . . *that* trade goes on day in day out, if you don't get any value from that you occasionally get the odd clinic thrown at you or projects thrown at you, but they've been working for *years*, they don't *want* charity. They've only accepted it because they've had little choice. (Tucker, 16 June 2005, fieldwork notes)

this corporate social responsibility concept . . . is just businesses complying with the law . . . most companies say 'oh, we'd better comply with the law' – and the world needs to celebrate that? (Tucker, 16 June 2005)

It is a stark fact that the price MNCs now pay for coffee is at a desperate 30 year low. Cafédirect has proved that even in such a crisis, we can pay more, offer upfront credit and development support to farmers – and still make profit. As a company, we face all the usual stresses of a conventional business – like cash flow, 'just in time' supply chain management, fluctuating interest and exchange rates. And on top of that, we meet stringent Fair Trade criteria that conventional business would not countenance. This is not just an alternative way of doing business. It transforms business ethics. (Newman, cited in Nicholls and Opal, 2005: 95)

These comments from several pioneers can be seen to reflect the radical vision and ambitions associated with game-playing. As these comments indicate, the pioneers dismiss conventional approaches to development and poverty as highly conservative. As part of a more radical empowerment of producers through business and trade, fair trade brand companies enable producers to develop and use new and greater capacities than the norm. As Tucker notes above, 'strong farmer businesses can do things . . . nobody has to do that for them . . . we don't have to provide that under charity if we put that value back by the way that we trade'.

In this way the attempt to maximise producer empowerment in global commodity value chains can be seen to mobilise a type of 'positive' rather than 'negative' form of freedom (see Berlin, 1958), a concept that emphasises the possibility of 'self-determination' and gaining new freedoms and capacities in one's life and future.[9] Berlin's (1958) distinction between positive and negative freedom offers an apposite parallel between fair trade's innovators (the 'game-players') and FLO/the LIs ('resisters') respectively:

the pioneers seek to create new enabling structures; FLO/the LIs tend to preserve producers' existing liberties – but also the constraints which attend those liberties. As respondents can be seen to suggest:

> The labelling people think they're leading the movement, but they're just the police force, they're there to do the job they're doing. They're not the leading element of the thing – do you want to be a police state or be led by the movement? (Tucker, 16 June 2005, fieldwork notes)

> a lot of the success and movement [in the USA] originally was built on activists – in church groups, community groups *et cetera*, and although there's *some* interest [among them] in working with . . . corporations, a lot of the excitement was about . . . mission-driven [fair-trade] companies. (Rosenthal, 6 July 2005, fieldwork notes)

These observations infer the pioneers' intent to shrug off conventional models altogether, an intent that clearly distinguishes them from FLO/ the LIs, who have modified Fairtrade to work within existing markets. The movement's innovators are building new market institutions and structures to empower those who are disadvantaged in the existing system, which bears significant implications for unleashing human capacities and potential. This empirical observation illuminates that, unlike resistance, game-playing does not subscribe to 'power over' to realise a mission for structural and institutional change.

Entrepreneurship studies do not explain this unique difference in innovative actors' approach to bringing about change. Most identify and describe particular behavioural and psychological traits, including a significant capacity for hard work, a determination to make the impossible possible, and inventiveness or imaginativeness to overcome seemingly insurmountable obstacles (Schumpeter, 1934; Drucker, 1985; Roberts and Weiss, 1988; Goyder, 1998; McGrath and MacMillan, 2000). Yet these descriptions do not offer much insight in the game-playing context on the question of game-players' relationship to power.

It is here that alternative power theories indicate the role of the 'power within' or 'self-empowerment' (see Townsend et al., 1999). The 'power within' refers to an internal capacity and 'strength' to question and reject social norms and values and to challenge constraints on one's life, and an ability to see social constraints as structural rather than personal (ibid.). For Rowlands (1998: 14), the 'power within' 'can be what enables the individual to hold to a position or activity in the face of overwhelming opposition, or to take a serious risk'. It is a 'sense of self and individual confidence and capacity' where 'internalised oppression' does not exist (Rowlands, 1995: 103). These kinds of internal resources attributed to 'power within' are echoed in fair trade pioneers' comments about their mission and vision:

> The future I see . . . is with these new ways of doing business that we're creating in the fair trade movement and with farmers, with new ownership structures of getting value back to poor farmers and poor communities and workers. . . . Are [conventional] companies going to genuinely change because [fair trade] is the way to do business, or are they going to become the dinosaurs of the future? Are they part of the new way of doing business? (Tucker, 16 June 2005, fieldwork notes)

As this comment illustrates, self-empowerment is the opposite of internalising these social forces which, for Gramsci (1971), is the means by which the social order maintains its durability. According to Williams et al. (cited in Rowlands, 1998: 14), the source of the 'power within' is 'self-acceptance and self-respect which extend . . . to respect for and acceptance of others as equals'.

The accounts from fair trade innovators above resonate with power theorists' ideas on how power can operate in liberating ways at the individual level. Moreover, they indicate the far broader consequences or impact of pioneers' exercise of 'power within' to push market boundaries, beginning a sequence of change that produces benefits for others. As game-players in the fair trade movement suggested:

> all the economists told us that it wasn't possible or economically viable, and that fair traders are a bunch of hippies who know nothing about this . . . you can have this conversation with them and they'll tell you that it's *really* not possible. I have an easy discussion with them. I say 'you see this Cafédirect product? That's what it does' . . . and what fair traders have done is to make the market work in a better way. (Tucker, 16 June 2005, fieldwork notes)

> when we started [with Equal Exchange], people in the industry, well pretty much everyone, said 'you can't *do* what you're trying to do', so by demonstrating that it was possible and that we could actually survive and grow a business, we made what had seemed impossible seem possible. (Rosenthal, 6 July 2005, fieldwork notes)

> everybody said what they say in each industry 'oh, we don't batch up the production runs, we won't be able to have a traceable supply chain . . . this is an industrial process, so it's got to be big'. And it's like 'well, why?' I'm going to find a market for a product, and if I can trace it, I can sell this product, if I can't trace it, I've got no product to sell. So let's work out how we can do it'. And so we found we could do it. Then they said 'you can't work with farmers, they can't organise themselves, they've got no communication systems, they're unreliable, blah blah blah . . . so you get through *that*. And then they go 'oh you'll never get it into the supermarkets with that, it's a very nice idea but it'll never work' . . . and you go to the supermarkets and they say 'well it tastes nice, reasonable price, it's a good idea . . . let's give it a go'. And so you sort of can't know until you try . . . . (Tranchell, 5 May 2005, fieldwork notes)

up until 5 years ago people were telling me, 'oh [fair trade] will never go above 3 or 5 per cent, just like the people at the Smithsonian Institute are now telling us 'ooh, it's not economically sensible', but we're *forging* ahead, we're there . . . but don't believe us, listen to the market where all the economists say that what people want is what's cheapest . . . . (Tucker, 16 June 2005, fieldwork notes)

These reflections show pioneers' refusal to accept defeat or to see their ideas as inferior or unworkable, even in the face of significant criticism. In fact, their success with 'convention-defying' models enables them to make a subsequent mockery of the naysayers – in this case market 'experts'. As Moscovici et al. (1994) and Schumpeter (1934) respectively observe, cultural and institutional repercussions flow from 'convention-defying' types of activity: not least, their mere existence challenges the perceived orthodoxy and universality of conventional models. This suggests that, as entrepreneurs of norms, game-players possess significant power in the process of social change. Their personal vision and strength (personal power) precipitates the empowerment of those oppressed by convention.

ON ORGANISATION

The second intriguing dynamic of power in the game-playing context relates to its organisation. Unlike the modern corporate behemoths that they seek to transform, fair trade pioneers' pursuit of 'positive' freedom is not evolving into new forms of market monopoly and oppression. Within the world of these dominant corporate structures, fair trade innovators utilise decentralised and egalitarian modes of networked business organisation, maintaining organisational modes conducive to their unique role and purpose as innovators. Their organisation parallels the small 'organic', 'disintegrated' networks comprised of 'weak ties' that are commonly associated with, and seen as necessary for, innovation (see Nooteboom, 2001; Achrol and Kotler, 1999; Schaper and Volery, 2002).

Interestingly, evolutionary economics tells us that in the evolution from innovation to market consolidation, a hierarchical and bureaucratic form of organisation supersedes the initial decentralised, egalitarian networked organisational structure. While the ultimate business structure may support the prerogative to secure market acceptance, it creates organisational impediments to capitalising on new ideas (see Nooteboom, 2001; Schaper and Volery, 2002; Achrol and Kotler, 1999; Robert and Weiss, 1988; McGrath and MacMillan, 2000). Chapter 5 told this story of static adaptation in knowledge and power. The accounts of fair trade pioneers' governance and organisational structures tell a different story of how power and knowledge evolve in politically radical ways.

An interesting observation concerning the subject of the fair trade game-players' innovation is that they innovate in business organisation/ ownership. From a Darwinian perspective of economic evolution, innovation is a trigger for potential diversity (competition) in a process similar to genetic variation: in any given industry (environmental niche), variation is stimulated when a firm adopts an innovation (such as a new technology) and then competes with rival firms in a struggle for survival. Those firms that do survive the struggle are the 'fittest'; they have adopted best practice (see Nelson and Winter, 1982). Analogous though it may be, a Darwinian view of the market does not discriminate between different interests in the market – such as whether it will be in the interests of a firm to adapt in a static or innovative fashion. The overriding assumption is that the interest of all firms is to mimic and seek to outperform the innovator at his/her own game. Nor does it account for the selection pressures exerted on firms by market institutions to conform to dominant models (see Chapter 7).[10]

Given the political structure to market relations, the Darwinian assumption that all firms will move to mimic new varieties is erroneous. For instance, the fair trade pioneers' radical ownership structures are their innovation. Adopting this innovation would not simply require change to the design of, or addition of a label on, a product. On the contrary, it would require significant restructure – actual transformation – of the traditional ownership structure and legal mandate of the modern corporation. The insight here is how issues of deliberate choice and the politics in organisational design are missing from an evolutionary account of how the business cycle and market evolution work. The following two sections respectively pursue these empirical insights to understand first the distinct way in which knowledge and power evolve in the context of game-playing (as opposed to resistance), and second, the basis on which organisational evolution in the game-playing context enables innovations to thrive without conforming to the *status quo*.

THE INNOVATION CONTINUUM: POLITICAL EVOLUTION IN ECONOMIC CHANGE

Evolutionary economists posit that the market is a learning process and entrepreneurship a problem-solving activity (see Harper, 1996). New innovations are a response to market 'feedback' on preceding innovations; the generation of variety is produced by learning (Ramazzotti, 2001: 75; Nooteboom, 2001: 41). For Nooteboom (2001: 41–2), 'innovation is not random', it is 'informed' and 'based on a search' of the effect of an innovation on the business environment. While emphasising the learning process that precedes and informs entrepreneurial activity, the above section signposted the inherent politics involved in the social production of that variety or, more specifically, the propensity for the innovation prerogative to be overcome by the desire for market power and profitability. As Schaper and Volery (2002) observe, while an 'entrepreneurial spirit' may initially predominate in new ventures, it is frequently overshadowed by organisational pragmatism and conservatism. In a political reading of the story, business models no longer serve as mechanisms for learning and re-innovation, as Harper (1996) and Nooteboom (2001) suggest, but instead become pathways to profit and economic power. Robert and Weiss (1988: 4) describe this traditional strategy as a means of 'defending' one's 'turf' and 'creating fiefdoms of power'.

While this story of reinstituting monopoly structures in the market (through static adaptation) tells of a more predominant market pattern, innovative adaptation is nevertheless a more noteworthy, and potentially significant, subject of analysis. It takes the form of testing new innovations in the market to refine knowledge, and to re-innovate on the basis of the insights gained. This is what Harper (1996: 37) refers to as the 'evolutionary conception of the entrepreneur's learning process'. Drawing on Popper's evolutionary theory of knowledge Harper (1996: 239) suggests that

> the entrepreneur's learning process essentially consists in going from problems to deeper problems and subproblems. In solving any particular market problem, the entrepreneur discovers new problems, as well as their ramifications and interconnections: 'Problems, after they have been solved and their solutions properly examined, tend to beget problem-children: new problems, often of greater depth and even greater fertility than the old ones'. (Popper, cited in Harper, 1996: 239)

In the fair trade context the liberating potential of knowledge that Popper conceptualises is brought to life. The pioneers' frustration with FLO and the Fairtrade certification system stems in part from the fact that FLO's model is inadequate for empowering producers structurally in the trading chain (for detail see Chapter 5). For them, large-scale traders are 'window-dressing' with Fairtrade and making a 'mockery' of fair trade. According to business theorists, entrepreneurs tend to be successful at remaining competitive in the market because they concentrate on the 'end result – the effect on the business environment – rather than on the product' or the 'managerial activity' (Robert and Weiss, 1988: 3). When they no longer have the desired result they 'up the ante' with a new innovation. As Drucker (1985: 210) writes, the entrepreneur 'aims at [permanent] leadership . . . of a new market or industry'. In order to maintain their leadership in the fair trade market and debate, fair trade pioneers are constantly looking to innovate to stay ahead of the game. As respondents expressed it:

> I always see it as a kind of challenging model, you have to challenge in order to get [others to change] . . . but if you want to challenge, you have to be able to move up [to the challenge] yourself, because you can't challenge others all the time with all of the same issues. It doesn't work like that. . . . and your influence . . . will diminish when the others are responding . . . from the moment you stop innovating you're already losing. You have to be innovative [otherwise] the gap [between you and other players], it might become too narrow and all of a sudden people might say, well what's the difference? (Uit de Bosch, former Project Coordinator, International Markets, Fair Economic Development Program, Interchurch Organisation for Development Cooperation, 13 April 2005, fieldwork notes)

> Fairtrade is an enormous innovation, and part of the strength [of innovating] is that we need to continue to innovate, because if everyone is trying to catch up with you, then you have to carry on setting the standard and showing them the way to do it. (Sophi Tranchell, Managing Director, Divine Chocolate Ltd, UK, 5 May 2005, fieldwork notes)

Uit de Bosch's description captures the emphasis that business management theorists place on the importance of innovation as a continuous strategy for competitive engagement. It is an 'offensive weapon' that enables smaller market players to topple 'better-financed' and established opponents. This dynamic is mimicked in the strategy of game-playing. Game-playing in the fair trade context can be seen to involve perpetual innovation, a perpetuity motivated by the need to maintain leadership in market contests. Game-players are vigilant about remaining the standard-setters of norms – a status that can be quickly lost. As Tranchell's comment illuminates, innovation in fair trade standard-setting is a strategic and powerful approach to producing change; it is the basis on which game-playing is capable of influencing the market and evading corporate capture.

In larger part, the pioneers' criticism derives from FLO/the LIs' unresponsiveness to the need for Fairtrade's renewal. The 'organisational inertia' that has developed in FLO threatens the certification system's survival and relevance (see Chapter 5). According to organisational theorists, the most life-threatening response in a phase of 'market growth' is for an organisation to 'go to sleep', since it carries imperfections or 'limits' that competitors will seek to outdo (Robert and Weiss, 1988; Drucker, 1985; Schaper and Volery, 2002: 244). Jeroen Douglas of Solidaridad interpreted FLO's growing weakness in these terms: 'the stronger people within FLO *know* what the limitations of their own model are . . . The imperfection of models is a law of nature. Any model has to live with that – that it's not *the* model.' The pioneers' creation of new fair trade brand models in response to FLO's 'limits' demonstrates the innovator's prerogative to (re-)innovate in the face of model limitations (see Chapter 5 and below). Herman uit de Bosch noted furthermore the risk that FLO/the LIs' organisational inertia poses to the survival of its own model:

> if they [FLO] don't become the innovators again – if they don't become *the* standard-setting initiative – they'll be forgotten and others will take their place. Innovations are coming more from the outside and not the inside [of FLO] right now . . . and if more things are changing around you, then you're not the innovator anymore, you're just one of the players. [FLO] is just one of the stakeholders, not the big guys setting the standards . . . instead of being on the defensive, instead of looking at what's coming towards them, they should be changing their position, their attitude. They could just accept their role [as mere players] at the moment, but then others will take over and in the end others will forget them. (13 April 2005, fieldwork notes)

This observation suggests the threat of organisational complacency associated with resistance and the risk that it poses to evolution: resisters lose leadership in the contest over market evolution by neglecting new information. This resonates with Drucker's (1985) idea of the ongoing need to set the trend and 'up the ante' to maintain market leadership. Innovation ensures authorship in the norms of the marketplace ('the big guys setting the standards'). The evolutionary trajectory of knowledge in this context (towards perpetual innovation) highlights game-playing's significance for social change.

The fair trade pioneers have exercised market leadership throughout the movement's history. For example, at the end of the 1980s, several game-players in the movement acknowledged that the then prevailing alternative trade model of non-profit trade shops had a limited market (Douglas, 12 April 2005, fieldwork notes). While the Max Havelaar system was subsequently created by fair trade pioneers to overcome this limitation, the pioneers have innovated again in the wake of this system's weaknesses for producer empowerment in international markets. Here are Pauline Tiffen's reflections on the motivation for fair trade brands:

> [the brands] were designed to achieve a few things. One was – when we started Cafédirect, it was designed to give small-scale producers who had really worked *hard* to learn how to access the market, somebody to sell to, someone to call their own . . . Because you know that old adage 'you can lead a horse to water but you can't make it drink' – the thing about Transfair and the trade-marking models – . . . [is] it made it possible for conventional companies to buy directly from small farmers and get some kind of reward for that . . . but it didn't make [conventional companies] *do* it with many small-farmer organisations, especially the weaker ones with which they just didn't want to get involved. They tended to pick the ones that were more capable, more able anyway. And that's

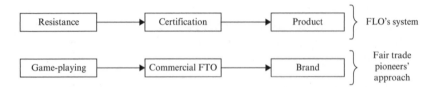

Figure 6.7   Different approaches to pursuing change adopted by the resisters and the game-players (the latter approach is informed by the limitations of the former approach)

> not very developmental . . . In some ways [the fair trade brand model] was a developmental outlet in terms of farmer opportunity . . . And then it was one of those things that was born out of total frustration not from genius at all. I realised quite early on that [the brand] was where you made money . . . it was like 'ooooh, brands' . . . everybody at the time thought I was insane but now of course it looks more obvious . . . . (19 August 2005, fieldwork notes)

Tiffen's comment highlights how the newer fair trade innovation in brands stems directly from practical insights gained from experimenting with earlier models ('I realised quite early on that [the brand] was where you made money'), and the realisation that the certification system did not alter this underpinning power inequality. Figure 6.7 shows that FLO's model has become stuck at the level of product development and certification – it does not tackle the political structure of agricultural value chains. Given the limited scope for empowerment by paying producers a marginally higher price for the crop they sell, the pioneers' model has sought to transcend this model with new business models that harness brand power, giving producers systematic control over and collaboration in company activities and profit. As explained earlier, the fair trade pioneers are free from the constraints of FLO's system to continue innovating despite – and because of – FLO's stagnation. Fair trade brands have aimed to succeed commercially with radical fair trade business structures and missions in order to retain market leadership in setting the terms of (fair trade) market competition.

Figure 6.8 shows in turn how the innovation in business organisation advances producer empowerment in the fair trade market. Since their commercial models are not designed to rely on, but rather compete directly with, conventional brand companies, fair trade innovators are at liberty to pursue this more radical mission with their business models, undeterred by MNCs' more conservative interest in fair trade. The innovators, unlike FLO, have not based their growth on MNCs' market power but instead on their unique difference as a fair trade company.

Yet the pioneers did not stop there. Following the innovation in the first

Figure 6.8   *The evolution of fair trade models (fair trade pioneers have bypassed MNCs' capture of FLO's system by introducing fair trade brand companies)*

fair trade brand, Cafédirect, the fair trade pioneers continued to experiment in producer empowerment through fair trade. The result was more radical company ownership structures in subsequent fair trade brands designed for other industries, such as Divine Chocolate Ltd. Divine Chocolate Ltd has experimented with, and shown the viability of, a more unorthodox governance structure than Cafédirect (which Cafédirect is beginning to adopt). As Tranchell found:

> What was *different* about our model [Divine Chocolate Ltd] was that we were the next model along in that producers were actually going to own shares. So although Cafédirect was set up clearly for the benefit of farmers, it wasn't *owned* by them, they weren't *empowered* by it, they were merely financially rewarded by it, which obviously didn't empower them in the same way. (5 May 2005, fieldwork notes)

This comment reflects the pioneers' motivation to (re-)innovate to overcome the limitations of existing models. Figure 6.9 captures the inherent evolution in knowledge that is not only required for this process of continual innovation but also dependent on continued innovation. This continuum of innovation marks the game-players' unique approach to change.

Even more recently the pioneering FTO 'LightYears', based in Washington, DC, has bypassed not only FLO's neglect of producer ownership and value chain integration, but also its resistance to pushing the issue with conventional firms in the system, by launching a new model of fair trade with Ethiopian coffee producers and their Government. With the support of LightYears, the Ethiopian Government registered an

Max Havelaar ——→ Cafédirect ——→ AgroFair ——→ Divine Chocolate ——→ Kuyichi

| Cert. system | 1st fair trade brand | Brand company co-owned by farmers (fruit sector) | Brand company co-owned by farmers (chocolate sector) | Brand company co-owned by farmers (cotton/textiles sector) |

| (1989) | (1991) | (1996) | (1998) | (2000) |

Note: The fair trade pioneers innovated in the Fairtrade certification system, then in fair trade brands, corporate governance structures and expansion of these radical models across different industry sectors. These companies remain the only 100 per cent fair trade businesses and brands in their respective industries.

Figure 6.9   Continuum of innovation

application in March 2005 with the US Intellectual Property Office for trade mark ownership of the names of three of its regions (Sidamo, Harrar and Yrgacheffe). These names are renowned in the coffee industry for producing high-quality beans, which Starbucks uses (but does not legally own) in marketing its 'Black Apron Exclusives' line to add a premium of around US$26 to standard coffee pack prices. Ethiopian producers, however, are reported to receive less than US$1 (net) in return, and estimate that, if they owned the trade marks for the three regions, they would receive roughly US$88 million per year (Faris, 5 March 2007).

Since Starbucks would incur royalty fees and be subject to terms and conditions if Ethiopia gained ownership of the names, Starbucks lobbied the US Intellectual Property Office to reject Ethiopia's application, which it did. Starbucks has argued that Ethiopia should opt for geographic certification rather than trade mark rights for its regional names, yet certification guarantees only that the product came from the region; it does not give the owner of the certification exclusive right over the names in brand marketing (Faris, 5 March 2007). Thus other distributors, such as Starbucks, could continue to use the names in its marketing without permission, and without licensing fees to the name's owner (ibid.). After a drawn-out legal battle, an international NGO-led media campaign against Starbucks, successive out-of-court negotiations between Starbucks and the Ethiopian Government, and the Government's concession of a royalty-free licence for Starbucks' future use of the names, Ethiopia's 'ownership' of the trade names has been 'recognised' by the global coffee roaster (Reuters, 28 August 2007). Developing-country governments stand to benefit from significantly greater economic returns if the ownership structures of trade marks – from which superior added-value in agricultural commodities derives – are redefined in their favour. The point that LightYears has shown – to an international audience – is that, while conventional firms such as Starbucks are content to stock some Fairtrade coffee, the company is unwilling to empower producers in structural terms through company co-ownership or advance Ethiopia's developmental agenda to secure greater value from the international coffee trade.

Through fair trade pioneers' strategy for change we can see the game-player's steps in the symbiotic dance of evolution (see Chapter 5). When resisters enable monopolies to re-form, game-players are motivated to innovate to break up these power blocs. The empirical accounts above show that, while more conservative organisational actors and individuals may be co-opted, game-players remain a source of innovation who consistently surpass predecessors' limitations. This means that the movement's more radical elements cannot be silenced in the market by more conservative nodes (such as IFAT; see Chapter 7). In addition, the networked govern-ance structures of this movement appear to allow for continued innovation and multidirectional challenges to *status quo* players who cannot buy off or control the entire movement by capturing one entity or node (see Chapter 5). Networks cannot be captured, hence fair trade supports a networked dyna-mism that allows the movement to remain functional and relevant overall in the face of external attempts to undermine it. This institutional structure and dynamic between the two strategies of resistance and game-playing denotes an evolutionary resilience which Chapter 7 examines in further detail.

This empirical story illuminates how knowledge evolves and is gov-erned in the context of game-playing. It highlights the decidedly political nature of innovation intended to alter market power structures. Harper (1996: 38) construes the market as an 'institutional learning mechanism', yet the story of fair trade pioneers in this chapter – complemented by that of FLO/the LIs in Chapter 5 – refines this interpretation by showing that actors with divergent market interests 'learn' and behave according to their situatedness. Specifically, the desire to recognise new ideas and informa-tion is not universal, nor is the subsequent desire to initiate innovation (see for example Chapter 5; see also Robert and Weiss, 1988; Schaper and Volery, 2002). Perpetual innovation in an information-rich environment enables game-players to retain leadership in steering the future direction of evolution, however uncertain that future may be. This ongoing learning strategy equips them with the tools of influence. As Nooteboom (2001: 45) remarks:

> while we can think of many logically possible future worlds, we not only lack knowledge on their likelihood, but we have no way of knowing whether we have thought of all possible futures, and we cannot be certain the futures we have thought of contain the actual future . . . the future is difficult to predict because

actions will have unforeseen consequences and there will be strategic reactions to our actions from others. We are playing games whose participants, strategies and payoffs are revealed only as the game is played, and then shift in the process. The future will be different from any of the ones imagined, but nevertheless one may have developed a platform for viable strategies, with capabilities in place to execute them. This discovery goes beyond a search among existing options, to include the creation of new options.

Nooteboom's observation supports a central argument in this book: the act of innovation liberates new knowledge and as such is a source of power. More than this, the game-player exercises an ongoing capacity to influence change through perpetual innovation. This is insightful for post-liberal thinking on power, which seeks to better understand how social actors exercise agency to bring about change. In the strategy of perpetual innovation, learning and its application plays a key role in the process of change. Yet how does game-playing affect broader change processes? This line of enquiry continues below where we consider how fair trade innovators have achieved success and impact with fair trade brands. This gives insight into how the game-player's 'power within' triggers broader – collective – processes of empowerment.

SOCIAL CONNECTIONS: THE POWER TO MATERIALISE IDEAS AND CREATE SCALE

According to McGrath and MacMillan (2000), underpinning the success of any innovation is 'leadership', the 'process of persuasion or example by which an individual or leader induces a group to pursue objectives held by the leader or shared by the leader and his or her followers' (Gardner, cited in Goyder, 1998: 15). In the context of entrepreneurship, Goyder (1998: 15) posits that

> Without leadership the entrepreneur cannot create and continually develop organisations which deliver a new product or service. Without leadership the entrepreneur cannot hope to inspire colleagues to unprecedented levels of achievement in delivering solutions to the customer . . . Leaders point out to people what they have in common, appealing to that part of their make-up that wants to belong and contribute, and help a group to realise together a potential that they would never achieve as competing individuals.

McGrath and MacMillan similarly view as 'essential' the 'act of bringing other people into the entrepreneurial process' (McGrath and MacMillan, 2000: 340). In their observations the authors note that successful innovators:

engage the energies of everyone in their domain . . . [and] involve many people – both inside and outside the organisation – in their pursuit of an opportunity. [Successful entrepreneurs] create and sustain networks of relationships rather than going it alone, making the most of the intellectual and other resources people have to offer . . . . (Ibid.: 3)

The main thrust of these ideas on 'leadership' is that success requires enroll-ing others; entrepreneurs corral human resources to realise their ideas for innovation. As McGrath and MacMillan (2000) emphasise, in order to mate-rialise their ideas, entrepreneurs depend on others to actively support them. The materialisation, let alone success, of innovation cannot occur without this. The point is that a new model is not powerful in and of itself. Rather, it is a potential source of power that only collective action can produce.

Two interrelated insights are revealed by the suggestion that leadership with an innovation enables innovators to successfully affect the business environment. First, the necessity of network leadership to generate power resonates with the social connections model (see Chapter 1). This concep-tual scheme is based on Latour's view of power as a product of enrolling many actors to exercise influence. This enrolment activity parallels busi-ness theorists' concept of 'entrepreneurial leadership'. On the one hand, the social connections model is at one with the concept of entrepreneurial leadership because it depicts how innovations depend on 'networking net-works' to generate new power flows (see Chapter 5). On the other hand, and in parallel with the notion of leadership above, the social connections model portrays how new models act as the power circuit from which new sources of power flow. That is, only by engaging with the model can indi-viduals and groups realise new forms of (positive) freedom. This concep-tual scheme of empowerment is illustrated in Figure 1.1 (p. 21).

This scheme can be seen as fair trade pioneers' political paradigm, their 'lens' on power in the social world. Their strategy for building and growing FTO brands is indicative of the power that 'networking networks' (exercis-ing leadership) activates. As fair trade pioneers indicated:

with farmers, Twin decided to launch a brand, which to most people seems totally crazy – 'in one of the most powerful sectors in the world you're going to launch a brand with your farmers?' but Twin then got Oxfam, who had their alternative shops, they had their campaigners, then hooked up with Traidcraft who had the church networks, and Equal Exchange who had the independ-ent wholefood stores network, and they jointly created the company called Cafédirect. And the farmers gave the first 3 containers [of coffee] on loan, because they trusted the idea. Then Oxfam campaigned, they campaigned with it, the Wholefoods stocked the thing, Oxfam shops stocked the thing, and it finally got into the supermarket. And that was the growth of Cafédirect. Now that brand 12–14 years later is the fastest growing coffee brand in the UK by value, it's just . . . sold shares in it to the public, and the producers own it . . . (Tucker, 16 June 2005, fieldwork notes)

the Fairtrade Towns idea has been a fantastic way to bring together loose groups of people who wouldn't have otherwise come together, because what happens is in towns outside London, you get activists together, but they don't meet retail people, and so retail people don't have any confidence that there might be people who will use these [products] and the activists – religious activists, political activists – don't necessarily cross paths and come together . . . so by starting to bring them together and building a critical mass you can actually create a level of awareness that's quite exciting. (Tranchell, 5 May 2005, fieldwork notes)

These comments animate the notion of 'entrepreneurial leadership' as the crucial factor in determining the market success of innovation. The first comment shows how a bold idea to destabilise the oligopolistic structure of the chocolate industry was made possible by enrolling the energies of a number of networks (such as Oxfam, Traidcraft and Equal Exchange). The second highlights Goyder's (1998) point that entrepreneurs engage diverse groups for a common goal or purpose in a way that sublimates those actors' own (competing) interests ('loose groups' of activists and retailers 'who wouldn't have otherwise come together'). The descriptions above illustrate that fair trade pioneers' ability to materialise and make a success of the fair trade brand innovation has hinged on viewing power as the product of social connections between diffuse or 'loose groups' acting in concert to generate new sources of power. Indeed, since the fair trade pioneers do not possess established market power or abundant financial resources, they have had to network networks in order to gain scale (see Chapter 4). This echoes McGrath and MacMillan's (2000) idea that entrepreneurs 'sustain networks of relationships' and mobilise them to make innovation possible and successful. Fair trade's game-players have exercised network leadership to make a success of their models (game-players' role in market evolution as network leaders is examined in Chapter 7).

The insight about the power and scale produced by the networking process resonates with post-liberal scholars' concept of the 'power with' (see Townsend et al., 1999; Rowlands, 1998; Eyben et al., 2006). This is the second insight, which relates to collective power. Alternative power theorists describe 'power with' as a 'capacity to achieve with others what one could not do alone'. It 'involves a sense of the whole being greater than the sum of the individuals, especially when a group tackles problems together' (Williams cited in Rowlands, 1998: 14). As Rowlands (ibid.) says of 'power with', 'one person standing up against an unjust law is unlikely to achieve much on their own; many people working together, however, are more likely to provoke change'. In this sense, fair trade pioneers' network leadership and strategy of networking networks can be seen to serve the role of enrolling and concentrating a source of 'power with' – a collective capacity and sensibility to cause significant effects on the environment for collective benefit. The concept of how power operates in the context of game-playing resonates with business theorists' view that new ideas are not successful unless supported by multiple networks.

At the same time, as depicted in the social connections model, in a hostile and politically conservative environment game-players and those support-ing their work are not reliant on those with market power; nor are they unable to exercise influence without these actors. Game-playing leads the creation and expansion of new structural arrangements through models that will liberate human capacities and power. These models do not evolve in a conservative direction but instead provide ongoing leadership in the contest to shape the markets of the future.

CONCLUDING COMMENTS

This chapter has analysed the pioneers in the fair trade movement, includ-ing their historical evolution and unique role in the movement. The chapter detailed their discrete entrepreneurship manifested in innovations in business organisation and ownership, first in the Max Havelaar certi-fication system, then in commercial ownership and organisational design in brands across different industries. The mini-portraits of the pioneers' models – such as Divine Chocolate Ltd, AgroFair, Equal Exchange (USA) and CTM Altromercato – offered purchase on the way in which the 'game-players' organise knowledge and power: that is, in decentralised, egalitar-ian network relationships that are highly amenable to the free flow of information and new ideas needed for continued innovation (Achrol and Kotler, 1999; Schaper and Volery, 2002; Nooteboom, 2001). Moreover, the nature of their innovation indicated the inherent politics that belie this organisational and governance design.

While the assumption is that innovations become less innovative and entrepreneurial as they grow in size (Schaper and Volery, 2002; Nooteboom, 2001; Achrol and Kotler, 1999), the story of the movement's 'game-players' illustrated that they thrive as market agitators – expressed as a state of con-tinuous innovation to break up stable power structures. This observation offered the insight that the pattern of organisational evolution in markets is more deliberate a development than is portrayed in evolutionary accounts of markets. Some actors – namely game-players – consciously organise power in ways that promise that more radical markets power relations will evolve.

Changing big business

The story of innovative adaptation in fair trade validates the concerns of post-liberal scholars over the significant potential for social agency that overly structural accounts of power neglect. Game-players are not constrained by inherited social practices and subjectivities. Rather they exhibit a significant capacity to reject and transform existing norms. Norm entrepreneurship is the game-player's strategic weapon to procure and maintain a position of market leadership (see Drucker, 1985). While innovation itself is a seemingly spontaneous occurrence (albeit informed), it confers permanence on game-players' leadership in guiding the future of the market, or at the very least their capacity to influence that future (see Nooteboom, 2001).

As revolutionaries who remain radical over time – that is, who elude capture and pacification – game-players themselves must initiate the construction of the radical models of social and economic organisation in their mind's eye. Conservative actors will not willingly mimic the game-players' *avant-garde* models, hence game-players must create markets for these models. Business theorists term this propensity to initiate the creation of innovation 'entrepreneurial leadership' (Goyder, 1998; McGrath and MacMillan, 2000), or what I call 'networking networks' (see Chapter 4). It essentially refers to the process of enrolling many groups of actors to exercise influence (see Latour, 1986). By generating flows of 'power with', network leadership enables game-players to materialise and expand their models without conforming to the *status quo* in order to do so. The insight offered by the empirical stories in this chapter was into the sequence that game-playing triggers: game-players' 'power within' sets in train the generation of 'power with'. These models, while capacious in their potential to bring forth change with new structures, are mere conduits for the power generated in the enrolment process. The social connections model – as a conceptual scheme of this process of empowerment from the individual level of the game-player to the collective level across societies – provided an explanatory basis for the operation of power in the game-playing context.

Together with Chapter 5, this chapter has explicated the symbiotic, evolutionary dance between game-playing and resistance. While the resister waits for the game-player to take the 'lead' with innovation in a new model and then revels in market stability, the game-player thrives on market volatility to get the resister dancing. Yet game-players make an additional move in guiding their dancing partner around the dance floor: the game-player can change the rhythm of the music. That is, when the resister becomes too familiar with one dance – to the point of 'going to sleep' (Robert and Weiss, 1988) – the game-player changes the music to put the resister on his/her toes again. In economic terms, game-players can force the pace of evolution, causing broader institutional transformation. We now turn to explore this institutional move through an analysis of the developments in the movement's governing institutions, FLO and IFAT.

NOTES

1. Numerous FTOs are structured to return maximum income to producers above and beyond meeting Fairtrade minimum prices and premiums. For instance, as part of its 'Gold Standard Fair Trade policy', Cafédirect invested 86 per cent of its working capital in 2006 (and £574 000 in 2004–05) into initiatives for producer capacity-building (Cafédirect, 2005, 2006).
2. For brevity, not all fair trade's pioneering firms are included in this book. Those included here are several leading and illustrative examples.
3. In 2006, AgroFair's Oké-labelled bananas gained access to marketing and distribution through a new fair trade company called Oké USA. Oké USA is owned by AgroFair, Equal Exchange (US pioneer in fair trade coffee) and Red Tomato (Boston-based non-profit organisation that helps family farmers in New England to access markets, founded by co-founder of Equal Exchange). AgroFair farmers benefit from this owner-ship structure through ownership of company equity in addition to fair trade minimum prices and premiums.
4. The AgroFair Foundation provides grants and loans to producer groups for quality improvement projects. New AgroFair producers are offered membership in AgroFair's producer cooperative (CPAF), and own a share percentage according to the value of the crop they deliver to AgroFair. Growers from Peru, Burkina Faso and the Dominican Republic have benefited from this arrangement thus far.
5. Sainsbury's in the UK surpassed the Coop since then. The company observes that further growth in the volume of AgroFair bananas demanded is unlikely to grow due to EU protectionism, hence overall growth in the company will depend largely on AgroFair's other products, particularly citrus fruits (AgroFair, 2004: 4).
6. Additional cotton farmer cooperatives working towards becoming part of Kuyichi are situated in Tunisia, Turkey and India (Kuyichi, 2007b).
7. This system, set up by Solidaridad, is an umbrella label used by fashion brands to com-municate their preference for organic cotton production and factory manufacturing operating a social code of conduct. The label does not guarantee that a garment or col-lection is 100 per cent 'clean and socially responsible', but it does ensure that the 'door to the production process is wide open' (MADE-BY, 2007). This is achieved by a company linking its production data to the MADE-BY tracking system, which enables consumers to see where a garment was manufactured (MADE-BY, 2005b).
8. The company raised capital through an alternative share issue in which shares are not listed on an exchange but rather with the brokering (social investment) bank, Triodos, which linked willing buyers and sellers through its matched bargaining system, Ethex.
9. Negative liberty does not expand or challenge those bounds but merely prevents inter-ference with an individual's or group's existing bounds of freedom.
10. The rapid market adoption of the M-form of organisation pioneered by DuPont and other corporate giants in the late nineteenth and early twentieth centuries was due in large part to the rapid development of associated institutions that supported the model of mass production (Nelson, 2001: 26).

7.   Governance as 'creative destruction'

While Chapter 4 documented the unique networked growth of the fair trade, Chapter 5 illuminated that in less than two decades MNCs have found their way into the Fairtrade certification system and, via the LIs, are moulding it to their own market interests. These insights demonstrate how using markets to design new institutions for development is subject to quite rapid evolutionary shifts. It highlights the tenacity and power of MNCs to pacify threats to the existing market structure and shape those threats according to the (dominant) institutional rules of the game. In this chapter we explore how the movement's pioneers (the 'game-players') and the broader movement are addressing the growing influence of MNCs and commercial prerogatives in the Fairtrade system. This helps elucidate the institutional means by which game-players overcome market absorption.

According to Schumpeter (1934), entrepreneurs are economic revolutionaries. Their innovations stimulate 'gales of creative destruction' which render existing ideas, technologies and skills obsolete and replace them with new market institutions and structures. These gales punctuate the history of economic progress.[1] Evolutionary economists liken the innovation process to Darwinian genetic variation to view the market as a mechanism for selecting the 'fittest' among competing species (see especially Nelson and Winter, 1982). As in nature, selection mechanisms 'favour one variety over another, from which one species is eliminated and the other prevails based on its adaptability'. Innovation (genetic variation) is a source of selection pressure, in response to which weaker species adopt the comparatively superior traits of the 'fittest' species (Nelson and Winter, 1982: 9; Casson, 1990: xvii; Foster and Metcalfe, 2001: 1–2).[2]

Yet in fair trade's recent history in mainstream markets, MNCs have not evolved into a new organism with the gene structure of Fairtrade. Rather, the movement's 'resisters' have adapted the Fairtrade gene to mimic the dominant (ideological) model (see Chapter 5). Put simply, a Darwinian account of market evolution is too simplified to the extent that it neglects the real-world political strategies such as symbolic imitation (the pretence of model imitation)[3] and static adaptation that dominant species and institutions use to protect and manufacture the cultural perception of their evolutionary 'fitness'.

Together, symbolic imitation and static adaptation are, respectively, salient institutional responses to, and evolutions in, model innovation that game-players must address if they are to succeed in transforming the existing system. Understanding how game-players address these market conditions to bring about social transformation requires consideration of the role of (formal) institutions in the process of selection. If innovations are accompanied by new institutions that create the conditions for them to thrive (see Nelson, 2001), how game-players operate at an institutional level becomes pertinent to understanding the complete act of causing 'gales of creative destruction'.

As a starting point for this analysis, the evolutionary process can be seen as shaped by the relationship between institutions,[4] knowledge[5] and power. Institutions reflect bodies of knowledge, which in turn define the scope of possible action and interaction (Nooteboom, 2001). In this way institutions exert significant influence over the models that are 'in use and being developed' (Nelson, 2001); whose knowledge institutions they favour and whose they suppress is a mechanism for shaping the market environment. In a post-industrial society in which power relations are based on the ownership and control of knowledge (Bell, 1978), this institutional mechanism is fundamentally political: it defines and controls the bounds of human potential and imagination (see Hayward; 1998; Gaventa and Cornwall, 2006). In this context, the survival of an innovator's new model appears to be largely influenced by his/her capacity to shape and influence institutional spaces where knowledge production occurs (see Gaventa, 1993). Evolutionary economists do not map the political trajectory that explains how the innovative actors in fair trade (its 'game-players') operate at an institutional level.

The key insight in this chapter is that institutions act as a source of selection pressure that actors harness to shape the pace and direction of evolution. Chapter 5 and the first section of this chapter highlight the way in which resisters produce a benign pressure on the dominant market model by building institutional models of knowledge governance that suit the *status quo*. The main analysis that follows in this chapter is of how game-players respond to institutional opposition to changes in the organisation of power (knowledge) relations. This analysis reveals strategies that are additional to business model innovation and relate to institutional network leadership. Given the institutional obstacles that innovations experience in attempting to change the market environment (see Chapter 5), this chapter integrates an analysis of power (as knowledge) to understand how the institutional component of 'gales of creative destruction' are achieved. While evolutionary economics proposes that a market 'environment' does the selecting between market models, this chapter shows that through politics, this environment – and the institutional selection pressures that it exerts

– can be changed. While institutional power is not available to institutionally weak actors, networks are, and they are a key mechanism for forcing institutional evolution in the selection environment. Through networks, game-players change the politics of the institutional environment to force the pace of evolution.

STATIC ADAPTATION: RELIEVING SELECTION PRESSURE VIA INSTITUTIONAL ORTHODOXY

For Popper (1963), 'disagreement' is a prerequisite for the growth of knowledge, which, for evolutionary economists, speaks of the importance of democracy for evolution (see especially Loasby, 1999; see also Harper, 1996). 'Democracy' is not, however, a uniform or static construction of collective decision-making; nor are democratic institutions inherently immune to abuse or unable to suppress disagreement (see Dzur and Olson, 2004; Przeworski, 1998; Gaventa, 1993, 2006a; Parkinson and Roche, 2004). Governance, especially the governance of knowledge in the post-industrial complex, is not a level playing-field (see Drahos with Braithwaite, 2002; Gaventa, 1993; Bell, 1978; Hall, 1981).

Popper's implicit political philosophy to increase knowledge for the purpose of change is none the less rooted in a 'deliberative' school of democratic theory. Deliberative democracy refers to a model of democratic decision-making governed by public discussion and collective reasoning rather than bargaining and aggregating preferences (as in 'representative' democracy) (see Dryzek, 2000; Elster, 1998; Goodin, 2003; Dzur and Olson, 2004).[6] This model assumes the participation of those affected by the decision-making process (i.e. participatory democracy), and focuses specifically 'on the nature and quality' of participation in the political process (Gaventa, 2006b).[7] It also intends to effectively pool a diversity of knowledge and expand its boundaries by overcoming structural information asymmetries that would otherwise narrow decision-making processes (see Cohen in Bohman and Rehg, 1997; Dryzek, 2000; Dzur and Olson, 2004). Furthermore, its proponents suggest that the unique emphasis on values found in a deliberative model of democracy (Dzur and Olson, 2004) is a vehicle for social transformation in individual and collective knowledge and awareness, and for fostering new capabilities and power (Habermas, 1975; Lewin, 1946; Hall, 1981; Rahman, 1991; see Eyben et al., 2006).

Just as democracy is not immune to abuse, neither is a deliberative form of it. Specifically, the institutional spaces in which deliberative governance materialises are not 'value-free' (Cornwall, 2002; Gaventa, 2006a; Gaventa and Cornwall, 2006). Rather, the boundaries of what is possible in 'spaces' or 'nodes' of governance, who may enter them, and which discourses are acknowledged, are issues that speak to the power relations that define and shape space (Lefebvre, 1991; Cornwall, 2002; Gaventa, 2006a). As Lefebvre (cited in Gaventa, 2006a: 26) observed, 'Space is a social product . . . it is not simply "there", a neutral container waiting to be filled, but is a dynamic, humanly constructed means of control, and hence of domination, of power.' As a consequence, under the guise of 'democratic' institutions and in spite of 'deliberative' or 'participatory' procedures, deliberation can fall short of its philosophical ideal of transforming the self-interest and levelling the differential power relations that exist more widely in society. Parkinson and Roche (2004: 507) suggest, for instance, that 'people may initially agree to engage with each other, but if they perceive they are not having their way, they will choose other means of engagement in which they calculate their chances of winning to be higher'. In particular, actors will choose other spaces and 'shift' forums (see Braithwaite and Drahos, 2000). As Dzur and Olson (2004: 102) observe, 'sharp differences [emerge] between "weak" and "strong" . . . spheres, where the former merely voice or acclaim positions whereas the latter truly have the power to enact collective decisions'. The latter are 'closed spaces' (Gaventa, 2006a: 26) where 'decisions [are] made by actors behind closed doors without any pretence of broadening the boundaries of inclusion'. In short, actors construct and exploit institutional 'spaces', or 'nodes', to achieve certain outcomes (see for instance Burris et al., 2005).[8]

FLO'S INSTITUTIONAL EVOLUTION

These challenges for democratic governance have arisen in FLO's development as a formal institution.[9] As we saw in Chapter 5, FLO's institutional structure has come to reflect prevailing market discourse at the expense of the broader collective of fair trade producers and traders using the Fairtrade certification system (see Figure 5.2, p. 105).

Within this complex governance structure, the circle in bold depicts the ultimate decision-making power of the Meeting of Members (MoM) wherein the market-driven interests of a 'small cadre of people' have coalesced. Several respondents observed this concentration of interests in the MoM and the MoM's decision-making power within FLO's model, commenting that the MoM, not the board meeting, is the ultimate decision-making forum for FLO's operations (see Chapter 5). This is not surprising since the LIs have historically been FLO's legal 'owners'.[10] Even though the MoM has had effective control over FLO, the Board (until 2004) has been dominated by (market-oriented) LIs. The LIs have held a majority over producers and traders in the FLO Board's decision-making because, according to FLO's Constitution, the Board's President is elected by (and from among) the LIs and holds a casting vote on decisions. Despite their dominant influence over decisions that affect the lives of thousands of producers and communities, the six LI Board Directors have been chosen from among the LIs themselves and not by this wider stakeholder group. In this context, the MoM has provided an alternative forum through which business model LIs have pursued their interests on controversial issues unimpeded, sometimes in contradistinction to decisions made by the Board (see Chapter 5).

This series of developments in FLO's political organisation illuminates the politics behind building and evolving new institutions to support new models. As the story of FLO so far has shown, the LIs' design of FLO has enabled them to exercise 'power over' Fairtrade's development through a monopoly on knowledge production. Dzur and Olson (2004) have noted that distributional discrepancies in knowledge and decision-making power in society may reassert themselves in new institutions (see also Parkinson and Roche, 2004; Cornwall and Gaventa, 2006: 126). The nodal dynamics in the FLO institution reflect underpinning power relations. For instance, when one node (such as the FLO Board) has made decisions or set policies that are incompatible with a market-driven agenda, market-oriented LIs have activated alternative 'closed spaces' (i.e. the MoM) to override the authority and validity of the decisions produced by the FLO Board. By comparison with the LIs' closed spaces, producers and FTOs participate in what Cornwall (2002) calls 'invited spaces'. 'Invited spaces' purport to open up governance processes to broader participation, yet as the reality of the FLO Stakeholder Forum shows, 'invited spaces' do not have the decision-making influence of 'closed spaces' (depicted by the dashed circle in Figure 5.2, p. 105).[11] Rather, the Forum has served as a periodic meeting ground for those actors who are critical of, and disillusioned by, FLO's decision-making on highly controversial issues – and a platform for voicing their collective disapproval of FLO (Deighton, 20 April 2006, fieldwork notes; Earley, 23 June 2005, fieldwork notes). As one respondent put it, 'there's a huge criticism about FLO now from producers . . . [that] there is participation [of producers in FLO's system], but when it comes to *decision*-making, they [producers] are in a minority, because the National Initiatives have this majority'. Comments from producers and traders illustrated their exclusion from FLO's decision-making processes:

> Small producers expect to seriously participate in FLO's governance; not only
> from the top-down [in the FLO Board] but bottom-up as well. If FLO is for

everyone, then everyone should be involved in its decision making. We know that some of the National Initiatives (NI) think that FLO is theirs – and in their defence, the [legal] statutes [of FLO] say so. Nevertheless, the small producers don't think this is right. They believe that all 'Fair Trade' actors should be the owners of the system, rather than the NIs that, according to the small producers, have taken over FLO's ownership. The small producers say that FLO's bylaws (statutes) should be changed in order to achieve wider participation in its decision making. (Denaux, 25 November 2004)

We (Producers) got really upset when we got to know that Nestlé became [a] member of FLO. They [Nestlé] are one of the biggest exploiters in the coffee field and are paying rotten prices to the farmers. The amount of Fairtrade coffees they [Nestlé] are proposing to do is almost nothing, but [Nestlé] have created a smoke screen [by becoming a member of FLO] to get rid of the protest movements against the policies of Nestlé *et cetera*. It is sad to see this happening also because of the complete lack of democratic decision making in FLO. They [LIs] never consulted the producer/farmer organisations [about the deal with Nestlé]. (VanderHoff Boersma, 23 December 2005, fieldwork notes)

the fair trade movement [in Italy], including Transfair Italy [the Italian LI], has been shocked about the news that the Fairtrade Foundation in UK has given the Fairtrade label to Nestlé . . . in the last three weeks, there are mountains of comments internally and in the newspapers, which are discussing, mostly very critically, this issue. (Dalvai, 9 November 2005, fieldwork notes)

We thought this fair trade would help us escape the practices of companies like Nestlé. How can it be that they are now a fair trade company, buying a tiny amount, while their practices on the whole remain as exploitative as ever? (Manji, cited in Tucker, 2006)

These comments indicate how, despite their majority on the Board, the LIs have bypassed formal governing mechanisms and fora to achieve their aims without the consensus of the entire Board or wider membership. This has had the effect of making the Board powerless or symbolic in function when its decisions have been incompatible with the market-driven LIs' interests, yet serviceable when there is agreement over decisions. These accounts support Gaventa's (1993) argument that mere 'participation' in institutional discourse is ultimately meaningless: without a change in power relationships, 'participation' might add a more democratic face to the *status quo* and the 'illusion of inclusion', but it does not penetrate the underpinning structural relations that ultimately determine whose knowledge prevails (Gaventa and Cornwall, 2006; Gaventa, 1993). As Gaventa posits, 'While participatory, it is still based upon gaining access to and control over knowledge that has already been codified by others. It is an access to a paradigm which the people had little part in creating' (Gaventa, 1993: 37).

In this sense, the strategy of resistance can be seen to reinforce dominant market conditions through controlling new institutions' knowledge production. This is Berlin's (1958) 'negative liberty' in action: the movement's resisters have preserved producers' existing range of possibilities and opportunity within conventional markets but not significantly expanded their human freedoms. On the contrary, they have circumscribed this potential with their own situatedness in capitalist market institutions (see Chapter 5).

Empirically, the fair trade movement's 'resisters' have mobilised institutional knowledge production as an instrument of 'power over' by influencing operational decisions on issues such as new product development,[12] Fairtrade minimum price changes,[13] and the certification of plantation farms (see Paulsen, 2005). Using the last as an illustrative example, FLO has begun the practice of certifying plantations because the market-oriented LIs view this policy as necessary to meet conventional traders' demands for large volumes. In their view, insufficient supply or a policy of no plantations within the system could potentially restrict the growth of Fairtrade products in the mainstream market (see Paulsen, 7 July 2005).[14] Some conventional traders have also approached LIs with the proposition of having their own plantations certified by FLO (such as Chiquita approaching Transfair USA). Respondents highlighted how these decisions over the development of the Fairtrade certification system circumscribe the possibility of producer empowerment, whether as a decision favouring conventional market power structures or one determined heavily by LIs rather than producers:

> in the past, the FTOs have supported the producers to be able to export by themselves. Now, with FLO activities growing fast, they do not have the time to empower producers and bring them to a level [at which they can] export directly. Therefore exporters are needed. Often the exporters are very large companies which in the past have not had any interest in supporting the small [producer], and most probably still do not have an interest. Often the interest of FLO authorised exporters is 'business' and that's it. The most critical thing I see in this development is that the small producers are again dependent and have not changed [their market power] to grow by themselves. (Dalvai, 2 February 2007, fieldwork notes)

> not only have partnerships between buyers and producers been reduced in the [FLO] fair trade movement, they're no longer assumed to be direct. 'As soon as the buyer and the seller do not know each other, a completely different relationship exists. Traditional fair trade relationships required a personal relationship. Without this, the buyer puts price or supply pressure on the middle person, who often must transfer this pressure to the seller'. (Harris, President, Cooperative Coffees, cited in Hood, 22 February 2007)

> it does seem that Transfair [USA] is investing an awful lot in trying to solve the problem of 'how is it that Chiquita can make a go in the Fairtrade [banana]

market?', instead of trying to solve the problem of 'how is it that existing [small-scale] Fairtrade banana coops can make it in this market?' I think that that's wrong-headed . . . if they [Transfair] continue to go forward [with this] in the way that they are, they will find that they won't get support [from the movement]. (Gorman, 12 July 2005, fieldwork notes)

I would like to not give up the idea that you can still do things with more small-holders, and that delivers more benefits to some of the poorest people on the planet. And that's actually what we're talking about, because it's [fair trade] about empowerment in the relationship – do you properly deliver that in your plantation model?. (Tranchell, 5 May 2005, fieldwork notes)

The impression I have of information on tea and banana plantations is that the owner has become a very good patron: gives medicine, school opportunity, spends money for betterments of housing of workers etc. Instead of a 'revo-lutionary workforce' the system could create benign patron–worker relations which takes away the bargaining possibilities because 'the boss is so good for us'. Most workers do not have a clue that the boss is creating a good image with money from Fairtrade. What did we gain: better situation for the workers, but no empowerment. (VanderHoff Boersma, cited in Paulsen, 7 July 2005: 5)

As these comments highlight, the market-driven LIs' decision to support the certification of plantations is not a universally evident course of action for expanding fair trade markets, but rather a complex political question.[15] For the movement's 'game-players' and FTOs, for instance, certifying MNCs' plantations is an acquiescent response to market pressures to conform. It is 'the path of least resistance': LIs supply the volumes the market demands by allowing the certification of plantation farms, but in their haste to conform, divert investment and attention away from smallholder groups who have high potential but who need the initial capacity-building support to get their products on the market.[16] It also blurs Fairtrade's focus on marginalised small-scale producers who are often displaced specifically by large-scale plantation- and commercial-farm operations.[17]

As sociologists and political scientists would tell us, part of the reason that industrial evolution does not follow a spontaneously occurring pattern is that social perceptions of prevailing social/cultural narratives are subject to change (see Chapter 1; see also Eyben et al., 2006: 5; Navarro, 2006). As socially constructed phenomena, dominant business models and the rules they operate under do not possess an intrinsic strength or 'value' as evolutionary economists would suggest (see Nelson and Winter, 1982), but have been successful in institutionalising a particular discourse. Chapter 2, for instance, documented the ways and means of the highly sophisticated modern advertising industry to effectively manufacture the cultural value of global brands. In this sense, market actors use institutions to influence and define the perceived value of models to increase their capacity to succeed. In the case of the Fairtrade system, we see how success is largely influenced by the institutional environment that actors create to support the growth of a particular model. Through control over knowledge production (in the form of rules, standards, policies and the like), the market-oriented LIs' institutionalisation of a market-oriented version of Fairtrade has diminished the validity of the more radical fair trade proposition and thus its perceived evolutionary strength and potential (see Navarro, 2006; Gaventa, 1993: 29–30).

The experience of mainstreaming Fairtrade demonstrates how new models can face political threats to their survival from the institutions that emerge to support their growth; emergent institutions can weaken a new model's chances of surviving in its original form, and can alter the model rather than question the legitimacy and value of the current 'rules of the game' (see Loasby, 1999).[18] In this sense, evolutionary 'fitness' in markets is contingent on the (political) capacity of new institutions not only to promote their own institutional rules over time, but also (and importantly) to withstand pressure from markets to conform to the *status quo*. The integration of power dynamics into an analysis of the process of selection in this section leads to a more nuanced and complex account of the evolutionary process as dependent on the organisational design of institutional knowledge relationships (as power relationships), which prescriptions of 'disagreement' or 'democracy' do not get at (see for example Popper, 1963; Loasby, 1999). This point is significant: how power relationships are organised, who designs them, and who governs their evolution are issues that play a defining role in determining the direction and pace of change. More therefore needs to be said of the necessary conditions for democracy to prevail both over time and in a genuine – or non-symbolic – manner. The following sections examine such conditions by looking at how the movement's pioneers and the broader movement have navigated and responded to FLO's conservative political trajectory.

GOVERNING 'MARKET TRANSFORMATION': DELIBERATIVE NETWORKS AND THE 'PEOPLE'S SCIENCE'

According to Gaventa (1993), when 'the people' become disempowered within and by dominant institutions, a strategic response is to develop and mobilise their shared narrative as a countervailing (collective) power. As he proposes, 'A . . . strategy evolves as the powerless develop, create, and systematize their own knowledge, and begin to define their own science'

(Gaventa, 1993: 37). As we have seen, creating and owning new governance institutions that reflect their own knowledge system (Gaventa, 2006a: 26)[19] involves collective deliberation and decision-making, and an institutional structure that perpetuates this dialogic process over time to evolve knowledge and action (see Rahman, 1991). How institutional structures supporting the 'people's science' evade capture becomes a pertinent factor in the analysis if new institutions, however democratic or deliberative they originally intend to be, can ultimately reinforce structured power relations (see Gaventa, 2006a). For this reason, deliberative democratic theorists have tended to concentrate on principles for designing power relationships such as equity between participants, equal speaking time, and participation in decision-making (see for example Parkinson and Roche, 2004). While important, this is less helpful for understanding how actors will or might respond when, despite the application of design principles, structured power relations resurface as those institutions evolve.

Regulatory and organisational theorists have contributed to this enquiry. For Hayek (1960), a well-known theorist of knowledge governance in markets, the abundant and diffuse distribution of human knowledge within complex social systems possesses its own mysterious ('spontaneous') capacity for synthesis, a process that centralised institutional control and organisation only frustrates. However, regulatory scholars of 'networked' and 'nodal' governance show that it is not spontaneous; it is in fact purposively produced through multiple nodes in a dense network configurations (see Burris et al., 2005; Shearing and Wood, 2003; Braithwaite, 2004). From an organisational perspective, like Hayek, Achrol and Kotler (1999) observe that the 'network organisation' is superior to hierarchy and centralisation for governing dispersed knowledge:

> The network organisation is . . . a superior learning organisation . . . [compared with] hierarchy [which] creates strong ties within and among functional units. Strong ties cause members to think and act alike, and thus, information that flows in the system becomes largely redundant over time. In contrast, networks create dense but weak ties with members with different functions, interests and knowledge bases. Each link transmits new and different information, and for the network as a whole, this means superior knowledge assimilation. (Ibid.: 147)

The key idea here is that the decentralised and networked governance of knowledge is superior to hierarchy precisely because it levels power relationships among nodes or participants *vis-à-vis* knowledge creation and its use. The network organisational structure that Achrol and Kotler describe reflects the distinct operation of power in networked knowledge governance – there is no source of authority or hierarchical organisation but instead nodes that coordinate and facilitate information flows.

Networked knowledge governance is collective knowledge governance. Philosophically, these ideas resonate with deliberative/popular democracy wherein collective knowledge is pooled and used in ways that benefit the collective. As Chambers unites:

> From planning, issuing orders, transferring technology and supervising, they shift to convening, facilitating, searching for what people need, and supporting. From being teachers they become facilitators of learning. They seek out the poorer and weaker, bring them together, and enable them to conduct their own appraisal and analysis, and take their own action. The dominant uppers 'hand over the stick', sit down, listen and themselves learn. (Cited in Gaventa and Cornwall, 2006: 123)

The political emphasis on the majority in deliberative governance is analogous to the above regulatory ideas that emphasise both the shift from the 'centre' to the constituent parts of the whole system in the ownership and production of new knowledge, and its distinctly non-hierarchical design. Institutionally, this organisational shift redefines power: the horizontal production of knowledge reallocates and redefines power as a collectively produced and owned resource.[20] As Gaventa (1993: 38) suggests, '[the] popular production and recovery of . . . knowledge is . . . a means of gaining strength'. These ideas on the design of collective governance as deliberative and networked are brought to life below in an examination of IFAT's institutional development and dynamic responses to FLO. As we shall see, this institutional design is (becoming) 'a resource for challenging the hegemony of the dominant ideas' (Gaventa, 1993) and illuminates the role of organised deliberative networks in setting up the preconditions for new, countervailing selection pressures that force the pace of social change.

IFAT'S INSTITUTIONAL GOVERNANCE[21]

Together with the other 290 Fair Trade Organizations (FTOs) that exist in 67 countries, the fair trade game-players (see Chapter 6) form a global network of trading organisations represented by the International Fair Trade Association (IFAT). IFAT's mission is to 'improve the livelihoods and well-being of disadvantaged producers by linking and promoting FTOs, and speaking out for greater justice in world trade' (IFAT, 2006a). IFAT was established in 1989 to bring together existing fair trade networks and FTOs around the world, and more significantly, to foster stronger representation and leadership from Southern producer organisations in this global network. IFAT's three main areas of work include developing the market for fair trade, building trust in fair trade (through the FTO Monitoring System), and advocacy (speaking out for greater justice in world trade). In so doing, IFAT has played a crucial role in nurturing the development of, and connections between, FTOs that do not have FLO certification (see Nicholls and Opal, 2005). This work has been invaluable for increasing marginalised small-scale producers' power in the market: organising small-scale producers into cooperatives maintains the viability of cooperative business structures and alleviates the structural atomisation and social dislocation they experience (ibid.). IFAT has also supported the development and capacity-building of Southern regional and national producer groups.

To date, the fair trade movement has been Northern-centric in its strategic development and lacked Southern participation and influence (see Nicholls and Opal, 2005: 253). In this context, IFAT's organisational prerogative to strengthen producer voices and ownership in the institutional governance of fair trade has been a defining and progressive feature of the institution (Dalvai, 13 April 2005, fieldwork notes; see also Nicholls and Opal, 2005: 253). Producer-respondents described IFAT as a 'strong ally' for farmers and that 'because of the strong impact of the South in [IFAT's] approach, [IFAT] is not only flexible in its approach but also has a strong attachment to the cause of the South' (VanderHoff Boersma, 7 January 2006, fieldwork notes). By contrast, FLO has maintained a Northern perspective and standardised implementation of fair trade (Denaux, 25 November 2004). Carol Wills, former Executive Director of IFAT, conveyed IFAT's producer-oriented institutional outlook in her comment that 'IFAT will never agree to something [with FLO] that it [IFAT] believes will let down the small producer' (cited in Nicholls and Opal, 2005).

By contrast with the hierarchical and centralised organisation of FLO (see Chapter 5), IFAT's institutional governance structure reflects its South-centric outlook (see Figure 7.1). IFAT's structure has sought to reflect 'the networked nature of the fair trade movement and operations with a small Secretariat . . . and a number of sub-Committees and international working groups' (IFAT, 2003: 7). This democratic organisation comprises several key groups, each of which contributes to the overall networked structure and its functions. Firstly is IFAT's General Assembly comprised of five regions (Asia, Latin America, Africa, Europe and CAJUNz – Canada, Australia, Japan, the USA and New Zealand).[22] Two-thirds of the IFAT membership comprises Southern members from Asia, the Middle East, Africa and South America. IFAT members in Asia, Africa and Latin America have established regional platforms including the Asia Fair Trade Forum (AFTF) (2001), the Cooperative for Fair Trade in Africa (COFTA) (2005), the Associacion Latino Americana de Commercio Justo (2006), as,

IFAT

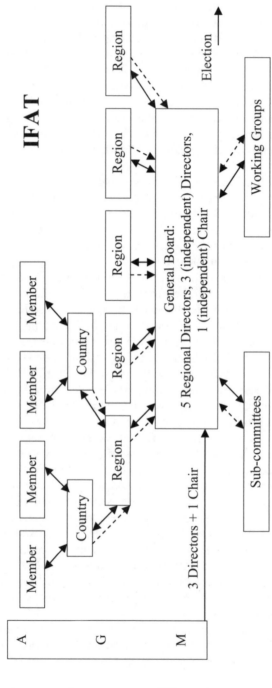

Source: IFAT, personal communication.

Figure 7.1 IFAT governance structure

soon, will European members (Wills, 26 February 2007, fieldwork notes). At present, regional networks are autonomous bodies with full control of their decision-making in relation to regional activities such as networking, market access, promotion of trade between IFAT members, fundraising, advocacy, capacity-building and promotion of membership (IFAT, 2006e).[23] The membership also includes national network platforms, which have developed rapidly and exist in most countries in which IFAT has members, including ECOTA Fair Trade Forum (EFTF) in Bangladesh, Fair Trade Group Nepal, Associated Partners for Fair Trade Philippines, Fair Trade Forum India and Kenya Federation for Alternative Trade (KEFAT). Local-level Members, Provisional Members and Individual and Organisational Associates participate in both national and regional platforms.[24] In order to emphasise this networked governance structure which spans micro-local networks feeding into national, regional and international network connections, IFAT aims in coming years to further 'support its members to create regional forums in order to boost cooperation and collaboration in each region' as well as to 'continue to encourage the creation of more national networks' (IFAT, 2003: 7–10).

These regional and national developments illustrate IFAT's deliberate decentralisation of its institutional structure in order to strengthen regional – rather than central/'Northern' – bases of the fair trade movement (IFAT, 2003). One respondent stated, for example, that IFAT had undergone a 'process of regionalising much more to build up regional platforms in order to decentralise control to these groups' (Deighton, 20 April 2006, fieldwork notes). This process has occurred most strongly in the South rather than in the North in response to the growing proportion of IFAT's Southern members, involving the establishment of Southern secretariats and their networks (Shimizu-Larenas, 9 June 2006, fieldwork notes). These decentralised bases have enabled enhanced functioning in each region since then; for instance, regional issues affecting producer groups can be responded to directly and more accurately from these local platforms (Shimizu-Larenas, 9 June 2006, fieldwork notes). IFAT is seeking to support this organic development based on the belief that 'the development of the regions will strengthen IFAT globally and make it more effective in pursuing its goals' (IFAT, 2006e: 2).

Given their predominance among IFAT members, Southern region representatives make up the majority of IFAT's Board (each of whom are members of their regional Boards or Councils).[25] The Board is the second key group in IFAT. It is a voluntary Board comprising five regional member Board Directors, three independent Directors and one (independent) President, all of whom are chosen at the AGM by, and from among, IFAT's General Assembly (comprised of Members, Provisional Members, and Individual and Organisational Associates) to lead IFAT. Convening two to three times per year (Wills, 26 February 2007, fieldwork notes), the Board develops and implements the directive agreed by the IFAT membership at each biennial AGM;[26] makes policy; and decides on membership applications. IFAT's Secretariat is the third group.[27] The Secretariat is a contact point for members worldwide, facilitating and coordinating members' initiatives and activities, and uses its position at the centre of a global network to make links between, and disseminate information to, individuals, groups and networks (IFAT, 2006c).[28]

In distinct contrast to FLO's institutional form, IFAT can be seen to have established institutional arrangements in a horizontal networked structure for mutual governance between producers and traders over global fair trade. IFAT's governance is structured around inclusive spaces that tie together a series of interdependent networks. The design of this networked institutional structure also appears to be highly deliberative and porous, with many voices and ideas given a hearing through IFAT's multiple nodes and networks. There are numerous layers and nodes of interconnected participation and influence for actors in IFAT's governance structure at local, national, regional and international levels. As one example, biennial international and regional conferences are meeting places for networking and debate for IFAT members who personally meet with one another and discuss issues of concern. They are (formal) venues 'for debates, discussions, seminars and Fair Trade fairs' (IFAT, 2007a: 1–2).[29] Moreover, the membership (the majority) controls and determines IFAT's institutional direction and major decision-making through the AGM.

IFAT's structural and processual emphasis on producer empowerment can be interpreted as a genuine shift in the governance of knowledge and its production. According to Gaventa (1993: 31), any attempt to genuinely alter *status quo* power relations in the post-industrial complex involves a shift not only in the content of prevailing knowledge, but also by and for whom it is produced. In Figure 7.1, the direction of the arrows indicates the flow of knowledge/information from member organisations/associates that create a forward driving force for the Secretariat and Board. In other words, the membership's vision and knowledge directs and propels the institution. These decentralised nodal inputs of information can be translated as diffuse inputs of power that produce a collective power ('power with') to bring about change.

Importantly, these nodes of information and action are illustrative examples of Gaventa's (2006a) idea of 'created' spaces, or Cornwall's (2002) 'organic spaces', which are 'claimed by less powerful actors' and 'created more autonomously by them'. For Cornwall (2002), these nodes 'emerge out of sets of common concerns or identifications' and 'consist of spaces in which like-minded people join together in common pursuits'. IFAT can be seen to have emerged, grown and become an institution built on many spaces or nodes created autonomously by like-minded actors with similar concerns and values. This institutional design places structural value on the knowledge of this community.

From a 'power over' perspective, in complex systems an authoritative, controlling actor is needed in order to create and maintain political order (Wood and Shearing, 2007: 8–9; see for example Hobbes, 1991). From this view, the decentralisation of power and control risks fragmentation and a loss of control. The story of IFAT so far does not conform to this prediction about power and governance: the IFAT Secretariat does not 'control' the network, but simply facilitates and coordinates the activity and learning of producers and serves the needs of this constituency. Similarly, the Board functions to implement the directive that the membership collectively defines at AGMs. Further, the empirical accounts above indicate that IFAT is gaining strength through increasing decentralisation. In these ways, governing power can be seen to reside with 'the people' (i.e. the membership) in IFAT, not an authoritative central node or actor. This supports Chambers's advocacy of decentralised systems of knowledge governance as a means of increasing the power of the majority. By building new capacities among emergent nodes to network, lobby, organise, gain market access and new skills, IFAT can be seen to generate new power flows and 'positive freedom' (Berlin, 1958) among producers and producer networks.

In the absence of an authoritarian node that holds 'power over' IFAT, the way in which the IFAT structure maintains cohesion offers empirical insight into the micro-processes of, and institutional design for, coordinating and nurturing horizontally distributed power. As Wills suggested:

> It's being in an international voluntary membership association of like-minded organisations and having opportunities to meet and share experiences and learn from each other, to learn from special workshops that are put on all over the world all the time, to be part of your national and regional set up, to meet people from other parts of the world . . . It's very difficult to say what networks really bring, but I think the value of networks has been grossly under-estimated by a lot of people. We can be in touch with each other in a matter of seconds round the world; it's very self-supportive, self-sustaining and people help each other out in all kinds of situations – producers and traders. (Cited in Nicholls and Opal, 2005: 254)

> the networks and networking hold the movement together. People are so tied up in their own enterprises, with their own internal organisational challenges, that the fair trade networks offer a breathing space where people can go to talk about the issues that concern them with likeminded friends and work out how to move forward together. (4 November 2005, fieldwork notes)

These comments offer insight into IFAT's cohesiveness. Wills vividly describes networks of deliberation that 'hold the movement together' and make for a 'self-sustaining' system. Deliberative networking – through physical and virtual conversation, discussion and deliberation – is the lifeblood of IFAT's governance structure and acts as social glue. Coordination thus becomes a constant, highly deliberative process of networking. Deliberative networking allows for a type of deliberative conversation about values ('like-minded friends work out how to move forward together'). Not only are deliberative networks sites of discussion, debate and collective problem-solving over diverse issues that produce novelty in information flows ('people are so tied up . . . with their own internal organisational challenges'), but they are also spaces in which members' sense of collective purpose in fair trade is reaffirmed. This reflects the values-oriented nature of deliberative governance (see Dzur and Olson, 2004) which, in networked structures, binds the overall network. In short, deliberative networks play a central role in the evolutionary governance of alternative majority-knowledge systems.

IFAT'S MODEL

At an ideological level, the rapid growth of FLO-certified products in mainstream markets and FLO's growing institutional influence has created a hostile environment for IFAT's alternative understanding of fair trade. As FTOs and pioneers saw it:

I emphasise [to] FLO that they [should] recognise that Fair Trade Organisations . . . have a different status [from MNCs within FLO's system], that they [FTOs] are not just another big company but are doing something different. I don't want Fair Trade Organisations to have the same status in FLO as Chiquita – at the moment it is like that . . . FLO still does not recognise this. Especially the Board [of FLO], they do not care about it. (Dalvai, 13 April 2005, fieldwork notes)

IFAT tried several times in the past to get the FLO Board to recognise IFAT members – FTOs – as different from conventional traders. Each time we've heard no response. Not even 'no'. Just nothing. FLO doesn't really view IFAT as relevant. (IFAT Regional representative, fieldwork notes)

Equal Exchange is one of the leading [fair trade] organisations pushing back against Transfair's direction – which they have really embraced – this notion of corporation reform – which has somewhat *abandoned* the Fair Trade Organisations . . . (Rosenthal, 6 July 2005, fieldwork notes)

It's the added value and power that fair trade brings to producers – beyond just getting a better price – that is under threat. The certification of huge privately owned plantations (as opposed to small farmers' co-ops) for new products, the recent introduction of a substantial licence fee charged to producers wanting to qualify for the mark, the alleged squeezing of non-accredited producers (who perhaps can no longer afford the licence fee) out of potential marketplaces – all these developments raise questions as to whether fair trade's move into the mainstream is still meeting poor producers' aspirations. (Tucker, 2006)

We are the centres of excellence for trading, and our leadership is being challenged. Fair trade is currently being redefined at the product level, displacing the definition at the organisational level, so the FTO Mark needs to be strengthened. (IFAT, 2006i: 13)

These comments resonate with Gaventa's (1993: 37–8) observation that the legitimacy of alternative discourses will 'constantly . . . [be] devalued and suppressed by the dominant science'. Until the 'powerless' build their own institutions and 'science', genuine influence in governance remains elusive. IFAT's recent experiences are testimony to this. In 2004 the IFAT community sought to strengthen the credibility and value of fair trade and FTOs with the outside world by launching the IFAT FTO Mark (see Figure 7.2).

Figure 7.2   IFAT Fair Trade Organization (FTO) Mark

The development of the FTO Mark acknowledges the desire and need among FTOs to differentiate the unique value of their business models from conventional traders selling Fairtrade-certified products and to gain international recognition of their value (Dalvai, 13 April 2005, fieldwork notes). The FTO Monitoring System provides a certification mark for 100 per cent FTOs, organisations whose core function is fair trade.[30] The FTO Mark represents a symbol of FTOs' collective knowledge of a way of doing business and trade that produces developmental outcomes. As one respondent commented:

So it's not like Carrefour, or now Chiquita, or like McDonalds, or like Starbucks, which have some of their products which are Fairtrade . . . *we* as Fair Trade Organisations have *100 per cent of our business* as fair trade . . . We are not just selling some Fairtrade products, there are many responsibilities and activities we do in supporting a producer organisation. There are many producer organisations which without us . . . would be very insignificant and small . . . So we are part of the fair trade family, together with FLO, but there is something more [that we do]. If you look at the fair trade definition 'fair trade is . . . ', and then 'Fair Trade Organisations are supporting producers, campaigning to change international rules, and, and, and'. This is not what the normal traders – all the FLO commercial licensees – do, they are not doing this. (Dalvai, 13 April 2005, fieldwork notes)

Dalvai's point is that FTOs have a unique capacity to trade in a way that produces organisational developmental and new human capacities ('there are many activities that we do in supporting a producer organisation . . . which without us would be very insignificant and small'). He describes a skill and knowledge which conventional traders involved in FLO's system do not possess and have no interest or institutional incentive within FLO's institutional system to emulate ('We are not just selling some Fairtrade products') (see Chapter 5). As Dalvai emphasises, FTOs play a very different role in fair trade markets that challenges the institutional *status quo* supported by FLO and conventional MNCs ('This is not what the normal traders – all the FLO commercial licensees – do, they are not doing this'). In fact, FLO's reassertion of the institutional rules by which conventional MNCs play creates a disincentive for them to change (see Chapters 2 and 5).

Given MNCs' unique knowledge and skill in producing developmental outcomes through business, the FTO business model – symbolised by the FTO Mark – carries a unique market value. An important aspect of this model, which contrasts with FLO's certification system, is its participatory nature,[31] which involves a three-tiered process for guaranteeing quality based on self-assessment, peer review (second-party conformity assessment) and a sample external verification (see Figure 7.3).

The first level involved in the audit of an FTO seeking certification is a Self-Assessment Report, whereby an FTO assesses its performance against the standards developed in 2001 at the IFAT biennial conference in Tanzania. IFAT members are obliged by the IFAT Constitution to conduct a Self-Assessment Report every two years, which involves consultation with stakeholders, setting improvement targets, and feeding this information to IFAT (specifically, the Registration Sub-Committee). The second step in the auditing process is a Peer Review whereby an FTO shares its Self-Assessment Report with its trading partners. This provides an opportunity for the trading partners to corroborate, and comment on, the self-evaluation contained in the Self-Assessment Report. Third, external verification of FTOs is based on random selection of a percentage of IFAT members. An independent external inspector assesses and verifies the self-assessment procedure of an FTO to ensure the credibility and reliability of the FTO's Self-Assessment Report. This external verification involves

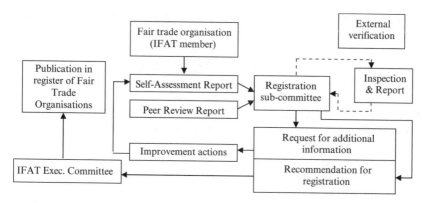

Figure 7.3   IFAT registration process of FTOs

interviewing trading partners, cross-checking documents and conducting on-site procedures/facilities (IFAT, 2004).[32] The IFAT Registration Sub-Committee oversees the FTO Monitoring System process and puts forward recommendations for registrations to the Board. Members awarded Registration are entitled to use the FTO Mark. Organisations carrying the FTO Mark include fair trade's innovators such as Cafédirect, CTM Altromercato and Divine Chocolate Ltd (see Chapter 6).

This participatory governance system shows how the creation, judgement and allocation of the market value of a producer or trader is co-produced through 'relational' mechanisms of governance rather than a traditional approach that utilises mechanisms of 'authority' and 'control' (see Normann and Ramirez, 1993). Traders support producers in developing organisational capacities and business skills that enable them to build viable business models in the marketplace. More than this, both producers and traders have created the FTO standards, they assess each others' performance and progress, and in so doing are involved in the allocation of the Mark. A recent review of the FTO Monitoring System highlighted that the system's strength was based on the 'democratic process through which it evolved'. The review noted that the System is grafted on to IFAT's structure, itself 'comprised of a network of members who know each other well, and are thus able to participate in monitoring each other in a peer review system, keeping costs down' (IFAT, 2006d: 2). Research on IFAT's Monitoring System also suggests that the advantage of this participatory model from a developmental perspective is that it more easily targets producers in greatest need, is more responsive to mutually identified issues and needs, and it maximises the value returned to producers by removing the expense of independent labelling organisations' monitoring and certification costs (Tallontire, 2002).[33]

Interestingly, by comparison with FLO's 'independent' product certification based on third-party conformity assessment, IFAT's participatory
system is criticised for its lack of 'stringency' (Nicholls and Opal, 2005:
102). Yet, as we have seen above, FLO's seemingly impartial model of
certification is no less immune to political influence; the market-oriented
LIs have exerted significant influence over issues of product standard
and policy development, price-setting and the preferential allocation of
the certification Mark to large conventional market players (see Chapter
5). Additionally, producers criticise FLO's system as one governed by
Northern LIs who 'do' Fairtrade to Southern producers and 'control' certification in an authoritarian and top-down manner (Wills, 29 April 2005,
fieldwork notes; Bretman, 3 May 2005, fieldwork notes; Renard, 2005).
Given the power that a monopoly on knowledge production confers,
one respondent suggested that IFAT's participatory process for developing the FTO standards and system offers an example for FLO of how to
empower producers, by developing standards on the basis of producers'
direct involvement and decision-making (Van Beuningen, 11 April 2005
fieldwork notes).

In this way it can be seen that IFAT's model of standard-setting, monitoring and institutional capacity-building plays an important role in challenging FLO's 'hegemony of ideas' in terms of the ideas themselves and
the relational mechanisms of authority and control that underpin them.
These developments in IFAT can be seen as creating a significant countervailing influence, an alternative 'power with', to FLO's control over fair
trade markets. As Gaventa (2006a: 27) suggests, gaining power 'in one
space through new skills, capacity and experiences, can be used to enter
and affect other spaces'. Below, we shall look more closely at how IFAT's
membership is mobilising its collective power to 'enter' and 'affect' FLO.

THE POLITICAL STATE OF FAIR TRADE TODAY

According to fair trade pioneers, the fair trade movement is currently at
a 'crossroads' and the pioneers are assessing whether to make a decisive
'split' from FLO and the LIs (Rosenthal, cited in Hood, 22 February 2007).
Since creating the initial certification system, the pioneers have gone on to
build successive highly successful '100 per cent fair trade' companies and
support the development of a large-scale international network of FTOs
(see Chapter 6). Yet the market they have built has become populated with
conventional traders whose business models do not subscribe to or mimic
fair trade principles but who have none the less gained access to the fair
trade market by selling a token amount of Fairtrade-labelled products. For

the pioneers, moving conventional traders into Fairtrade is an important part of changing the market, but as North (cited in Hood, 22 February 2007) pointed out, 'You want them to get on board at a high-bar level, and not at a low-bar level . . . Unfortunately we've seen the tokenism . . .'. Importantly, it is the LIs and FLO that have enabled this tokenistic response from MNCs:

[FLO and the LIs have] taken their eye off the ball on some of the broader goals and [focused] solely on growth . . . In so doing they have sold the label too cheap to transnational companies. . . . (Earley in Hood, 22 February 2007)

Fair trade is a European phenomenon. It's just replacing the middleman, so that now middle-class NGOs can get a piece of the capitalist action. Perhaps 'fair trade' is a description of the colour of their skin? (Manji, cited in Tucker, 2006)

there are competing models of social change. There's the Fair Trade Organisations' model of social change which is transforming what it means to be in business and who you're accountable to as a business. Those [companies] would be Equal Exchange and many other small mission-driven [fair trade] companies. Then there's the corporate reform model of social change, which is Transfair USA signing up Starbucks to do 1 per cent of their coffee as Fairtrade, chipping away bit by bit – but working with large companies. (Fair trade pioneer, fieldwork notes)

These divergent political trajectories between resistance and game-playing suggest significant complexity in the process of market evolution. Change is not simply an issue of innovating once, or a number of times, in new business models. Rather, it is an ongoing game to ensure that innovations have the cumulative political effect of annihilating dominant institutions and models; and this involves not only business model innovation (Chapter 6) but also institutional gaming. At this institutional level, the pioneers in fair trade have begun to implement a networked strategy to 'reclaim' their leadership status, their vision of fair trade, their 'movement' (Rosenthal, cited in Hood, 22 February 2007). This networked strategy is empirically demonstrable in two key ways, reflected in what one respondent described as 'two schools of thought' among the IFAT/FTO community (Deighton, 20 April 2006, fieldwork notes).

The first is a strategy of network cooperation with FLO. This involves harmonising the respective IFAT and FLO certification systems in a total quality management system (TQMS) whose purpose it is (in part) to protect the fair trade market from competing 'fair trade' labels.[34] This objective is in the interests of both FLO and IFAT. However, while FLO seeks legal protection of the term 'Fairtrade' to retain consumer trust (Zonneveld, cited in

Nicholls and Opal, 2005: 247), IFAT's counter-argument to the legalisation of the Fairtrade Mark is that it would simultaneously exclude significant numbers of IFAT members from the fair trade market.[35] Some fair trade producers are FLO certified and others are not. Those that do not have FLO certification are typically makers of handcrafts, other non-food products such as toys or music, or producers of semi-processed foods or micro-quantities that are unviable for FLO certification (Wills, 29 April 2005, fieldwork notes). For this reason FLO's system is inaccessible to the majority of IFAT producers, and perceived as too complex, costly and bureaucratic for developmental purposes (David, 2007: 3). Several trader FTOs such as Italy's CTM Altromercato and the USA's Just Coffee have exited FLO's system, despite being highly committed traders in the movement.

In this context, the logic of the TQMS is that if the FLO and IFAT systems could be harmonised to include all producer and trader FTOs (whether or not they are registered as Fairtrade producers or traders), legal protection of the fair trade term would be possible. Thus the TQMS aims to produce an 'efficient, low-cost Fair Trade certification and registration system which is accessible to small-scale handicraft producer groups, small-holders, as well as to employee-based operations' (IFAT, 2007b).[36]

By contrast with the strategy of networked governance with FLO over the fair trade market is IFAT's growing ideological fissure with FLO which threatens to fragment the movement. A number of IFAT members view FLO as a constraint on, and impediment to, their capacity to bring about market change:

> The integrated monitoring system is incredibly difficult because not all Fair Trade Organisations are sure they want to be associated with the FLO certification mark because it's carried by the likes of Starbucks and others and our members say: 'We are not Starbucks and we don't want to be associated in the minds of consumers with the Starbucks of this world. We believe that those organisations giving the impression that they are Fair Trade somehow dilute Fair Trade'. (Wills, cited in Nicholls and Opal, 2005: 246)

> We parted ways with Transfair USA [TFUSA] over a year ago because we believed that we could do a better job guaranteeing fair trade standards with other allies in the fair trade movement. We believe that TFUSA does a great job with many aspects of their mission, in particular the marketing of fair trade to the public. However, we also feel that many of TFUSA's licensees are watering down the ethic of fair trade and misusing the TFUSA label at the expense of committed fair traders. We, and other 100 per cent fair trade roasters like Cafe Campesino, Dean's Beans, and Larry's Beans, have moved on to try to raise the bar for the industry. (Earley, 23 June 2005, fieldwork notes)

That fair trade pioneers and FTOs have begun to 'move on to try to raise the bar for the industry' dovetails with the second network strategy and 'school of thought' within the IFAT community: network mobilisation outside FLO to force the pace of change in corporate behaviour. This involves mobilising IFAT members to strengthen independent alternative network structures and constituencies at national, regional and international levels. These emerging advocacy-based constituencies – deliberative networks – are publicly and actively agitating and organising for new fair trade governance structures and a more 'principled' version of fair trade (see for example Hood, 22 February 2007; Tucker, 2006; Low and Davenport, 2005). Fair trade pioneers described the power of the strategy of organising and agitating deliberative networks in an attempt to influence FLO and the LIs:

> [the wider movement] took a collective leap in organising and ambition. The movement here badly needed and needs some counterbalance to Transfair. The NGOs [advocating fair trade] are also coming together in a new way . . . Transfair has brought fair trade to a whole new level [in the USA] and they have done so in a manner that has alienated many producer organisations and activists. They [Transfair] are working to change their ways and mend the rift . . . (Rosenthal, 26 October 2005, fieldwork notes)

> Much like producer groups, we [fair traders and our supporters] need to organise groups, realising what our power is in the movement, and open up the certification aspect to a more democratic process . . . It's very undemocratic and not transparent – there's no accountability . . . Transfair USA is run like a corporation . . . It has a CEO . . . [and] a board appointed by the CEO. It has no democratic accountability. (Earley, in Hood, 22 February 2007)

> there's a whole group of people [in the fair trade movement] who have come together to critique – and raise their voices about – what actually comes down to *governance*. Because if we don't like the way something is run, or what's being decided, one thing to say is 'well how is this thing being decided?', 'who's making these decisions? . . . who do you represent?' (Tiffen, 19 August 2005, fieldwork notes)

As part of this dynamic critique, various networks of students, trader FTOs and producer FTOs have written letters of disapproval to FLO, as well as published press and internet articles that question and express concern over the decisions made by the LIs and FLO. E-zines and conference spaces have been established to debate the 'dilution' of fair trade and the influence of conventional MNCs in the system in which the pioneers' voices feature strongly (see *New Internationalist*, 2006; DevNet, 2006). Academic papers, short documentary films and newspaper articles by various journalists are proliferating on the issue of the 'corporatisation' of the fair trade market, and shared around internet networks (see Ransom, 17 October 2005; Bezençon and Blili, 2006; Low and Davenport, 2006;

Hood, 22 February 2007; Fridell et al., forthcoming). These multiple inputs of critical information, research and new ideas into deliberative networks are fuelling further debate and action in ways that impact on FLO and the LIs.

By agitating and mobilising networks of deliberation, the wider movement is gaining increasing capacity to influence the external environment. For example, regional networks within FLO's Stakeholder Forum, such as the Latin American and Caribbean Network of Small Fair Trade Producers, CLAC, have threatened to leave FLO if it does not give producers a seat at the decision-making table and address their needs. 'This is a really significant sign that CLAC wants out [from FLO]', observed one respondent; 'CLAC represents thousands of producers across Latin America'. The CLAC has since also applied for FTO registration with IFAT (Deighton, 20 April 2006, fieldwork notes).

Market-oriented LIs have also faced critical debate and an FTO exodus from national and regional fair trade networks as FTOs strengthen coalitions and networks to counter the LIs' domination over the national fair trade market and message (Equal Exchange, 7 October 2005; Ransom, 17 October 2005; Tucker, 2006). In the USA, Equal Exchange and other fair traders are continuing to publicly criticise Transfair USA's motivation for giving the Fairtrade Mark licence to several MNCs, and for encouraging Fairtrade certification of coffee plantations (in which small-scale producers represent the majority).[37] This critical debate about LIs – and because of them, FLO – has also been cross-national in direction. The Italian fair trade platform and 'backbone' of the Italian fair trade movement, AGICES, together with Transfair Italy, has come out in opposition to the UK's Fairtrade Foundation for awarding Nestlé the Fairtrade Mark license for its 'Partner's Blend' brand[38] (Dalvai, 9 November 2005, fieldwork notes).

These empirical developments illustrate how power, knowledge and skills built in alternative nodes (such as IFAT/FTO networks) are mobilised to disrupt dominant institutions (such as FLO) (see Gaventa, 2006a). In response to the unstable political environment and internal and external critique of FLO these counter-movements have produced, FLO/LIs have moved to change FLO's governance structure (see Figure 7.4). As several LI respondents claimed:

> The problem with [FLO] is that it's not a democracy, it's not balanced . . . so the future of Fairtrade is . . . how are we going to broaden [fair trade] . . . that's the eternal problem of NGOs is how are we going to involve *other* stakeholders than the classical ones in our decision making processes . . . we are quitting the monopoly and we don't know what to do with this . . . this is *difficult*. This is *really difficult* . . . (Former LI Director, fieldwork notes)

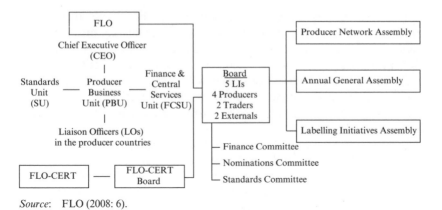

Source: FLO (2008: 6).

Figure 7.4   FLO's new governance structure (as of 2007)

what's becoming untenable is where there's *so* much decision making [by LIs] in the North about issues and policies, and sometimes it still feels . . . like everybody signs up to this definition about fair trade being a partnership and blah blah *blah*, but it actually often feels like Fairtrade is something that comes from something we do in the North *to* people in the South, we don't do it *with* them. (LI staff member, fieldwork notes)

things can't continue where NIs either have – or are perceived to have – all the power within the system. Producers have not felt sufficiently trusting of NIs because they felt NIs were being drawn only by the market, and that NIs did not trust producers because the NIs felt that producers were being very ideologically motivated in all the decisions. It's a multi-stakeholder Board, but we've reduced the number of NIs on that Board recently so that there is now no one stakeholder group which can out-vote everyone else altogether – as was the case in the past with NIs. Before, there was a Board of twelve members, six of them NIs, with the casting vote for the President who could only be elected by the NIs – that obviously was a blocked system. We do need to put that in the perspective of who the members of FLO were *before*, and where they were coming from, and to what extent they were relatively wary about opening up the system and potentially having decisions taken which they felt could be damaging to their markets . . . So we've now installed a Board which is the highest decision-making body which can *no longer be trumped* by the MoM. And what that means is actually a change in the structure and the *ownership* structure, which means that NIs will no longer be the sole owners of the organisation defining the standards and policies – FLO. *That* is the crux of the matter, changing the governance system. It is fundamental to dealing with all the different questions about how we work with multinationals and with plantations and what the place of those different actors within the system is. (Former FLO President, fieldwork notes)

These comments illuminate the evolution in FLO's Northern, 'top-down' structure in response to a changing (more critical) political environment. According to one observer, the changes that FLO has made to its Constitution (in 2006) can be 'qualified as historic in the sense that they enshrine FLO as a truly multi-stakeholder organisation with producers, traders, NIs and independents coming together constituting FLO's most senior decision-making body' (Shimizu-Larenas, 9 June 2006, fieldwork notes).

For the first time in FLO's organisational history, FLO's membership in the new structure extends beyond the LIs to include producers, traders and independents. At least one representative from Fairtrade producer networks in each of Asia, Africa and Latin America now sits on the FLO Board. The current Board Chair is not an LI representative, and future election of Board Chairs must give preference to an independent Board Director (FLO, 2006b: 10; FLO, 2007a: 7). Whether these structural developments in FLO's governance produce noteworthy change to FLO's operations and policies remains to be seen (Meckel, 30 March 2007, fieldwork notes). Already some have suggested that it has done little to resolve the tension between producers/FTOs and FLO (Raynolds and Murray, 2007: 229).

MOBILISING DELIBERATIVE NETWORKS 'WITHIN' AND 'WITHOUT': FORCING (INSTITUTIONAL) 'CREATIVE DESTRUCTION'

Even so, the accounts and analysis here suggest that the external environment in which FLO and the LIs now operate is being shaped by deliberative networks of FTOs. Given the propensity for institutions to be captured by conservative interests and for those institutions to become new forms of constraint, the movement's pioneers can be seen to possess a unique skill in network leadership, a capacity to leverage deliberative networking to destabilise *status quo* institutional structures. The fair trade pioneers (the 'game-players') are radical entrepreneurs of norms and leaders of networks. They are intent on market transformation, disrupting established models and institutions in order to succeed. Together with the last section, the developments in fair trade discussed here show that structural change necessitates a highly deliberative environment found in horizontal network structures that make optimal use of new knowledge (see Achrol and Kotler, 1999).

The role of networks in forcing the pace of economic evolution is little explored in the evolutionary economic literature. This analysis offers deeper understanding of the political structures and micro-processes that market evolution requires. Game-players' mobilisation of them plays a pivotal role in influencing the process of economic transformation. Deliberative networks in particular cannot be tamed by the dominant political environment. As a series of multiple and ongoing conversations about shared values, deliberative networks contribute a rapidly evolving counter-knowledge and source of power to the process of social change. Game-players lead deliberative networks to destabilise the market environment which *status quo* actors prefer, in so doing forcing the pace of change.

CONCLUDING COMMENTS

This chapter has explored the strategic countermovement of IFAT/FTOs and pioneers in response to FLO's increasing corporatisation. It has illuminated how social movement actors use institutions to force the pace of change. While evolutionary economists propose that a market environment conducts the selection between different market models, this chapter has shown that politics changes the institutional pressures exerted on the market environment through networks. Drawing on Braithwaite's (2009) defiance framework, the analysis revealed a set of micro-processes involved in the strategy of game-playing that are additional to model innovation. This captured how institutionally weak actors exercise power – by exploiting network politics to alter selection pressures. The chapter first charted the political evolution of FLO to show how institutional evolution affects the capacity for new innovations to succeed by exerting conservative selection pressures on the market. It then analysed the pioneers' counter-strategy in this environment: mobilising deliberative networks to force change to institutional selection pressures. As foundations of alternative institutions (for which IFAT provided illustration), deliberative networks play a key role in shoring up new – untapped – sources of collective power, or in other words, collective knowledge. Their porous networked structure and values orientation supports the development and rapid evolution of a majority-knowledge system that, when agitated and mobilised strategically by the game-players, forces the pace of change in the external environment.

Predicting the future success of the game-players to bring about market transformation is difficult. The story of FLO would suggest that, if FLO continues on its current course, then fair trade is likely to fail in achieving its broader mission. Supporting this is the fact that, historically, agenda globalisation follows a non-linear dynamic: agendas can regress as much as they can progress (see Braithwaite and Drahos, 2000). However, the story

Table 7.1   Comparative retail value of Cafédirect and Nestlé in the UK market

UK hot drinks brand company	2001 % retail value	2002 % retail value	2003 % retail value	2004 % retail value	2005 % retail value
Nestlé	22.1	21.2	21.4	20.8	20.4
Cafédirect	0.2	0.2	0.3	0.4	0.5

Source: Global Market Information Database (GMID), 14 August 2006.

of IFAT and fair trade pioneers suggests the converse: due to the challenge they present to FLO's evolution, and due to similar future challenges, fair trade will be rescued through constant evolutionary pressure. While the analysis in this book comes down in favour of fair trade's evolutionary potential, the simple empirical example of the gap between Cafédirect and Nestlé's retail value in the UK nevertheless shows that the road ahead of the movement's pioneers is long (see Table 7.1).

For an atypical business model that now, after 15 years, is the fourth-largest coffee brand in the UK, Cafédirect is doing remarkably well (see also Chapter 6).[39] Yet to succeed in the long term to transform conventional big business, fair trade's 'game-players' will need to continue to recreate the institutional framework within which their models operate, as they have done in recent years with FLO.

It is perhaps, then, the notion of incremental progress that best suits game-playing's transformative potential: social change occurs in a series of ebbs and flows (or small, cumulative victories or losses) rather than one revolutionary moment (Drucker, 1985: 253). This is particularly the case in a networked world in which the governance and realisation of outcomes is nodally produced (Johnston and Shearing, 2003). Irrespective of the challenge of predicting the course of change, this chapter has provided an empirically based account of the micro-processes by which game-players respond to institutional resistance and point the way to the economic future.

NOTES

1. Historical examples of Schumpeter's gales of creative destruction, whereby revolutionary innovations have transformed the way in which societies, let alone economies, operate: steam power from the late eighteenth century to the 1840s; the railway from the 1840s to the 1890s, electric power in the 1890s–1930s; the motor car and oil from

the 1930s to the 1980s; information technology to the present (computers, software, telecommunications).

2. As Casson (1990: xvii) writes, 'variation occurs within a population of firms when one of them adopts a new managerial practice or a new technology . . . The industry constitutes an environmental niche in which the struggle [for survival] goes on. Imitation constitutes a social mechanism by which the characteristics of the successful innovation are transmitted to rival firms. In the long run, only the fittest firms in the industry – those using best practice techniques – earn a normal rate of profit and so survive.'

3. Symbolic imitation, like symbolic regulation, is a regulatory measure that projects meaning and significance but in reality involves little change to existing behaviour. Its effect is to placate public concern. For classic works on symbolic regulation, see Edelman (1964) and Gusfield (1963).

4. The term 'institution' is defined in different ways by different disciplines (see Goodin, 1996) and an extensive analysis of the term is not the purpose of this book. In economics, institutions refer to the 'rules of the game' (North, 1990), whereas sociology employs a much broader conception of 'social institutions' as a 'stable, valued, recurring pattern of behaviour' (Huntington, cited in Goodin, 1996: 21). In the sphere of economics, the market is one such social institution: it 'regulates the production, distribution and consumption of goods and services within any society' (Eisenstadt, cited in Goodin, 1996: 22). In addition are 'formal institutions', namely formally constructed bodies or organisations that arise to govern and stipulate rules of conduct in a social institution. This book regards IFAT and FLO as formal institutions governing the rules and evolution of the fair trade market (a social institution). Formal institutions significantly influence the social institutions they govern by shaping the (social) institutional incentive structure that causes some innovations (modes of activity) to succeed and others to fail (Goodin, 1996: 29).

5. Broadly conceived, 'knowledge' includes 'any mental activity including perception and value judgements' and social actors 'perceive, interpret and evaluate the world according to mental categories (mental frames or mental models)' (Nooteboom, 2001: 42).

6. Deliberative democracy is an evolving concept with multiple approaches (Parkinson and Roche, 2004: 507).

7. 'Participatory' and 'deliberative' democracy are generally understood as having distinct focal points and criticisms (see Gaventa, 2006b). While participatory democracy emphasises more direct involvement of citizens in, and deeper engagement with, substantive political issues, deliberative democracy focuses on the quality and nature of collective participation such that citizens address public problems by reasoning together about how best to solve them (Cohen and Fung, cited in Gaventa, 2006b). To the extent that deliberation assumes participation, there is significant overlap and similarity between the two approaches (see Cornwall and Gaventa, 2001). It is not possible, nor the focus of this book, to investigate these distinct literatures. Rather, the intention is to draw on the most empirically relevant ideas from both literatures in order to understand how different actors and institutions use both approaches as political strategies to own, control and govern knowledge.

8. This chapter uses the concept of 'spaces' (Gaventa, 2006a) and 'nodes' (Burris et al., 2005) interchangeably. Gaventa (2006a: 26) describes 'spaces' as 'opportunities, moments and channels where citizens can act to potentially affect policies, discourses, decisions and relationships that affect their lives and interests'. To the extent that these are physical locations and opportunities for affecting the process of governance, the idea of 'spaces' can be seen to parallel what Burris et al. (2005: 37) define as a 'node' within the context of networked governance: 'a site of governance which mobilises diffuse knowledge, capacity and resources that reside within networked arrangements'.

9. This section deals with empirical material on FLO's governance before the FLO Board Meeting of November 2006 at which the Board made structural changes to its governance structure. The analysis in this section reflects this former state. The changes made to FLO's governance are examined in the final section of this chapter.

10. This legal structure has been changed in response to the tensions that this chapter

examines. The details of these changes to FLO's Constitution are analysed in the final section. The presentation of relatively outdated data here is deliberate and for the purpose of tracing the chronology of FLO's political evolution, which illuminates the theoretical story in the book.

11. Chapter 5 documented the removal of producers from the governing body of the Max Havelaar labelling organisations when FLO was established.

12. The market-oriented LIs' influence over product development has at times directed FLO's resources towards developing standards for products that dominant market players view as potential consumer markets but which are of limited developmental impact for small-scale producers (Douglas, 12 April 2005, fieldwork notes).

13. Based on a study commissioned by the Latin American and Caribbean Network of Small Fair Trade Producers (CLAC) in FLO's Stakeholder Forum revealing the increased cost of production since 1994 (when coffee prices were last set), the CLAC requested at the FLO Board Meeting of November 2006 a rise in the Fairtrade Minimum Price for both organic and non-organic coffees, and the Fairtrade Premium. The Board endorsed the request, commissioning the Standards Unit to undertake a review of Fairtrade coffee prices and for the Standards Committee to make a decision (see FLO, 2007b, 2007c). The price-rise request was denied by the Standards Committee for the time being on the basis of a lack of consensus among different stakeholder groups about the need for a price rise. Making the same request of IFAT traders, producers began to receive a higher price from FTO-trader partners on the basis that 'after 14 years of the same price, a price increase is justified' (Dalvai, 7 February 2007, fieldwork notes). Supporter groups from the broader fair trade community have publicly criticised the decision, pointing to the power relationships among the Standards Committee as the basis for the decision (USFT, 2007b), and have threatened a 'backlash' if the decision is not revoked (see for example USFT, 2007a).

14. Whereas in some product sectors such as coffee, global production is based heavily on small-scale farming, in other sectors such as tea or bananas, plantation-based production is the norm. Hence, in the eyes of market-driven LIs, FLO should adopt 'flexibility' when it comes to its standards for different product sectors to suit market conditions (see Paulsen, 7 July 2005).

15. As noted in Chapter 5, FLO has begun certifying plantations in increasing number in industries where small production exists such as bananas and tropical fruits – in contradiction to its original policy (see Raynolds, 2007; Wilkinson and Mascarenhas, 2007a; Renard and Pérez-Grovas, 2007). While corporate traders have pushed the interest in certification of plantations (see Chapter 5), so too have plantation farmers, who question their exclusion from Fairtrade simply because they are not small farmers or their national or local contexts do not sit comfortably with smallholder farming (see Kruger and du Toit, 2007; Wilkinson and Mascarenhas, 2007b). Nevertheless, both small and plantation farmers challenge the 'Northern' monopoly on decision-making on this controversial issue.

16. FTOs have demonstrated and continue to demonstrate small producers' potential (see Chapter 6).

17. In Chapter 5 I noted that FLO's certification of plantations creates one of two entry barriers to small producers seeking access to Fairtrade markets.

18. Loasby (1999) infers the difficulty entrepreneurs face in attempting to make their models affect the institutional environment: 'most imaginative conceptions which succeed are substantially changed along the way . . . selection is mainly rejection, but . . . it sometimes takes the form of adaptation and redesign, leading to another set of trials, which may result in further adaptation, or eventual rejection'. Loasby's point is that innovations will fail to penetrate the broader institutional environment more than they will succeed outright. In other words, the norm is for institutions to remain intact and for innovations to adapt.

19. Similar to Gaventa's notion of the 'people's science' is O'Malley's (1996: 313) concept of 'indigenous governance' which locates governance 'in the everyday, voluntary interactions or commonalities of interest of . . . individuals'.

20. This idea corresponds with the notion of social capital as a collective good: social capital

is not the possession of an individual nor is it an individual trait. However, social capital is of benefit to individuals (see Putnam, 2000; Lin, 2001; Szreter, 2001).

21. A brief version of IFAT's institutional structure was presented in Chapter 3.

22. IFAT's membership includes 'members' (FTOs, fair trade networks and fair trade support organisations), 'associates' (donor organisations and national/international agencies that support trade justice efforts), 'individual associates' (scholars, writers and the general public who have an interest in and intention to promote fair trade) and 'honorary members' (individuals of notable service to humanity, society or the fair trade movement specifically). Only IFAT 'members' have voting and speaking rights at IFAT AGMs. Whether producer cooperatives and associations, export marketing companies, importers, retailers, national/regional fair trade networks or financial institutions, all share a commitment to fair trade principles and IFAT's mission as part of their formal membership of the global network (IFAT, 2006h).

23. At IFAT's 2007 AGM a review of its governance structures resulted in an approved 'Agenda for Change', which stipulates that the regional networks are part of the body of IFAT and thus there is no need for a Memoranda of Agreement between them and the IFAT Secretariat. Each region has a director on the main IFAT Board (Wills, 20 January 2008, fieldwork notes).

24. Formal sub-committees are appointed by the Board to further specific projects of impor- tance to the entire membership and make recommendations to the Board: advocacy, finance, market access and development, standards and monitoring, and membership accreditation (IFAT, 2003: 8). IFAT members with knowledge in these particular areas are invited to join sub-committees, their 'expertise' deployed as a collective resource to benefit the broader membership (IFAT, 2007a: 2). The international working groups are likewise voluntary groups of IFAT members who work together on relevant projects through long-distance phone and email communication. They advance specific projects in market development, advocacy, and strengthening the Monitoring System to build credibility for fair trade (IFAT, 2007a). IFAT members' level of volunteering is very high and an organisational strength, and the means by which many of IFAT's opera- tions are conducted (IFAT, 2006f).

25. This provides the formal link between international and regional nodes (Wills, 26 February 2007, fieldwork notes).

26. The election of IFAT Board representatives also takes place at the AGM.

27. The Board appoints the Executive Director of the IFAT Secretariat, who appoints any other central office staff recruited to carry out IFAT business. At the time of writing, the Executive Director combines the role of General Secretary with that of Chief Finance Officer and fund-raiser (Wills, 26 February 2007, fieldwork notes). The Secretariat employs four office staff based in Culemborg (the Netherlands), and more broadly, three staff and four formal volunteers.

28. IFAT promotes information-sharing and relationship-building. For instance, it pub- lishes *Trade Post*, a quarterly members' newsletter; an annual database of information on members (the IFAT Member Directory); a fortnightly members e-news updates; and maintains a section of its website for members' information. As the organisation states, 'IFAT is about building partnerships within the Fair Trade movement. We encourage our members to get into the habit of regular communication – share your news, your stories, your experience . . . ' (IFAT, 2007a).

29. At international conferences (held in odd-numbered years), the entire international membership of IFAT is invited, and the AGM is held for full members of IFAT to take decisions on key issues and collectively decide future priorities and direction for IFAT. The regional conferences, in even-numbered years, take place in Europe, Asia, Africa, Latin America and North America/Pacific Rim, where members in those regions meet to discuss and debate issues of especial regional relevance as well as issues raised for discussion and feedback by working groups and sub-committees (IFAT, 2007a).

30. The FTO Mark is a monitoring system for companies/organisations, not products (IFAT, 2006j). As such, the FTO Mark can be used to promote the organisation's Fair Trade status in marketing activities and on organisational resources such as letterheads,

posters, websites and facilities, but not on products. While many FTOs produce products that do carry the Fairtrade Mark, these organisations also produce a wide range of other fair trade goods for which FLO does not have standards, handcrafts being one example (IFAT, 2006j). As a further example, some FTOs sell non-certified handcrafts as well as products for which Fairtrade product standards exist but do not seek FLO certification for this latter group of products (such as CTM Altromercato in Italy). This latter group of products has none the less been produced and traded according to fair trade principles and terms, which is signified by the organisation's FTO status.

31. Participatory monitoring focuses on involving the 'least powerful, visible and assertive actors in evaluation'. It emphasises a process of learning (at individual, organisational and institutional levels) in which self-evaluation enables individuals to assess and further their own organisational capacities, a process through which individual and collective learning produces a responsiveness to the needs and contextual specificities of individuals' circumstances (Estrella and Gaventa, 1997). It is for these numerous benefits *vis-à-vis* development that participatory monitoring and evaluation have become increasingly popular as an alternative to a traditional, 'top-down' approach to monitoring and assessment (ibid.).

32. An FTO seeking the FTO Mark cannot apply for certification until it has been operating for at least two years.

33. Chapter 3 documented FLO's change in legal structure, which saw it split into two organisational structures. Specifically, certification became independent and separate from the rest of the organisation for the purpose of impartiality in monitoring and assessment. One consequence of this change, noted in Chapter 5, has been the introduction of producer certification fees associated with independent labelling, which has presented a significant barrier to entry for small-scale producers.

34. While the focus of their cooperation is through the harmonisation of the two systems, FLO and IFAT are also engaging in cooperation under the auspices of F.I.N.E.

35. Another is the commercial aspect of certifying the handcrafts that IFAT members produce. Such items already have markets – through world shops, gift shops and so on. Consumers buying these products do not need guarantees that the product is fair trade since the trust is in the shop's brand itself. As Luuk Zonneveld, President of FLO, observed, 'The additional cost and administration involved in certification of these goods would not be off-set by an additional increase in sales' (cited in Nicholls and Opal, 2005: 246–7).

36. At the time of publication the TQMS has been advanced by the Sustainable Fair Trade Management System (SFTMS) which features in part a product labelling component for handcrafts and potentially for any other product (see Commons, 2008).

37. See North, 10 February 2006; 2003b.

38. AGICES, 11 November 2005.

39. The company now intends to enter into the US market and take on the US coffee monolith, Starbucks (Fortson and Veevers, 2007).

Conclusion: game-playing – the key to global empowerment

In putting together the pieces of fair trade's story over the last four chapters, this book has developed an alternative theory of power about social change. Power theories have traditionally favoured deterministic and/or liberal notions of power and empowerment. Alternative power theories, combined with Braithwaite's sophisticated psychological framework of defiance, highlight the inadequacy of such a lens for understanding power in modern times.

Fair trade's development in the last two decades has been rapid, bringing both the advancement and appropriation of fair trade principles. Its grassroots base of support has been largely responsible for this growth – a labyrinth of networks all networking the fair trade message and contributing to its development. The Fairtrade certification system's expansion has capitalised on the organic spread of fair trade's social roots. Yet under the direction of (market-driven) LIs, FLO's development has been shaped by an eager pursuit of 'mainstream' corporations and markets, opening the movement up to a series of political and philosophical fault lines.

As Chapters 6 and 7 showed, it is in this context that fair trade's pioneers in particular are of critical importance, both practically and conceptually (as game-players). Their ongoing disruption of institutional attempts to co-opt fair trade – both at the level of new innovations in business organisation and leading deliberative networks within FLO – will see the movement survive and prosper. The FTO brand model, in which farmers are co-owners of both company assets and trading processes and decisions, is an important one for FLO to promote. In FLO's reluctance to do so – and its institutional and policy discrimination against FTOs – fair trade's innovators have again bypassed FLO's system in recent times with an innovation that publicly thrusts the issue of producer-value ownership in international trade on to the corporate agenda. In this development we can perceive new futures in fair trade in which producer ownership prevails in both the process and structures of empowerment models.

And what of the conceptual significance of fair trade's story? The movement's emergence and growth has occurred in a context of unprecedented global power in the hands of global corporations that manipulate global subjectivities by harnessing market resources and institutional mechanisms (such as TRIPs). As we saw in Chapter 2, this power affects the global coffee market – a heavily structured environment in which three or four roasters dominate and world market prices have been in crisis.

Given these structural constraints, how do traditionally 'weak' actors use markets to trigger change in producers' circumstances and capabilities? Market evolution is a dynamic process, and thus difficult to capture and analyse. Contemporary social scientists with an interest in alternative theories of power have explored the politics of change when power is in the hands of structurally disempowered people. This book has applied these ideas – and others – to the market context. By focusing on, and elaborating, Braithwaite's concept of regulatory game-playing, the story of fair trade helped to reveal the micro-foundations of market-based social change in which agency, and its connection to large-scale market outcomes, can be more completely explained.

Chapter 4 illuminated the centrality of networks to the process of change. The potential of networks to spread new ideas and action is attributed to scattered, 'weak' network relationships as opposed to centralised, hierarchical or 'strong' ones (Granovetter, 1973; see also Putnam, 2000). From a Latourian perspective, the potential of such ties has everything to do with the power of numbers. Weak ties enrol a greater number and diversity of people into their composition than do strong ones (Granovetter, 1973). By strategically exploiting networks, social actors are able to achieve their aims (Braithwaite and Drahos, 2000; Burris et al., 2005). While Hayek suggested that this process of network coordination and resulting social order was a spontaneous affair, the fair trade movement's experience supports regulatory scholars' more recent insights of the heavy political hand that secures particular market outcomes and structures. Chapter 4 showed a sophisticated network strategy that social actors exploit to trigger expanding circles of enrolment (COE): networking networks, which means activating existing networks to support a particular idea and set of actions.

In this process, fair trade activists have exercised the cumulative power of many smaller and diffuse sites of human action, rather than exerting power through a centralised bureaucracy in which power is concentrated. The fair trade pioneers have innovated in the act of social protest, creating a market tool for consumers to reveal their (political) preferences via the market. By engaging with this system or tool (to produce, trade and consume in new ways), individuals and groups have acquired the 'power to' affect markets. The pioneers and activists have linked or harnessed individual 'power to' to generate collective, indeed transnational, 'power with'. This is the social connections model of power in action; large-scale effects originate with the act of game-playing by multiplying others' engagement with their models.

Given the political implications of networking networks, fair trade's network networkers – the fair trade 'missionaries' – are of particular conceptual significance. Indeed, a fundamental condition of the success of game-players' innovative models is that the model has sufficient normative appeal to motivate actors to take direct action. Skilled in the art of persuasion, fair trade missionaries keep collective action alive and expanding: they spread the knowledge and message about game-players' models across diverse networks and 'translate' the meaning of those models in new contexts. The movement's intensive investment of human resources into constant network networking (a many-to-many model of marketing) has achieved this. Networks enable action and unleash marginalised discourses as long as two-way flows between nodes are socially and institutionally sustained. In this context, 'power over' recedes in theoretical relevance and accuracy as an explanation of outcomes by comparison with other categories of power developed here: the 'power with', the 'power to', the 'power within'. The social connections model of producing new power structures adequately captures this sequence of how power operates to alter the capacity of individuals and groups to influence the structures that constrain their lives. In summary, this chapter indicated the following conditions for causing large-scale change through markets:

1. a social connections view of the world is a precondition for agency to change structure;
2. game-players draw on the 'power within' to create models that connect networks;
3. network networkers help new groups to translate new models into direct action and access 'power to';
4. networks offer a source of 'power with'; and
5. networking networks leads to large-scale diffusion and change.

While this strategy for scale has enabled the Fairtrade market to expand, evolutionary economists and business theorists highlight the simultaneous waning of the system's market power to influence market actors; innovations possess only a temporary power in the market, which is lost relative to a so-called 'natural' organisational evolution into a hierarchical and vertically organised business structure that inhibits innovation (Nooteboom, 2001; McGrath and MacMillan, 2000; Robert and Weiss, 1988). Chapter 5 showed that the market power of fair trade's initial innovation in certification has been weakened by resisters' vulnerability to co-option over time (see Braithwaite et al., 2007: 292). However, resisters are not homogeneous

in this regard. The heterogeneity among them in this case reflects different
dimensions of agency (Bevir and Rhodes, 2005; Nygren, 1999) situated along
an ideological spectrum ranging from the radical to the conservative – some
resisters for instance were aware of, and struggled to cope with, their organisational contradictions and sought to move beyond the *status quo*. Situated
within capitalist market institutions, resisters find it difficult to completely
shrug off the constraints and pressures of existing regulatory frameworks to
instead envisage and pursue radically different ideas and approaches; they
perceive prevailing norms, structures and institutions as ultimately the only
'realistic' way in which to achieve scale with new models.

Chapter 6 showed that 'resisters' set in train the institutional sequence
of static adaptation through the governance and implementation of
game-players' models. Forming 'strong ties' (knowledge hierarchies) in
FLO's governance from the outset (which mimic prevailing liberal modes
of decision-making control), the pragmatic market-oriented LIs shaped
FLO's institutional evolution to enable the rapid uptake of the model by
conventional traders. Through FLO's financial and governance model
resisters harnessed the power of brand corporations in Western consumer
markets as a type of 'power with' to assert institutional 'power over'
others. This 'power with' was premised on MNCs' institutional 'power
over' resisters, or in other words, resisters' institutional dependence on
MNCs for growth: the LIs that embraced brand corporations' power and
its inherent belief system exerted the greatest power over FLO. LIs that did
not embrace the pragmatic market worldview, or did so to a lesser degree,
were weak in FLO.

Second, fair trade's experience highlighted that the evolution of FLO's
governance model in support of the conservative discourse of market-
oriented LIs was possible even in networked configurations: in networked
structures, resisters constructed nodal hierarchies as mechanisms of 'power
over'. While it is not a new insight that nodally coordinated networks can
produce negative or inequitable outcomes (see Burris et al., 2005), the
movement's experience shows that for networked governance to live up
to its reputation as a superior means of acquiring new and diffuse information and coordinating action, a precondition is that two-way flows of
information between nodes of contextual knowledge within the network
are socially and institutionally sustained.

Networks can never be completely captured: they allow for continued
innovation. This was shown empirically in the fair trade case study. The
fair trade pioneers began to innovate in brand companies that conferred
greater market power on small-scale producers to exert greater political
pressure than FLO's model on *status quo* traders to change. This development and dynamic showed that the organisational phase of consolidation

is produced by actors who seek to institutionalise new models in the existing market structure, not annihilate those dominant institutions. Network structures allow game-players the freedom to innovate in response to – and in the context of – resisters' institutional capture. This chapter also illuminated how social actors use networks and nodes strategically to begin and engage in institutional sequences to achieve outcomes. This illuminates the significance of a nodal and networked conception of governance for explaining social outcomes and the way in which social actors perceive and operate in their social environment.

Overall, Chapter 5 added complexity to our understanding of how power operates in the process of market change. 'Power over' is not as easily annihilated in the market environment as Schumpeter's notion of entrepreneurship implicitly proposes. For instance, actors located in existing institutional structures (resisters) recreate structures of 'power over' within new institutions, yet even among resisters there is heterogeneity (i.e. some accept traditional market norms more readily than others do). Different actors pursue different ideological and organisational pathways that protract and make complex the market battle between hegemonic discourses and the empowerment of alternative ones in the market. The ability to accommodate and capture these real-world differences and dynamics of power in conceptual terms highlights the value of Braithwaite's conceptual framework of defiance. In sum, the chapter revealed the actors and some of the processes that precipitate and evolve new market processes:

1. resisters play the role of triggering new institutional sequences in evolution;
2. resisters harness new forms of power that trigger new institutional trajectories;
3. these new forms of power are generated by using 'power with' *status quo* actors;
4. harnessing 'power with' institutional actors re-produces 'power over';
5. new forms of institutional 'power over' stymie market transformation, leading to new political tensions;
6. game-players create new models under conditions of market equilibrium to disrupt that equilibrium; and
7. nodes of resistance and game-playing coexist symbiotically in market-based attempts to bring about change.

Chapter 6 pursued the analysis of the fair trade movement's innovators. These actors are on a mission to achieve radical change through markets. Braithwaite's 'game-player' is a novel and unique social actor with entrepreneurial qualities and capabilities: he/she redefines and innovates in regulatory rules, transcends social norms, and thinks and acts boldly, 'outside the square'. Linking the concept of game-playing with post-liberal power theorists' notion of 'power within', the analysis of the fair trade movement's innovators revealed how power operates in the game-playing context and indicated greater potential for agency in the process of social change than is traditionally captured in the literature on power.

Rather than follow the same political and economic trajectory as resistance, game-players respond to market concentration by innovating to ensure that alternative narratives continue to be liberated from those that dominate. In this way, game-playing ensures that the process of genuine empowerment continues. Business theorists describe the perpetuity of the act of innovation as the entrepreneur's 'offensive' weapon to topple dominant, better-financed opponents (Drucker, 1985; Robert and Weiss, 1988; McGrath and MacMillan, 2000), or, in other words, to escape the constraint of 'power over'. The fair trade pioneers' ongoing search for, and exploitation of, new knowledge gives them continuing power to unleash alternative narratives and new capacities that work to break up market monopolies (expressed in the 'continuum of innovation'). Their inbuilt propensity to innovate and gain new knowledge puts them ahead of recalcitrant and resistant corporations in defining the terms of future markets.

Importantly, this challenged the notion that the evolution in business structures towards a hierarchical design is 'natural'. The chapter highlighted that there was nothing temporary about game-playing since continued innovation is the game-players' source of power. Game-players are politically resilient and their individual power, which manifests in new models, triggers subtle processes of social change by suggesting the possibility of alternative ways of acting and thinking (Moscovici et al., 1994).

Chapter 6 also offered further explanation of the broader cultural and institutional repercussions of game-playing. It is one thing to come up with a new and controversial idea, but materialising it – and in grand proportions – is another matter. This begged the question of how entrepreneurial actors actually materialise their models with such success as to annihilate dominant market actors and structures. Something of an explanation has been offered by business theorists who emphasise that an entrepreneur's success with an innovation depends on their 'leadership' of networks – entrepreneurs need to enrol the active support of their networks (Goyder, 1998; McGrath and MacMillan, 2000). We saw this process in action in the game-playing context – game-players' strategy and understanding of power mimics the idea of network leadership and enrolment for market success.

Strategic networking enables game-players to materialise their models. Their 'power within' enables individuals and groups to exercise 'power with' others, but game-players ultimately depend on their 'power with' to trigger change. This is a Latourian expression of power wherein ultimate power lies with collective action, not an individual; intense enrolling and enlisting is needed (Latour, 1986). The analysis of game-playing in this chapter demystified the agency and power in entrepreneurship to trigger market transformation and documented its methodology for change:

1. the basis of game-players' power is a unique 'power within';
2. the 'power within' begins a sequence of change that produces benefits for others;
3. game-playing involves perpetual innovation;
4. innovation – and the organisational structures that support it – is a purposive political act to exploit marginal discourses. It is not naturally occurring;
5. the social connections framework is game-players' map of the world and how to liberate new sources of power; the 'power within' is a prerequisite for others' power and is dependent on these new sources of 'power with' to bring changes in markets; and
6. game-players link perpetual innovation with network entrepreneurship to trigger new sequences of broader socio-political and economic behaviour.

In light of FLO's/the LIs' capture and MNCs' recalcitrance to genuinely mimic the fair trade pioneers' new business governance structures, Chapter 7 turned to examine how game-playing works to influence the institutional environment in a hospitable direction for their models. Evolutionary economists such as Nelson and Winter (1982) portray selection as something that the market 'environment' conducts; the environment makes a selection between competing 'species'. However, the accounts in Chapter 7 indicated that, rather than genuinely imitate and transform, dominant MNCs (facilitated by the movement's 'resisters') instead activate institutional strategies such as static adaptation and symbolic imitation to keep the existing order intact. An evolutionary account of markets lacks an appreciation of institutional power and the politics of institutional selection pressures and their role in producing market outcomes.

The empirical insight that emerged from this chapter was that market actors harness institutions as new sources of selection pressure to support themselves to thrive in evolutionary struggles. The analysis of the evolution of the Fairtrade system revealed that actors harness spaces or nodes where institutional knowledge is produced in order to influence selection pressures in their favour. This illuminated how the battles for evolutionary 'selection' are anything but natural in their outcome: selection is an ongoing political contest over the ownership of institutional knowledge.

This insight became the basis of an important contribution to understanding evolution in institutions and their relationship to market evolution: through politics, the selection environment can be changed. Evolutionary economists have paid insufficient attention to the role of networks in evolutionary processes and the politics of institutional selection. As we saw, game-playing involved strategic leadership of deliberative networks to force the pace of change in the market environment. Deliberative networks are social networks that, physically and virtually, nurture a type of deliberative conversation about shared concerns, values and issues that cannot be silenced. This is an evolving and responsive politics in (networked) action. Institutions of deliberative networks reflect collective ownership of institutional knowledge on which game-players draw to force change in the selection environment.

These empirical insights contributed to the development of an understanding of how the market environment is changed by networks to favour alternative business models and market principles. Through deliberative networks new majority-knowledge systems develop, and can be used to destabilise the political environment. Networks give institutionally weak actors power to bring change in dominant institutions. This is because networks and networked institutions are construction sites for building the capacities and strength of marginalised narratives to cause change in the market. Game-players deliberately engage in and provoke deliberative networks, stimulating lively debate to disrupt the *status quo*. The chapter captured the empirical expression of this process in the fair trade pioneers' strategic agitation of fair trade activist and FTO networks, involving increasing discussion that questioned, deliberated and reaffirmed the movement's shared principles and led to their mobilisation.

The inability of hierarchical institutions to completely capture networks and placate their disruptive influence makes established institutions vulnerable to shifts in network politics. This capacity to effect institutional change was demonstrated in FLO's institutional evolution in response to the wider movement's mobilisation of networks of deliberation. The empirical point is not simply that discourse can be enabling for marginalised actors (O'Malley, 1996; Bevir and Rhodes, 2005; Dryzek, 2000), but that networks strengthen those discourses and can be harnessed to trigger political instability within institutions. Game-playing involves exploiting network capacities to force the pace of change. This sequence can be summarised thus:

1. Actors use institutions as new sources of market-selection pressure.
2. The pace and direction of evolution is affected by networks of deliberation.
3. Game-players are leaders of deliberative networks.

4. Deliberative networks are the structural and processual basis of institutions of collective knowledge ownership.
5. Deliberative networks cannot be captured and possess freedom from resisters.
6. Leadership of networks allows for constant change.
7. Capitalism requires deliberative institutional structures in order to evolve.

In its entirety, this book has aimed to offer a unique analysis of power for understanding how market actors bring about change. Using Braithwaite's conceptual framework of defiance, the book illuminates that modern 'power over' is neither immutable nor inevitably recreated in new discourses, while the potential for agency, by contrast, has been severely underestimated (see Bevir and Rhodes, 2005; O'Malley, 1996). A networked world enables power to be generated outside the existing institutional structure. Those with no organisational power or institutional control can transcend institutional power and the constraints of existing social structures through a unique set of dynamic strategies of business model innovation and network entrepreneurship. The former articulates alternative subjectivities while the latter harnesses the social resources with which to globalise them. Embodied in the act of game-playing, these strategies exploit the world of networked and nodal governance to free structures from their present institutional moorings. The game-player relies on a social connections view of power to trigger the process of change.

The product of free structures is a new type of power that can be referred to as 'power beyond' (or 'power over' existing structures). 'Power beyond' refers to the effect of creating new structures and institutions which no one individual can create alone, and which cannot be created by or through existing institutional structures. By working around – and independently of – institutional politics to build new structures, game-players are not reliant on those who exert 'power over' to be won over. Instead, game-players make possible the exercise of 'power beyond' by utilising network opportunities and connections to build models of empowerment as new sources and flows of power that cause large-scale change.

In this way, social structures can be considered as 'free'. The concept of 'free structures' injects into the notion of structure greater fluidity, latitude, opportunity and potential for ingenuity than is readily captured in existing theoretical accounts of power. 'Free' structures connote structures that can be changed because they are in the process of constant creation – or creative destruction – by social actors. At the heart of this process of human creation are game-players and game-playing, and it is in these conceptual terms that the micro-processes of market transformation can be understood.

Appendix: fair trade on the political agenda[1]

2006

- The European Parliament adopts a resolution on Fair Trade, recognizing the benefits achieved by the Fair Trade movement, suggesting the development of an EU-wide policy on Fair Trade, defining criteria that need to be fulfilled under Fair Trade to protect it from abuse and calling for greater support to Fair Trade (EP resolution 'Fair Trade and development', 6 July 2006).
- The French chapter of ISO (AFNOR) adopts a reference document on Fair Trade after five years of discussion.
- A Fair Trade Law is being discussed in Belgium.

2005

- Fair Trade Fair and Symposium in Hong Kong held during WTO's 6th Ministerial Conference in December.
- Opinion of the European Economic and Social Committee on Ethical Trade and Consumer Assurance Schemes, focusing on the need to protect consumers against misleading ethical claims (REX/196, 27 October 2005).
- A law is passed in France, proposing to establish a Commission to recognize Fair Trade Organizations (article 60 of law no. 2005-882, Small and Medium Enterprises, 2 August 2005).
- Communication from the European Commission on 'Policy Coherence for Development – Accelerating progress towards attaining the Millennium Development Goals' (COM(2005) 134 final, 12.04.2005). Fair Trade is mentioned as 'a tool for poverty reduction and sustainable development'.
- The European Parliament serves exclusively Fair Trade coffee and tea at meetings.
- French Deputy, Mr. Antoine Herth, issues the report '40 proposals to sustain the development of Fair Trade'.

2004

- The European Union adopts the 'Agricultural Commodity Chains, Dependence and Poverty – A proposal for an EU Action Plan', with a specific reference to the Fair Trade movement which has 'been setting the trend for a more socio-economically responsible trade' (COM(2004)0089).
- Fair Trade symposium at the XIth United Nations Conference on Trade and Development in São Paolo, Brazil. Rubens Ricupero, then UNCTAD Secretary General, said 'I am convinced that Fair Trade can only go in one direction: upwards. Because people understand increasingly the injustice of this world and want to do something against it.'

2003

- A Trade Fair and Sustainable Symposium in Cancun at the 5th WTO Ministerial Meeting show-cases the experience of Fair Trade.

2002

- Communication Trade and Development. Assisting Developing Countries to benefit from Trade (COM(2002) 513 final, 18.9.2002): 'The EU also intends to continue to work on fair trade and trade in environmentally friendly goods and organic products, particularly from developing countries.'

2001

- The Green Paper on Corporate Social Responsibility and the Communication on Social Development in the context of Globalization from the European Commission express an increasing legal recognition of the Fair Trade movement and its standards, in particular on labour practices.

2000

- The Cotonou Agreement, new Partnership Agreement between the African, Caribbean and Pacific states and the European Union, makes specific reference to the promotion of Fair Trade in article 23 g) and in the Compendium. Also, the 'Directive 2000/36/EC of the European Parliament and of the Council relating to cocoa and chocolate products intended for human consumption' suggests promoting Fair Trade.

- Public institutions in Europe start purchasing Fair Trade coffee and tea.

1999

- The European Parliament adopts a 'Communication from the Commission to the Council on "Fair Trade"' COM(1999) 619 final, 29.11.1999.

1998

- The European Parliament adopts the 'Resolution on Fair Trade' (OJ C 226/73, 20.07.1998).

1997

- The European Parliament adopts a resolution on the banana sector, calling on the Commission to facilitate access of new Fair Trade operators.
- The European Commission publishes a survey on 'Attitudes of EU consumers to Fair Trade bananas', concluding that Fair Trade bananas would be commercially viable in several EU Member States.

1996

- The Economic and Social Committee of the European Communities adopts an 'Opinion on the European "Fair Trade" marking movement'.

1994

- The European Commission prepares 'Memo on alternative trade' in which it declares its support for strengthening Fair Trade in the

South and North and its intention to establish an EC Working Group on Fair Trade.
- The European Parliament adopts 'Resolution on promoting fairness and solidarity in North South trade' (OJ C 44, 14.2.1994).

NOTE

1. Documents achievements from 1994 to 2006 only. Source: F.I.N.E. (2006).

References

PRIMARY SOURCES

AGICES (11 November 2005), *Pulling Fair Trade Leg*, available at http://www.babymilkaction.org/resources/yqsanswered/yqanestle07transfair.html.

BBC News (2 July 2006), *Nations unite for fair trade bid*, available at http://news.bbc.co.uk/2/hi/uk_news/wales/5138856.stm.

CTM Altromercato (30 January 2006), *Building a Strong National Association in Italy*, (powerpoint presentation), Bolzano, Italy.

Denaux, Guillermo (25 November 2004), New Office for Central America Outreach, *Welcome Letter to Luis Bran*.

Earley, Matt (11 February 2005), co-founder, Just Coffee, *Response to 'On Fair Trade Figleafs' article by Equal Exchange*.

Equal Exchange (2006), *Equal Exchange Corporate Governance Structure* (PDF file).

F.I.N.E. (2001), *Final Proposal for Improved Cooperation in Fair Trade. Fair Trade Definition and Strategic Aims*, available at www.eftafairtrade.org/definition.asp.

Kuapa Kokoo (2006), *Kuapa Kokoo Farmers' Trust and Fairtrade*.

Paulsen, O. (7 July 2005), *TNC-Owned Plantations in the Fairtrade Labelling System? with comments from Franz VanderHoff Boersma*, prepared for FLO Policy Considerations.

SECONDARY SOURCES

Abernathy, W. (1978), *The Productivity Dilemma: Roadblock to Innovation in the Automobile Industry*, Baltimore, MD: Johns Hopkins University Press.

Achrol, R. and P. Kotler (1999), 'Marketing in the network economy', *Journal of Marketing*, **63** (Special Issue), 146–63.

ActionAid (2003), *Competition Policy and the WTO*, available at: http://www.actionaid.org.

AgroFair (2006), *About AgroFair: Profile: Structure*, available at: http://www.agrofair.nl/pages/view.php?page_id=320.

AgroFair (2004), *The Oke Impact: 2004 Annual Report*, available at: http://www.agrofair.nl/pages/view.php?page_id=318.

Alcoff, L. (1990), 'Feminist Politics and Foucault: The Limits to a Collaboration', in A. Dallery and C. Scott (eds), *Crises in Continental Philosophy*, New York: SUNY Press, Chapter 6.

Allen, A. (2005), 'Feminist perspectives on power', *Stanford Encyclopaedia of Philosophy*, available at: http://plato.stanford.edu/entries/feminist-power.

Allen, J. (2003), *Lost Geographies of Power*, Malden, MA: Blackwell.

Aranda, J. and C. Morales (2002), 'Poverty alleviation through participation in fair trade coffee networks: the case of CEPCO, Oaxaca, Mexico', case study report prepared for Murray, D., L. Raynolds and P. Taylor (2003), *One Cup at a Time: Poverty Alleviation and Fair Trade Coffee in Latin America*, New York: The Ford Foundation.

Archer, M. (1990), 'Human agency and social structure: a critique of Giddens', in J. Clark, C. Modgil and S. Modgil (eds), *Anthony Giddens: Consensus and Controversy*, London: Falmer Press, Chapter 7.

Arendt, H. (1958), *The Human Condition*, Chicago, IL: University of Chicago Press.

Ayres, I. and J. Braithwaite (1992), *Responsive Regulation: Transcending the Deregulation Debate*, New York: Oxford University Press.

Bachrach, P. and M. Baratz (1970), *Power and Poverty: Theory and Practice*, New York: Oxford University Press.

Bacon, C. (2005), 'Confronting the coffee crisis: can fair trade, organic, and specialty coffees reduce small-scale farmer vulnerability in Northern Nicaragua?', *World Development*, **33**, 497–511.

Bain, J. (1956), *Barriers to New Competition: Their Character and Consequences in Manufacturing Industries*, Cambridge, MA: Harvard University Press.

Bakan, J. (2004), *The Corporation: The Pathological Pursuit of Profit and Power*, London: Constable and Robinson.

Bandura, A. (1982), 'Self-efficacy mechanism in human agency', *American Psychologist*, **37**(2), 122–47.

Bandura, A. (1986), *Social Foundations of Thought and Action: A Social Cognitive Theory*, Englewood Cliffs, NJ: Prentice-Hall.

Barber, R. (1966), 'Government and the consumer', *Michigan Law Review*, **64**(7), 1203–38.

Barnes, J. (1954), 'Class and committees in a Norwegian island parish', *Human Relations*, **7**, 39–58.

Barratt Brown, M. (1993), *Fair Trade: Reform and Realities in the International Trading System*, London: Zed Books.

Barrientos, S. and C. Dolan (eds) (2006), *Ethical Sourcing in the Global Food System*, London: Earthscan.

Barrientos, S. and S. Smith (2007), 'Mainstreaming fair trade in global production networks' in L. Raynolds, D. Murray and J. Wilkinson (eds), *Fair Trade. The Challenges of Transforming Globalisation*, New York: Routledge, Chapter 7.

Barsamian, D. (2000), 'Public relations: corporate spin and propaganda. An interview with Stuart Ewen', *Zmag*, available at: http://www.zmag.org/zmag// articles/barsamianewenmay2000.htm.

Bell, D. (1978), *The Coming of Post-industrial Society: A Venture in Social Forecasting*, New York: Basic Books.

Bellmann, C., M. Chamay, G. Dutfield, D. Vivas, A. Omer, C. Spennemann and T. Tesfachew (2005), *Resource Book on TRIPS and Development: An Authoritative and Practical Guide to the TRIPs Agreement* (ICTSD), available at: http://www.iprsonline.org/unctadictsd/docs/RB_2.14_update.pdf.

Benhabib, S. (1992), *Situating the Self: Gender, Community and Postmodernism in Contemporary Ethics*, New York: Routledge.

Benhabib, S., J. Butler, D. Cornell and N. Fraser (eds) (1995), *Feminist Contentions: A Philosophical Exchange*, New York: Routledge.

Berger, B. (1991), *The Culture of Entrepreneurship*, Richmond, CA: Institute for Contemporary Studies.

Berlin, I. (1958), 'Two concepts of liberty', an inaugural lecture delivered before the University of Oxford, 31 October.

Bevir, M. and R. Rhodes (2005), *Governance Stories*, London: Routledge.

Bezençon, V. and S. Blili (2006), 'Fair trade channels: are we killing the romantics?', *International Journal of Environmental, Cultural, Economic and Social Sustainability*, **2**(1), 187–96.

Bhagwati, J. (2005), *In Defense of Globalisation*, New York: Oxford University Press.

Binks, M. and P. Vale (1990), *Entrepreneurship and Economic Change*, Maidenhead, UK: McGraw-Hill.

Bohman, J. and W. Rehg (eds) (1997), *Deliberative Democracy. Essays on Reason and Politics*, Cambridge, MA: MIT Press.

Boorstin, D. (1974), *The Americans: The Democratic Experience*, New York: Vintage.

Bowles, S. and H. Gintis (1986), *Democracy and Capitalism: Property, Community and the Contradictions of Modern Social Thought*, London: Routledge & Kegan Paul.

Braithwaite, J. (1994), 'A sociology of modelling and the politics of empowerment', *The British Journal of Sociology*, **45**(3), 445–79.

Braithwaite, J. (2004), 'Methods of power for development: weapons of the weak, weapons of the strong', *Michigan Journal of International Law*, **26**(1), 298–330.

Braithwaite, J. and P. Drahos (2000), *Global Business Regulation*, Cambridge: Cambridge University Press.

Braithwaite, J., T. Makkai and V. Braithwaite (2007), *Regulating Aged Care. Ritualism and the New Pyramid*, Cheltenham, UK and Northampton, MA, USA: Edward Elgar.

Braithwaite, V. (1998), 'Designing the process of workplace change through the affirmative action act', in M. Gatens and A. Mackinnon (eds), *Gender and Institutions. Welfare, Work and Citizenship*, Cambridge: Cambridge University Press, ch. 7.

Braithwaite, V. (2009), *Defiance in Taxation and Governance: Resisting and Dismissing Authority in a Democracy*, Cheltenham, UK and Northampton, MA, USA: Edward Elgar.

Burris, S., P. Drahos and C. Shearing (2005), 'Nodal governance', *Australian Journal of Legal Philosophy*, **30**, 30–58.

Cafédirect (2004), *Cafédirect plc, 2003-2004 Annual Report and Accounts*, available at: http://www.cafedirect.co.uk.

Cafédirect (2005), *Cafédirect plc, 2004-2005 Annual Report and Accounts*, available at: http://www.cafedirect.co.uk.

Cafédirect (2006), *About Us*, available at: http://www.cafedirect.co.uk.

Caldwell, Z. and C. Bacon (2005), 'Fair trade's future: scaling up without selling out?', *One World*, 7 December, available at: http://us.oneworld.net/article/view/123087/1/.

Carr, E. (1946), *The Twenty Years Crisis, 1919–1939: An Introduction to the Study of International Relations*, London: Macmillan.

Casson, M. (ed.) (1990), *Entrepreneurship*, Aldershot, UK and Brookfield, VT, USA: Edward Elgar.

Castells, M. (1996), *The Rise of the Network Society*, Cambridge, MA: Blackwell.

Castells, M. (2000), *End of Millennium* (vol. 3), Oxford: Blackwell.

Cauthorn, C. (1989), *Contributions to a Theory of Entrepreneurship*, New York: Garland.

Certeau, M. de (1984), *The Practice of Everyday Life* (trans. S. Rendall), Berkeley, CA: University of California Press.

Chambers, R. (1997), *Whose Reality Counts? Putting the First Last*, London: Intermediate Technology Publications.

Chandler, A. (1962), *Strategy and Structure. Chapters in the History of Industrial Enterprise*, Cambridge, MA: MIT Press.

Chandler, A. (1964), *Giant Enterprise: Ford, General Motors, and the Automobile Industry: Sources and Readings*, New York: Harcourt, Brace and World.

Chandler, A., S. Bruchey and L. Galambos (eds) (1968), *The Changing Economic Order: Readings in American Business and Economic History*, New York: Harcourt, Brace and World.

Cheskin, L. (1959), *Why People Buy*, New York: Liveright Publishing Corporation.

Clegg, S. (1989), *Frameworks of Power*, London: Sage.

Cohen, R. and S. Rai (eds) (2000), *Global Social Movements*, London: Athlone Press.

Coleman, J. (1988), 'Social capital in the creation of human capital', *American Journal of Sociology*, **94** (Supplement: Organisations and Institutions: Sociological and Economic Approaches to the Analysis of Social Structure), S95–S120.

Commons, M. (2008), 'Fair trade products and supply chain certification. Consultation, round one', *The Organic Standard*, **86**(June), 13–14.

Coombe, R. (1998), *The Cultural Life of Intellectual Properties: Authorship, Appropriation and the Law*, Durham, NC: Duke University Press.

Cornish, W. and D. Llewelyn (2003), *Intellectual Property: Patents, Copyright, Trade Marks and Allied Rights*, 5th edn, London: Sweet and Maxwell.

Cornwall, A. (2002), 'Making spaces, changing places: situating participation in development', IDS Working Paper No. 170, Brighton: Institute for Development Studies (IDS).

Dahl, R. (1961), *Who Governs? Democracy and Power in an American City*, New Haven, CT: Yale University Press.

David, C. (2007), 'An alternative Fairtrade label for small producers to access mainstream markets' (project proposal), Asia Fair Trade Forum Inc./IFAT (personal copy).

Daviron, B. and S. Ponte (2005), *The Coffee Paradox: Commodity Trade and the Elusive Promise of Development*, London: Zed Books.

Dean, J.M. (2004), 'Conquering consumerspace: marketing strategies for a branded world' (book review), *The Journal of Consumer Marketing*, **21**(4), 360–61.

DevNet (Aotearoa New Zealand International Development Studies Network) (2006), 'Is fair trade really such a good idea?', available at: http://www.devnet.org.nz/forum/viewtopic.php?t=42.

Dicum, G. and N. Luttinger (1999), *The Coffee Book: Anatomy of an Industry from Crop to the Last Drop*, New York: The New Press.

Divine Chocolate Ltd (2005), *Chocolate Facts and Figures*, available at: http://www.divinechocolate.com.

Divine Chocolate Ltd (2006), *Divine Story in Full*, available at: http://www.divinechocolate.com.

Doherty, B. and J. Meehan (2004), 'Competing on social resources: the case of Day Chocolate Company in the UK confectionary sector' (unpublished paper), Liverpool John Moores University: The Management School.

Doppler, F. and A.A. González Cabañas (2006), 'Fair trade: benefits and drawbacks for producers', *Puente @ Europa*, **4**(2), 53–6.

Douglas, M. and B. Isherwood (2000), 'The uses of goods', in M. Lee (ed.), *The Consumer Society Reader*, Oxford: Blackwell, Chapter 6.

Drahos, P. (1996), *A Philosophy of Intellectual Property*, Aldershot, UK: Dartmouth.

Drahos, P. (2004), 'Towards an international framework for the protection of traditional group knowledge and practice' (draft paper prepared for the Commonwealth Secretariat), available at: http://www.unctad.org.

Drahos, P. (2005), 'Intellectual property rights in the knowledge economy', in D. Rooney (ed), *Handbook on the Knowledge Economy*, Cheltenham, UK and Northampton, MA, USA: Edward Elgar, Chapter 11.

Drahos, P. with J. Braithwaite (2002), *Information Feudalism*, London: Earthscan.

Drucker, P. (1966), *The Effective Executive*, New York: HarperCollins.

Drucker, P. (1969), *The Age of Discontinuity: Guidelines to our Changing Society*, New York: Harper & Row.

Drucker, P. (1985), *Innovation and Entrepreneurship: Practice and Principles*, New York: HarperBusiness.

Dryzek, J. (2000), *Deliberative Democracy: Liberals, Critics, and Contestations*, Oxford: Oxford University Press.

Dupont, B. (2006), 'Mapping security networks: from metaphorical concept to empirical model', in J. Fleming and J. Wood (eds), *Fighting Crime Together: The Challenges of Policing and Security Networks*, Sydney, Australia: University of New South Wales Press, Chapter 2.

Dzur, A. and M. Olson (2004), 'The value of community participation in restorative justice', *Journal of Social Philosophy*, 35(1), 91–107.

Economides, N. (1988), 'The economics of trademarks', *Trademark Reporter*, vol. 523.

The Economist (2007), 'Thinking out of the box: how African cocoa-growers are moving upstream into chocolate', 4 April, available at: http://www.economist.com.

Edelman, M. (1964), *The Symbolic Uses of Politics*, Urbana, IL: University of Illinois Press.

Eisenstadt, S. (1968), 'Social institutions: the concept', in D. Sills (ed.), *International Encyclopedia of the Social Sciences*, 14, 409–21. New York: Macmillan.

Elster, J. (ed.) (1998), *Deliberative Democracy*, Cambridge: Cambridge University Press.

Equal Exchange (2005a), *Twenty-Twenty Visioning: 2005 Annual Report*, available at: http://www.equalexchange.com/annual-reports.

Equal Exchange (2005b), *Fair Trade Coffee Pioneer Questions Nestlé's Entry into Market*, 7 October, available at: http://www.equalexchange.com/.

Estrella, M. and J. Gaventa (1997), 'Who counts reality? Participatory monitoring and evaluation: a literature review', IDS Working Paper No. 70.

Eyben, R., C. Harris and J. Pettit (eds) (2006), 'Power: exploring power for change', *IDS Bulletin*, 37(6), 1–10.

Fairtrade Foundation (2002), *Spilling the Beans on the Coffee Trade*, available at: http://www.fairtrade.org.uk.

Fairtrade Labelling Organisations International (FLO) (2005a), *Why FLO deals with Coffee*, available at: http://www.fairtrade.net/sites/products/coffee/why.html.

Fairtrade Labelling Organisations International (FLO) (2005b), *Delivering Opportunities: Annual Report 2004–5*, available at: http://www.fairtrade.net.

Fairtrade Labelling Organisations International (FLO) (2006a), *Building Trust: Annual Report 2005–6*, available at: http://www.fairtrade.net.

Fairtrade Labelling Organisations International (FLO) (2006b), *FLO 'New Model' Constitution (4th Draft)*.

Fairtrade Labelling Organisations International (FLO) (2007a), *Shaping Global Partnerships. Annual Report 2006/2007*, available at: http://www.fairtrade.net.

Fairtrade Labelling Organisations International (FLO) (2007b), *Standards Committee Statement on Fairtrade Coffee Price Review*, 19 January, available at: http://www.fairtrade.net/fileadmin/user_upload/content/Coffee_Statement.pdf.

Fairtrade Labelling Organisations International (FLO) (2007c), *Standards Committee Minutes. Item: Coffee Price Review 2006/2007*, 16 January available at: http://www.fairtrade.net/fileadmin/user_upload/content/Approved_SC_minutes_Jan_2007.pdf.

Fairtrade Labelling Organisations International (FLO) (2008), *An Inspiration for Change. Annual Report 2007*, available at: http://www.fairtrade.net.

Fair Trade Federation (FTF) (2006), *Fair Trade Federation website*, available at: http://www.fairtradefederation.org.

Faris, S. (2007), 'Starbucks vs. Ethiopia', *Fortune Magazine*, 5 March, available at: http://money.cnn.com.

Featherstone, M. (2000), 'Lifestyle and consumer culture', in M. Lee (ed.), *The Consumer Society Reader*, Oxford: Blackwell, Chapter 8.

F.I.N.E. (2006), *Business Unusual: Successes and Challenges of Fair Trade*, Brussels: F.I.N.E.

Fiske, J. (2000), 'The commodities of culture', in M. Lee (ed.), *The Consumer Society Reader*, Oxford: Blackwell, Chapter 25.

Fitter, R. and R. Kaplinsky (2001), 'Who gains from product rents as the coffee market becomes more differentiated? A value-chain analysis', *IDS Bulletin*, **32**(3), 69–82.

Fligstein, N. (1985), 'The spread of multidivisional form among large firms, 1919–1979', *American Sociological Review*, **52**, 377–91.

Follett, M. (1942), 'Power', in H. Metcalf and L. Urwick (eds), *The Collected Papers of Mary Parker Follett*, New York: Harper, Chapter IV, pp. 95–116.

Forrester, M. (2000), *Psychology of the Image*, London: Routledge.

Fortson, D. and L. Veevers (2007), 'The ethical espresso: Fairtrade firm to take on Starbucks', *The Independent*, 14 March.

Foster, J. and J.S. Metcalfe (2001), *Frontiers of Evolutionary Economics. Competition, Self-Organisation and Innovation Policy*, Cheltenham, UK and Northampton, MA, USA: Edward Elgar.

Foucault, M. (1977), *Discipline and Punish: The Birth of the Prison* (trans. A. Sheridan), New York: Vintage.

Foucault, M. (1979), *The History of Sexuality*, vol. 1 (trans. R. Hurley), New York: Vintage.

Fraser, N. (1989), *Unruly Practices: Power, Discourse and Gender in Contemporary Social Theory*, Minnesota, MN: University of Minnesota Press.

Freidmann, H. (1982), 'The political economy of food: the rise and fall of the postwar international food order', *The American Journal of Sociology* (Supplement: Marxist Inquiries: Studies of Labour, Class, and States), **88**, S248–S286.

Freire, P. (1996), *Pedagogy of the Oppressed*, London: Penguin Books.

Fridell, M., I. Hudson and M. Hudson (forthcoming), 'With friends like these: the corporate response to fair trade coffee', accepted journal paper for *Review of Radical Political Economics*, copy from authors.

Galbraith, K. (1976), *The Affluent Society*, Harmondsworth: Penguin Books.

Gardner, B. and S. Levy (1955), 'The product and the brand', *Harvard Business Review*, **69** (March/April), 33–9.

Gaventa, J. (1993), 'The powerful, the powerless and the experts: knowledge struggles in an information age', in P. Park, B. Hall and T. Jackson (eds), *Participatory Research in North America*, South Hadley, MA: Bergin and Garvey, Chapter 2, pp. 21–40.

Gaventa, J. (2006a), 'Finding the spaces for change: a power analysis', in R. Eyben, C. Harris and J. Pettit (eds), 'Power: exploring power for change', *IDS Bulletin*, **37**(6), 23–33.

Gaventa, J. (2006b), 'Triumph, deficit or contestation? Deepening the 'deepening democracy debate', IDS *Working Paper* No. 264.

Gaventa, J. and A. Cornwall (2001), 'Power and knowledge', in P. Reason and H. Bradbury (eds), *Handbook of Action Research: Participatory Inquiry and Practice*, London: Sage, pp. 70–80.

Gaventa, J. and A. Cornwall (2006), 'Power and knowledge', in R. Eyben, C. Harris and J. Pettit (eds), 'Power: exploring power for change', *IDS Bulletin*, **37**(6), 122–8.

Gereffi, G. (1994), 'The organisation of buyer-driven commodity chains: how U.S. retailers shape overseas production networks', in G. Gereffi and M. Korzeniewicz (eds), *Commodity Chains and Global Capitalism*, Westport, CT: Praeger, Chapter 5.

Gereffi, G. (1999), 'International trade and industrial upgrading in the apparel commodity chain', *Journal of International Economics*, **48**, 37–70.

Gereffi, G., J. Humphrey and J. Sturgeon (2005), 'The governance of global value chains', *Review of International Political Economy*, **12**, 78–104.

Gibbon, P. and S. Ponte (2005), *Trading Down. Africa, Value Chains, and the Global Economy*, Philadelphia, PA: Temple University Press.

Giddens, A. (1984), *The Constitution of Society: Outline of the Theory of Structuration*, Berkeley, CA: University of California Press.

Gilpin, R. (2001), *Global Political Economy: Understanding the International Economic Order*, Princeton, NJ: Princeton University Press.

Gladwell, M. (2000), *The Tipping Point: How Little Things can Make a Big Difference*, Boston, MA: Little Brown.

Global Exchange (2005), *Facts about Fair Trade and the Cocoa Industry*, available at: http://www.globalexchange.org/campaigns/fairtrade/cocoa/facts.html.

Golding, K. and K. Peattie (2005), 'In search of a golden blend: perspectives on the marketing of fair trade coffee', *Sustainable Development*, Special Issue 'Fair trade, business and sustainable development', **13**, 154–65.

Goodin, E. (ed.) (1996), *The Theory of Institutional Design*, Cambridge: Cambridge University Press.

Goodin, R. (2003), *Reflective Democracy*, Oxford: Oxford University Press.

Goodman, D. and M. Redclift (1991), *Refashioning Nature, Food, Ecology and Culture*, New York: Routledge.

Goodman, D., B. Sorj and J. Wilkinson (1987), *From Farming to Biotechnology: A Theory of Agro-Industrial Development*, Oxford: Basil Blackwell.

Goyder, M. (1998), *Living Tomorrow's Company*, Aldershot, UK: Gower Publishing.

References   217

Graham, C. and M. Peroff (1987), 'The legal side of branding', in J.M. Murphy (ed.), *Branding: A Key Marketing Tool*, London: Macmillan, Chapter 4, pp. 32–51.
Gramsci, A. (1971), *Selections from the Prison Notebooks* (ed. and trans. Q. Hoare and N. Smith), London: Lawrence & Wishart.
Granovetter, M. (1973), 'The strength of weak ties', *The American Journal of Sociology*, **78**(6), 1360–80.
Granovetter, M. (1983), 'The strength of weak ties: a network theory revisited', *Sociological Theory*, **1**, 201–33.
Gray, P. (1999), *Psychology*, 3rd edn, New York: Worth Publishers.
Green, D. (2005), 'Conspiracy of silence: old and new directions on commodities' (conference paper), Strategic Dialogue on Commodities, Trade, Poverty and Sustainable Development, 13–15 June, Faculty of Law, Barcelona.
Gusfield, J. (1963), *Symbolic Crusade: Status Politics and the American Temperance Movement*, Urbana, IL: University of Illinois Press.
Habermas, J. (1975), *Legitimation Crisis*, Boston, MA: Beacon Press.
Hall, B. (1981), 'Participatory research, popular knowledge and power: a personal reflection', *Convergence*, **XIV**(3), 6–17.
Hamilton, C. (2003), *Growth Fetish*, Crows Nest, NSW: Allen & Unwin.
Hanson, J. and D. Kysar (1990), 'Taking behaviouralism seriously: the problem of market manipulation', *New York University Law Review*, **74**, 630–749.
Harper, D. (1996), *Entrepreneurship and the Market Process: An Enquiry into the Growth of Knowledge*, London: Routledge.
Hartsock, N. (1990), 'Foucault on power: a theory for women?', in L. Nicholson (ed.), *Feminism/Postmodernism*, New York: Routledge, Chapter 7.
Haveman, H. (1992), 'Between a rock and a hard place: organisational change and performance under conditions of fundamental environmental transformation', *Administrative Science Quarterly*, **37**, 48–75.
Hayek, F. (1960), *The Constitution of Liberty*, London: Routledge & Kegan Paul.
Hayes, M. (2006), 'On the efficiency of fair trade', *Review of Social Economy*, **64**(4), 447–68.
Hayward, C. (1998), 'De-facing Power', *Polity*, **31**(1), 1–22.
Heffernan, W., M. Hendrickson and R. Gronski (1999), *Consolidation in the Food and Agriculture System*, Report to the National Farmers Union, University of Missouri, Columbia.
Held, V. (1993), *Feminist Morality: Transforming Culture, Society, and Politics*, Chicago, IL: University of Chicago Press.
Heydon, D. (1978), *Trade Practices Law: Restrictive Practices, Deceptive Conduct and Consumer Protection. Vol 1: Introduction and Restrictive Trade Practices*, Sydney: The Law Book Company.
Hoagland, S. (1988), *Lesbian Ethics: Toward a New Value*, Palo Alto, CA: Institute of Lesbian Studies.
Hobbes, T. (1991), *Leviathan*, New York: Cambridge University Press.
Holt, D., J. Quelch and E. Taylor (2004), 'How global brands compete', *Harvard Business Review*, September, 68–75.
Hood, G. (2007), 'Behind the label: as the fair trade movement evolves, farmers, activists and others fear that the meaning of the term will become corrupted', *Boulder Weekly*, 22 February, available at http://www.boulderweekly.com/archive/022207/coverstory.html.
Hudson, I. and M. Hudson (2003), 'How alternative is alternative trade? Alternative

trade coffee in the Chiapas region of Mexico' (draft/working paper), available at: http://fairtraderesource.org.

Hulme, D. and M.M. Turner (1990), *Sociology and Development: Theories, Policies and Practice*, New York: St Martin's Press.

Hutchens, A. (2007), 'Entrepreneurship, power and defiance: the globalisation of the fair trade movement', unpublished dissertation.

Hutchens, A. (forthcoming), 'Mainstreaming fair trade: fair trade brands and the problem of producer ownership' in K. MacDonald and S. Marshall (eds), *Fair Trade, Corporate Accountability & Beyond: Experiments in Globalising Justice*, Aldershot, UK: Ashgate.

International Fair Trade Association (IFAT) (2003), *The Whole World of Fair Trade: Strategic Plan 2003–2006*, available at: http://www.ifat.org.

International Fair Trade Association (IFAT) (2004), *Guidelines to Registering IFAT Members as Fair Trading Organisations*, available at: http://www.ifat.org.

International Fair Trade Association (IFAT) (2006a), *Mission Statement*, available at: http://www.ifat.org.

International Fair Trade Association (IFAT) (2006b), *Areas of Work*, available at: http://www.ifat.org.

International Fair Trade Association (IFAT) (2006c), *IFAT Organisational Structure*, available at: http://www.ifat.org.

International Fair Trade Association (IFAT) (2006d), *Discussion Paper for IFAT Regions on Membership and Monitoring* (prepared by A. Barrett and E. Davenport, IFAT Standards and Monitoring Sub-Committee).

International Fair Trade Association (IFAT) (2006e), *Memorandum of Agreement with IFAT Regions* (draft approved by IFAT Executive Committee).

International Fair Trade Association (IFAT) (2006f), *IFAT Strategic Plan 2007–2012* (powerpoint presentation).

International Fair Trade Association (IFAT) (2006g), *IFAT Membership Procedure and Policy Paper*.

International Fair Trade Association (IFAT) (2006h), *IFAT Constitution*.

International Fair Trade Association (IFAT) (2006i), *North America/Pacific Rim 2006 Regional Conference*, Christchurch, New Zealand, 4–6 August.

International Fair Trade Association (IFAT) (2006j), *About Fair Trade: Logos and Labels*, available at: http://www.ifat.org/index.php?option=com_content&task=view&id=3&Itemid=16.

International Fair Trade Association (IFAT) (2007a), *Welcome to IFAT* (Member Information Pack).

International Fair Trade Association (IFAT) (2007b), *Introduction to the Quality Management System (QMS)*, available at: http://www.ifat.org.

International Fair Trade Association (IFAT) (2008), *10 Standards of Fair Trade*, electronic resource, accessed 5 October 2008.

Jaffee, D. (2007), *Brewing Justice. Fair Trade Coffee, Sustainability, and Survival*, Berkeley, CA: University of California Press.

Johnston, L. and C. Shearing (2003), *Governing Security: Explorations in Policing and Justice*, London: Routledge.

Jung, H. (2006), 'Assessing the influence of cultural values on consumer susceptibility to social pressure for conformity: self-image enhancing motivations vs. information searching motivation', in L. Kahle and Chung-Hyun Kim (eds),

Creating Images and the Psychology of Marketing Communication, Mahwah, NJ: Lawrence Erlbaum Associates.

Just Business (2007a), *Cafédirect Company Case Study*, available at: http://www.jusbiz.org.

Just Business (2007b), *The Day Chocolate Company Case Study*, available at: http://www.justbiz.org/DAYchocolate.shtml.

Kabeer, N. (1994), *Reversed Realities: Gender Hierarchies in Development Thought*, London: Verso.

Kaplinsky, R. (2006), 'How can agricultural commodity producers appropriate a greater share of value chain incomes?', in A. Sarris and D. Hallam, *Agricultural Commodity Markets and Trade. New Approaches to Analysing Market Structure and Instability*, Cheltenham, UK and Northampton, MA, USA: Edward Elgar, Chapter 14.

Kaplinsky, R. and M. Morris (2001), *A Handbook for Value Market Chain Research*, Canada: IDRC.

Keohane, R. (1984), *After Hegemony: Cooperation and Discord in the World Political Economy*, Princeton, NJ: Princeton University Press.

Keohane, R. and J. Nye (2000), 'Introduction', in J. Nye and J. Donahue (eds), *Governance in a Globalising World*, Washington, DC: Brookings Institution Press.

Kirzner, I. (1985), *Discovery and the Capitalist Process*, Chicago, IL: University of Chicago Press.

Klein, N. (2000), *No Logo: Taking Aim at the Brand Bullies*, New York: Picador.

Kocken, M. (2003), *Fifty Years of Fair Trade*, available at: http://www.ifat.org.

Krasner, S. (1991), 'State power and the structure of international trade', in J. Freiden and D. Lake (eds), *International Political Economy: Perspectives on Global Power and Wealth*, 2nd edn, New York: St Martin's Press, Chapter 3.

Krier, J.-M. (2005), *Fair Trade in Europe: Facts and Figures in 25 European Countries*, Brussels: F.I.N.E.

Kruger, S. and A. du Toit (2007), 'Reconstructing fairness: Fair Trade conventions and worker empowerment in South African horticulture', in L. Raynolds, D. Murray and J. Wilkinson (eds), *Fair Trade. The Challenges of Transforming Globalization*, Oxford: Routledge, Chapter 12.

Kumar, K. (1995), *From Post-Industrial to Post-Modern Society. New Theories of the Contemporary World*, Boston, MA: Blackwell.

Kuyichi (2007a), *About Kuyichi*, available at: http://www.kuyichi.com.

Kuyichi (2007b), *Our Mission: Fair Trade*, available at: http://www.kuyichi.com.

Kuyichi (2007c), *Track&Trace*, available at: http://www.kuyichi.com.

Landes, W. and R. Posner (1987), 'Trademark law: an economic perspective', *Journal of Law & Economics*, **30**, 265–309.

Latour, B. (1986), 'The powers of association', in J. Law (ed.), *Power, Action and Belief: A New Sociology of Knowledge?* (Sociological Review Monograph 32), London: Routledge & Kegan Paul, Chapter 11, pp. 264–80.

Lefebvre, H. (1991), *The Production of Space*, London: Verso.

Leslie, D. and S. Reimer (1999), 'Spatialising commodity chains', *Progress in Human Geography*, **23**, 401–20.

Levi, M. and A. Linton (2003), 'Fair trade: a cup at a time', *Politics and Society*, **31**(3), 407–32.

Lewin, K. (1946), 'Action research and minority problems', *Journal of Social Issues*, **2**, 34–46.

Lin, N. (2001), 'Building a Network Theory of Social Capital', in N. Lin, K. Cook and R. Burt, *Social Capital: Theory and Research*, New York: Aldine de Gruyter, Chapter 1, pp. 3–29.

Lindsey, B. (2004), *Grounds for Complaint: Fair Trade and the Coffee Crisis*, London: Adam Smith Institute/Cato Institute.

Litrell, M. and M. Dickson (1999), *Social Responsibility in the Global Market: Fair Trade of Cultural Products*, Thousand Oaks, CA: Sage.

Loasby, B. (1999), *Knowledge, Institutions, and Evolution in Economics*, London: Routledge.

Low, W. and E. Davenport (2005), 'Postcards from the edge: maintaining the "alternative" character of fair trade', in W. Young and K. Utting (eds), 'Editorial: Fair Trade, Business and Sustainable Development', *Sustainable Development*, **13**, 143–53.

Low, W. and E. Davenport (2006), 'Mainstreaming fair trade: adoption, assimilation, appropriation', *Journal of Strategic Marketing*, **14**(4), 315–27.

Lukes, S. (1974), *Power: A Radical View*, London: Macmillan Press.

Lukes, S. (2005), *Power: A Radical View*, 2nd edn, London: Macmillan Press.

Lunney, G. (1999), 'Trademark monopolies', *Emory Law Journal*, **48**(2), 367–487.

Lury, C. (2004), *Brands. The Logos of the Global Economy*, Oxford: Routledge.

MADE-BY (2005a), *MADE-BY Annual Report*, available at: http://www.made-by.nl.

MADE-BY (2005b), *MADE-BY in short*, available at: http://www.made-by.nl.

MADE-BY (2007), *What does MADE-BY do?*, available at: http://www.made-by.nl.

Markusen, J., J. Melvin, W. Kaempfer and K. Maskus (1995), *International Trade. Theory and Evidence*, New York: McGraw-Hill, chs 4 and 5.

Martyn, T. (2007), 'Capturing the intangible: accessing marketing rents through farmer-own Brands', Masters dissertation, Faculty of Economics (Development Studies), London School of Economics (LSE) (unpublished), submitted 31 August, 2007.

McAlexander, J., J. Schouten and H. Koenig (2002), 'Building brand community', *Journal of Marketing*, **66**(1), 38–54.

McClelland, D. and D. Winter (1964), *Motivating Economic Achievement*, New York: Free Press.

McGrath, R. and I. MacMillan (2000), *The Entrepreneurial Mindset. Strategies for Continuously Creating Opportunity in an Age of Uncertainty*, Boston, MA: Harvard Business School Press.

McLaren, M. (2002), *Feminism, Foucault, and Embodied Subjectivity*, New York: SUNY Press.

McMichael, P. (2000), 'The power of food', *Agriculture and Human Values*, **17**, 21–33.

McNay, L. (1992), *Foucault and Feminism: Power, Gender and the Self*, Boston, MA: Northeastern University Press.

McWhorter, L. (1999), *Bodies and Pleasure: Foucault and the Politics of Sexual Normalisation*, Indiana, IN: Indiana University Press.

Mendez, V. (2002), 'Fair trade networks in two coffee cooperatives of western El Salvador: an analysis of insertion through a second level organisation', available at http://www.colostate.edu/Depts/Sociology.

Milgram, S. (1974), *Obedience to Authority*, London: Tavistock.

Miller, J. (1982), *Women and Power: Some Psychological Dimensions*, Wellesley, MA: Stone Centre.

Morgenthau, H. (1948), *Politics Among Nations: The Struggle for Power and Peace*, New York: Alfred A. Knopf.

Morissett, J. (1997), *Unfair Trade? Empirical Evidence in World Commodity Markets over the past 25 Years*, Washington, DC: World Bank.

Moscovici, S., A. Mucchi-Faina and A. Maass (eds) (1994), *Minority Influence*, Chicago, IL: Nelson-Hall Publishers.

Mouffe, C. (1992), 'Feminism, citizenship and radical democratic politics', in J. Butler and J.W. Scott (eds), *Feminists Theorise the Political*, New York: Routledge, Chapter 17.

Murdoch, J., T. Marsden and J. Banks (2000), 'Quality, nature, and embeddedness: some theoretical considerations in the context of the food sector', *Economic Geography*, **76**, 107–25.

Murphy, S. (1999), 'Market power in agricultural markets: some issues for developing countries', T.R.A.D.E. Working Papers No. 6, South Centre.

Murphy, S. (2002), *Managing the Invisible Hand. Markets, Farmers and International Trade*, Minneapolis, MN: Institute for Agriculture and Trade Policy (IATP).

Murray, D. and L. Raynolds (2000), 'Alternative trade in bananas: obstacles and opportunities for progressive social change in the global economy', *Agriculture and Human Values*, **17**, 65–74.

Murray, D., L. Raynolds and P. Taylor (2003), *One Cup at a Time: Poverty Alleviation and Fair Trade Coffee in Latin America*, New York: The Ford Foundation.

Navarro, Z. (2006), 'In search of a cultural interpretation of power: the contribution of Pierre Bourdieu', in R. Eyben, C. Harris and J. Pettit (eds), 'Power: exploring power for change', *IDS Bulletin*, **37**(6), 11–22.

Nelson, R. (2001), 'The co-evolution of technology and institutions as the driver of economic growth', in J. Foster and J.S. Metcalfe (eds), *Frontiers of Evolutionary Economics. Competition, Self-Organisation and Innovation Policy*, Cheltenham, UK and Northampton, MA, USA: Edward Elgar, Chapter 2.

Nelson, R. and S. Winter (1982), *An Evolutionary Theory of Economic Change*, Cambridge: Cambridge University Press.

Nelson, N. and S. Wright (1995), 'Participation and power', in N. Nelson and S. Wright (eds), *Power and Participatory Development: Theory and Practice*, London: Intermediate Technology Publications, pp. 1–18.

New Internationalist (1973), 'The baby food tragedy', No. 6.

New Internationalist (2006), 'Have your say on the future of fair trade', available at: http://interact.newint.org/have-your-say-on-the-future-of-fair-trade.

Nicholls, A. and C. Opal (2005), *Fair Trade: Market-Driven Ethical Consumption*, London: Sage.

Nooteboom, B. (2001), 'From evolution to language and learning,' in J. Foster and J.S. Metcalfe (eds), *Frontiers of Evolutionary Economics. Competition, Self-Organisation and Innovation Policy*, Cheltenham, UK and Northampton, MA, USA: Edward Elgar, Chapter 3.

Normann, R. and R. Ramirez (1993), 'From value chain to value constellation: designing interactive strategy', *Harvard Business Review*, **71**(4), 65–77.

North, D. (1990), *Institutions, Institutional Change and Economic Performance*, Cambridge: Cambridge University Press.

North, R. (2003a), 'Building mission into structure at Equal Exchange,' in M.

Kelly, 'The legacy problem: why social mission gets squeezed out of firms when they're sold, and what to do about it', *Business Ethics Magazine* **1**(2), available at: http://www.business-ethics.com.

North, R. (2006), 'On fair trade "fig leaves": Equal Exchange speaks out on abuse of the fair trade system', 10 February USFT listserv. Edited version published in *The Wedge Newsletter*, Feb.–March issue, available at: http://www.wedge.coop/newsletter/article/630.html.

Nussbaum, M. and A. Sen (eds) (1993), *Quality of Life*, Oxford: Oxford University Press.

Nygren, A. (1999), 'Local knowledge in the environment–development discourse. From dichotomies to situated knowledges', *Critique of Anthropology*, **19**(3), 267–88.

O'Malley, P. (1996), 'Indigenous governance', *Economy and Society*, **25**(3), 310–26.

O'Malley, P., L. Weir and C. Shearing (1997), 'Governmentality, criticism, politics', *Economy and Society*, **26**(4), 501–17.

Onyx, J. and P. Benton (1995), 'Empowerment and ageing: toward honoured places', in M. Mayo and G. Craig (eds), *Community Empowerment: A Reader in Participation and Development*, London: Zed Books, Chapter 5.

Organic Trader (2006), *Fair Trade: Who Grows Cocolo Chocolate: El Ceibo*, available at: http://www.cocolo.com.au/fairtrade.html.

O'Shaughnessy, J. and N.J. O'Shaughnessy (2002), *The Marketing Power of Emotion*, Oxford: Oxford University Press.

Osterhaus, A. (2006), 'World trade contradictions and the fair trade response', in F.I.N.E. (ed.), *Business Unusual: Successes and Challenges of Fair Trade*, Brussels: Fair Trade Advocacy Office, Chapter 2.

Oxfam International (2001), *International Commodity Research – The Coffee Market: a Background Study*, available at http://www.maketradefair.com/en/assets/english/BackgroundStudyCoffeeMarket.pdf.

Oxfam International (2002), *The Coffee Report – Mugged: Poverty in your Coffee Cup*, available at http://www.oxfam.org.uk/what_we_do/issues/key_papers.htm.

Oxfam International (2004), *Trading Away our Rights: Women Working in Global Supply Chains*, available at http://www.oxfam.org.uk/what_we_do/issues/key_papers.htm.

Packard, V. (1981), *The Hidden Persuaders*, New York: Penguin Books Ltd.

Parker, C. and J. Braithwaite (2003), 'Regulation', in P. Cane and M. Tushnet (eds), *Oxford Handbook of Legal Studies*, Oxford: Oxford University Press, pp. 119–45.

Parkinson, J. and D. Roche (2004), 'Restorative justice: deliberative democracy in action?', *Australian Journal of Political Science*, **39**(3), 505–18.

Pérez-Grovas, V. and E. Cervantes (2002), 'Poverty alleviation through participation in fair trade coffee networks: the case of Union Majomut, Chiapas, Mexico', available at: http://www.colostate.edu/Depts/Sociology.

Pimbert, M. (2001), 'Reclaiming our right to power: some conditions for deliberative democracy', in M. Pimbert and P. Wakeford (eds), *Deliberative Democracy and Citizen Empowerment*, London: IIED, Chapter 21.

Pimbert, M. and P. Wakeford (2001), 'Overview – deliberative democracy and citizen empowerment', in M. Pimbert and P. Wakeford (eds) (2001), *Deliberative Democracy and Citizen Empowerment*, London: IIED, Chapter 5.

Piore, M. and C. Sabel (1984), *The Second Industrial Divide. Possibilities for Prosperity*, New York: Basic Books.

Porter, M. (1980), *Competitive Strategy: Techniques for Analysing Industries and Competitors*, New York: Free Press.

Portes, A. (1998), 'Social capital: its origins and applications in modern sociology', *Annual Review of Sociology*, **24**, 1–24.

Przeworski, A. (1998), 'Deliberation and ideological domination', in J. Elster (ed.), *Deliberative Democracy*, Cambridge: Cambridge University Press, Chapter 6.

Putnam, R. (2000), *Bowling Alone: The Collapse and Revival of American Community*, New York: Simon & Schuster.

Putnam, R. (with R. Leonardi and Y.N. Raffaella) (1993), *Making Democracy Work: Civic Traditions in Modern Italy*, Princeton, NJ: Princeton University Press.

Rahman, M. (1991), 'The theoretical standpoint of PAR', in O. Fals-Borda and M. Rahman (eds), *Action and Knowledge: Breaking the Monopoly with Participatory Action-Research*, New York: The Apex Press and London: Intermediate Technology Publications, pp. 13–23.

Ramazzotti, P. (2001), 'Commentary: from evolution to language and learning', in J. Foster and J.S. Metcalfe, *Frontiers of Evolutionary Economics. Competition, Self-Organisation and Innovation Policy*, Cheltenham, UK and Northampton, MA, USA: Edward Elgar, Chapter 3.

Ransom, D. (2005), 'The wrong label?', *New Internationalist* (Special Features), 17 October, available at: http://www.newint.org/features.

Raynolds, L. (2000), 'Re-embedding global agriculture: the international organic and fair trade movements', *Agriculture and Human Movements*, **17**, 297–309.

Raynolds, L. (2002), 'Consumer/producer links in fair trade coffee networks', *Sociologia Ruralis*, **42**(4), 404–24.

Raynolds, L. (2004), 'The globalization of organic agro-food networks', *World Development*, **32**, 725–43.

Raynolds, L. (2007), 'Fair trade bananas: broadening the movement and market in the United States', in L. Raynolds, D. Murray and J. Wilkinson (eds), *Fair Trade. The Challenges of Transforming Globalisation*, Oxford: Routledge, Chapter 5.

Raynolds, L. and D. Murray (2007), 'Fair Trade: contemporary challenges and future prospects', in L. Raynolds, D. Murray and J. Wilkinson (eds), *Fair Trade. The Challenges of Transforming Globalization*, Oxford: Routledge, Chapter 13, pp. 223–35.

Raynolds, L., D. Murray and P. Taylor (2004), 'Fair trade coffee: building producer capacity via global networks', *Journal of International Development*, **16**, 1109–21.

Raynolds, L., D. Murray and J. Wilkinson (eds) (2007), *Fair Trade. The Challenges of Transforming Globalisation*, Oxford: Routledge.

Redfern, A. and P. Snedker (2002), 'Creating market opportunities for small enterprises: experiences of the Fair Trade movement', SEED Working Paper No. 30, Geneva: International Labour Organization.

Renard, M.-C. (2003), 'Fair trade quality, market and conventions', *Journal of Rural Studies*, **19**, 87–96.

Renard, M.-C. (2005), 'Quality certification, regulation and power in fair trade', *Journal of Rural Studies*, **21**, 419–31.

Renard, M.-C. and V. Pérez-Grovas (2007), 'Fair trade coffee in Mexico. At the center of the debates', in L. Raynolds, D. Murray and J. Wilkinson (eds) (2007), *Fair Trade. The Challenges of Transforming Globalisation*, Oxford: Routledge, Chapter 9.

Renkema, D. (2002), 'Coffee: the speculators' plaything', in European Fair Trade Association (EFTA), *EFTA Yearbook: Challenges of Fair Trade 2001–2003*, available at: http://www.eftafairtrade.org.

Reuters (2007), 'Starbucks, Ethiopia settle licensing dispute', 21 June, available at: http://www.reuters.com.

Rhodes, R. (1997), *Understanding Governance: Policy Networks, Governance, Reflexivity, and Accountability*, Buckingham: Open University Press.

Ricardo, D. (1976), *Principles of Political Economy and Taxation* (reprint), London: J.M. Dent.

Ricketson, S. and M. Richardson (2005), *Intellectual Property. Cases, Materials and Commentary*, 3rd edn, Chatswood, NSW: LexisNexis Butterworths.

Robbins, P. (2003), *Stolen Fruit: The Tropical Commodities Disaster*, New York: Zed Books.

Robert, M. and A. Weiss (1988), *The Innovation Formula. How Organisations Turn Change into Opportunity*, Cambridge, MA: Ballinger.

Rose, N. and P. Miller (1992), 'Political power beyond the state: problematics of government', *The British Journal of Sociology*, **43**(2), 173–205.

Rowlands, J. (1995), 'Empowerment examined', *Development in Practice*, **5**(2), 101–7.

Rowlands, J. (1997), *Questioning Empowerment: Working with Women in Honduras*, London: Oxfam Publishing.

Rowlands, J. (1998), 'A word of our times, but what does it mean? Empowerment in the discourse and practice of development', in H. Afshar (ed.), *Women and Empowerment: Illustrations from the Third World*, New York: St Martin's Press, Chapter 1.

Sawicki, J. (1991), *Disciplining Foucault: Feminism, Power, and the Body*, New York: Routledge.

Schaper, M. and T. Volery (2002), *Entrepreneurship and Small Business: An Asia-Pacific Guide*, 3rd edn, Guilford, Western Australia: Vineyard Publishing.

Schrank, A. (2004), 'Ready-to-wear development? Foreign investment, technology transfer, and learning by watching in the apparel trade', *Social Forces*, **83**(1), 123–56.

Schumpeter, J. (1934), *The Theory of Economic Development: An Inquiry into Profits, Capital, Credit, Interest and the Business Cycle*, Cambridge, MA: Harvard University Press.

Schumpeter, J. (1943), *Capitalism, Socialism and Democracy*, London: Allen & Unwin.

Schumpeter, J. (1949), 'Economic theory and entrepreneurial history', in Harvard University Research Center in Entrepreneurial History, *Change and the Entrepreneur: Postulates and Patterns for Entrepreneurial History*, Cambridge, MA: Harvard University Press, pp. 63–84.

Scott, C. (2004), 'Regulation in the age of governance: the rise of the post-regulatory state', in J. Jordana and D. Levi-Faur, *The Politics of Regulation*, Cheltenham, UK and Northampton, MA, USA: Edward Elgar, Chapter 7.

Scott, J.C. (1985), *Weapons of the Weak: Everyday Forms of Peasant Resistance*, New Haven, CT: Yale University Press.

Shah, A. (2006), *Poverty Facts and Stats*, 3 April, available at http://www.globalis-sues.org/TradeRelated/Facts.asp#fact1.

Shearing, C. and J. Wood (2003), 'Nodal governance, democracy and the new "denizens": challenging the Westphalian ideal', *Journal of Law and Society*, **480**, 400–419.

Shreck, A. (2005), 'Resistance, redistribution, and power in the fair trade banana initiative', *Agriculture and Human Values*, **22**, 17–29.

Simons, J. (1995), *Foucault & the Political*, New York: Routledge.

Slaughter, A.-M. (1997), 'The real new world order', *Foreign Affairs*, **76**, 183–97.

Slob, B. (2006), 'A fair share for coffee producers', in F.I.N.E. (ed.), *Business Unusual: Successes and Challenges of Fair Trade*, Brussels: Fair Trade Advocacy Office, Chapter 7.

Solomon, M.R. (2003), *Conquering Consumerspace: Marketing Strategies for a Branded World*, New York: Amacom.

Starhawk, M. (1987), *Truth or Dare: Encounters with Power, Authority and Mystery*, San Francisco, CA: Harper & Row.

Stevenson, H. and W. Sahlman (eds) (1991), *Introduction to the Entrepreneurial Venture*, Boston, MA: Harvard Business School Press.

Stevenson, H. and A. William (1986), 'Importance of entrepreneurship in economic development', in R. Hisrich (ed.), *Entrepreneurship, Intrapreneurship, and Venture Capital: The Foundations of Economic Renaissance*, Canada: Lexington Books, pp. 3–26.

Stevenson, H., M. Roberts, W. Sahlman, P. Marshall and R. Hamermesh (eds) (2006), *New Business Ventures and the Entrepreneur*, 6th edn, New York: McGraw-Hill/Irwin.

Sweney, M. (2001), 'Nestlé plots entry into fair trade coffee market', *Marketing*, No. 1, 6 May.

Szreter, S. (2001), 'A new political economy: the importance of social capital', in A. Giddens (ed.), *The Global Third Way Debate*, London: Polity Press, Chapter 21.

Tajfel, H. (ed.) (1978), *Differentiation between Social Groups: Studies in the Social Psychology of Intergroup Relations*, London: Academic Press.

Talbot, J.M. (1997a), 'Where does your coffee dollar go? The division of income and surplus along the coffee commodity chain', *Studies in Comparative International Development*, **32**(1), 56–91.

Talbot. J.M. (1997b), 'The struggle for control of a commodity chain: instant coffee from Latin America', *Latin American Research Review*, **32**(2), 117–36.

Tallontire, A. (2000), 'Partnerships in fair trade: reflections from a case study of Cafédirect', *Development in Practice*, **10**(2), 166–77.

Tallontire, A. (2002), 'Challenges facing fair trade: which way now?', *Small Enterprise Development*, **13**(3), 12–24.

Tallontire, A. (2006), 'The development of alternative and fair trade: moving into the mainstream', in S. Barrientos and C. Dolan (eds), *Ethical Sourcing in the Global Food System*, London: Earthscan, Chapter 2.

Taylor, P. (2002), 'Poverty alleviation through participation in fair trade coffee networks: synthesis of case study research question findings', available at: http://www.colostate.edu/Depts/Sociology.

Tiffen, P. and S. Zadek (1998), 'Dealing with and in the global economy: fairer trade in Latin America', in J. Blauert and S. Zadek (eds), *Mediating Sustainability: Growing Policy from the Grassroots*, Bloomfield, CT: Kumarian Press, Chaper 6.

Toffler, A. (1980), *The Third Wave*, New York: Morrow.

Townsend, J., E. Zapata, J. Rowlands, P. Alberti and M. Mercado (1999), *Women and Power: Fighting Patriarchies and Poverty*, London: Zed Books.

Traidcraft (2003), 'Fairtrade provides models for corporate social responsibility', *Traidcraft Policy Unit Briefing Series on Fair Trade*, available at http://www.traidcraft.org.uk.

Traidcraft (2004), 'Corporate social responsibility – does it make any difference?' *Traidcraft Policy Unit Briefing Series on Fair Trade*, October available at http://www.traidcraft.org.uk.

Tucker, A. (2006), 'Fair enough?', *New Internationalist*, No. 395, available at: http://www.newint.org/features/2006/11/01/fairtrade/, accessed 1 August 2008.

Twin Trading (2006), *About Us: An Incubator for Fair Trade Brands*, available at http://www.twin.org.uk.

United Nations Development Program (UNDP) (2005), *Human Development Report 'International Cooperation at a Crossroads: Aid, Trade and Security in an Unequal World'*, New York: UNDP.

United Students for Fair Trade (USFT) (Coordinating Committee) (2007a), *Letter to FLO Board on Minimum Price Issue Decision*.

United Students for Fair Trade (USFT), (e-zine) (2007b), *A Different Perspective on the Minimum Price Debate*.

Van Caenegem, W. (2003), 'Registered geographical indications. Between intellectual property and rural policy – Part 1', *The Journal of World Intellectual Property*, **6**(5), 699–719.

VanderHoff Boersma, F. (2002), 'Poverty alleviation through participation in fair trade coffee networks: the case of UCIRI, Oaxaca, Mexico', case study report prepared for D. Murray, L. Raynolds and P. Taylor (2003), *One Cup at a Time: Poverty Alleviation and Fair Trade Coffee in Latin America*, New York: The Ford Foundation.

VeneKlasen, L. and V. Miller (2002), *A New Weave of Power, People and Politics: The Action Guide for Advocacy and Citizen Participation*, Oklahoma City, OK: World Neighbours.

Vorley, B. (2003), *Food, Inc.: Corporate Concentration from Farm to Consumer*, London: IIED.

Weber, M. (1958), *The Protestant Ethic and the Spirit of Capitalism* (trans. T. Parsons), New York: Scribner.

Weber, M. (1978), *Economy and Society: An Outline of Interpretive Sociology* (trans. Fischoff et al.), Berkeley, CA: University of California Press.

Whatmore, S. and L. Thorne (1997), 'Nourishing networks: alternative geographies of food', in D. Goodman and M. Watts (eds), *Globalising Food: Agrarian Questions and Global Responses*, London: Routledge, pp. 287–304.

Wild, A. (2005), 'Coffee: good to the last drop?', *The Globalist*, 4 August, available at http://www.theglobalist.com/DBWeb/printStoryId.aspx?StoryId=4703.

Wilkinson, J. and G. Mascarenhas (2007a), 'Southern social movements and fair trade', in L. Raynolds, D. Murray and J. Wilkinson (eds) (2007), *Fair Trade. The Challenges of Transforming Globalisation*, Oxford: Routledge, Chapter 8.

Wilkinson, J. and G. Mascarenhas (2007b), 'The making of the fair trade movement in the South. The Brazilian case', in L. Raynolds, D. Murray and J. Wilkinson (eds) (2007), *Fair Trade. The Challenges of Transforming Globalisation*, Oxford: Routledge, Chapter 10.

Wills, C. (2006), 'Fair Trade: what's it all about?', in F.I.N.E. (ed.), *Business Unusual: Successes and Challenges of Fair Trade*, Brussels: F.I.N.E.
Wood, J. and C. Shearing (2007), *Imagining Security*, Devon, UK: Willan Publishing.
Young, I.M. (2004), 'Responsibility and global justice: a social connections model', paper presented at 'Global Justice' Conference, Bowling Green State University, Bowling Green, Ohio, 21–23 October.
Young, W. and K. Utting (eds) (2005), 'Editorial: fair trade, business and sustainable development', *Sustainable Development*, **13**, 139–42.
Zapata, E. (1999), '"Power with": getting organised', in J. Townsend, E. Zapata, J. Rowlands, P. Alberti and M. Mercado, *Women and Power: Fighting Patriarchies and Poverty*, London: Zed Books, Chapter 5, pp. 85–107.

PERSONAL INTERVIEWS (IN PERSON/EMAIL/ PHONE)

Atorf, Lars, (27 July 2005), Coffee Manager, Procter & Gamble.
Benesh, Melanie (22 June 2005), USFT Convergence 2005 co-Coordinator.
Bretman, Ian (3 May 2005), Deputy Director, Fairtrade Foundation UK.
Byrde, Rosemary (29 April 2005), Global Adviser on Fairtrade/Fair Trade, Oxfam Great Britain.
Casasbeunas, Constantino (5 May 2005), Policy Adviser, Oxfam International.
Coates, Barry (13 June 2005), Executive Director, Oxfam New Zealand.
Curnow, Joe (25 June 2005), USFT Convergence 2005 co-Coordinator.
Dalvai, Rudi (13 April 2005; 9 November 2005; 2 February 2007; 7 February 2007), Co-founder, CTM Altromercato, Italy/former Chair and Europe Regional Representative, Executive Committee, IFAT.
DeCarlo, Jackie (30 June 2005), author, *Fair Trade: A Beginner's Guide*, former Executive Director, Fair Trade Resource Network (FTRN).
De Clerck, Miguel (28 April 2005), Director, Max Havelaar Belgium.
Deighton, Paul (20 April 2006), Executive Director, New Internationalist/America and Pacific Rim Regional Representative, Executive Committee, IFAT.
Douglas, Jeroen (12 April 2005), Director of Fairtrade fruit and cotton, Fair Trade Programme, Solidaridad.
Earley, Matt (23 June 2005), Co-founder, Just Coffee.
Easson, Kimberly (15 July 2005), Director, Strategic Relationships, Transfair USA.
Eshuis, Fenny (11 April 2005), Executive Director, Max Havelaar Netherlands.
Ford, Sarah (14 July 2005), former Policy Director, Public Policy, Lutheran World Relief (LWR).
Gorman, Erin (12 July 2005), CEO, Divine Chocolate Ltd, USA/former Director, Fair Trade Program, Co-op America.
Guzzi, Jamie (10 May 2005), Fair Trade Chocolate Campaign Coordinator, Global Exchange.
Kocken, Marlike. Manager, European Fair Trade Association (EFTA), personal communication, 23 May 2005.
Leheup, Patrick (April 18 2005), Commodity Sourcing Manager for Coffee and Beverages, Strategic Business Unit, Nestlé.

Lingle, Ted (6 July 2005), Executive Director, Specialty Coffee Association of America (SCAA).

Meckel, Martina (30 March 2007), FLO Member Communications Officer.

Mecklenburg, Sue (12 July 2005), Vice-President, Sustainable Procurement Practices, Starbucks.

Meyer, Martin (27 June 2005), Corporate Affairs, Kraft Europe.

Miltenburg, Stefanie (30 June 2005), Sara Lee DE.

Novey, Joelle (5 June 2006), Membership Coordinator, Fair Trade Federation (FTF USA).

Osterhaus, Anja (3 April 2005), Coordinator, Fair Trade Advocacy Office.

Pare, Simon (4 July 2005), former Research & Development Division, Max Havelaar France/former President, Fairtrade Labelling Organisations International (FLO).

Paulsen, Olaf (14 April 2005), Former Director, Standards & Policy Unit, Fairtrade Labelling Organisations International (FLO).

Petchers, Seth (19 July 2005), Coffee Program Manager, Oxfam America.

Peyser, Rick (22 June 2005), Social Advocacy & Media Relations, Green Mountain Coffee Roasters, USA.

Rosenberg, David (7 April 2005), Director, Utz Kapeh.

Rosenthal, Jonathan (6 July 2005; 26 October 2005), Co-founder, Equal Exchange.

Schmitz-Hoffman, Carsten (10 June 2005), Secretariat Coordinator, Common Code for the Coffee Community (CCCC).

Sellers, Steve (10 May 2005), former Chief Operating Officer (COO), Transfair USA.

Shimizu-Larenas, Marietta (9 June 2006), Assistant to the Director, International Fair Trade Association (IFAT).

Tiffen, Pauline (19 August 2005; 25 October 2005), former Director, Third World Information Network (TWIN)/founder, Cafédirect and Divine Chocolate Ltd/Director, Strategic Planning, LightYears IP/Board Director, Fair Trade Federation (FTF) USA.

Tranchell, Sophi (5 May 2005), Managing Director, Divine Chocolate Ltd, UK.

Tucker, Albert (16 June 2005), Managing Director, Third World Information Network (TWIN).

Uit de Bosch, Herman (13 April 2005), former Project Coordinator, International Markets, Fair Economic Development Program, Interchurch Organisation for Development Cooperation (ICCO).

Van Beuningen, Coen (11 April 2005), Humanist Institute for Development Cooperation (HIVOS).

VanderHoff Boersma, Francisco (23 December 2005; 7 January 2006), UCIRI cooperative and founder, Max Havelaar.

Wills, Carol (29 April 2005; 4 November 2005; 26 February 2007; 20 January 2008), Former Executive Director, International Fair Trade Association (IFAT).

Index